St. Olaf College Libraries

Gift of LaVern Rippley

Ethnicity and Sport in North American History and Culture

Recent Titles in
Contributions to the Study of Popular Culture

Ethnicity and Sport in North American History and Culture

Edited by
GEORGE EISEN
and DAVID K. WIGGINS

Contributions to the Study of Popular Culture, Number 40

GREENWOOD PRESS
Westport, Connecticut • London

Library of Congress Cataloging-in-Publication Data

Ethnicity and sport in North American history and culture / edited by
George Eisen and David K. Wiggins.
p.   cm.—(Contributions to the study of popular culture,
ISSN 0198–9871 ; no. 40)
Includes index.
ISBN 0–313–28814–3 (alk. paper)
1. Minorities in sports—United States—History.   2. Minorities in
sports—Canada—History.   3. United States—Popular culture.
4. Canada—Popular culture.   I. Eisen, George.   II. Wiggins, David
Kenneth.   III. Series.
GV709.5.E84   1994
796.1′9—dc20   93–50538

British Library Cataloguing in Publication Data is available.

Library of Congress Catalog Card Number: 93–50538
ISBN: 0–313–28814–3
ISSN: 0198–9871

First published in 1994

Greenwood Press, 88 Post Road West, Westport, CT 06881
An imprint of Greenwood Publishing Group, Inc.

Printed in the United States of America

The paper used in this book complies with the
Permanent Paper Standard issued by the National
Information Standards Organization (Z39.48–1984).

10 9 8 7 6 5 4 3 2

To Marvin Eyler, Maxwell Howell, Joan Hult, and
Gerald Redmond, four individuals who encouraged us
and countless other students to pursue the study of sport history

Contents

Preface

The idea for this anthology was first discussed by the two of us several years ago during a conference in Las Vegas, Nevada. While catching up on the latest news and savoring cups of coffee during one of the breaks from conference sessions, we both determined during the course of our conversation that one of the most glaring gaps in the literature was the lack of research dealing with the involvement of ethnic groups in North American sport. This anthology attempts to help rectify this gap by providing twelve original essays that discuss the sport participation of various ethnic groups in both the United States and Canada. It is our hope that this collection will raise important questions, provide pertinent information, and encourage other scholars to pursue research on sport and the ethnic experience.

We would like to take this opportunity to thank those people who helped us with this project. We are very appreciative of the assistance we received from Greenwood Press. We are also very grateful for the help provided us by Susan Pufnock, Sandy Slater, and Anne Bonanno of George Mason University. Finally, we wish to express our gratitude to each of the contributing authors for their patience and unwavering support in completing this project.

Introduction

George Eisen

There are many voices that describe to us the building of America. The past century and a half has often been considered one of the most tumultuous epochs in American history. With unbridled optimism and staunch belief in a better life, and fueling an economic expansion on a scale unheard of before, waves upon waves of impoverished human masses arrived at the gates of America. A brilliant meeting and meshing of old-line Anglo-Saxon cultural and political values and vibrant new ideas from the Old Continent took place in this one hundred and fifty year time span. During these same years, a steady migration of African-Americans, escaping an economic blight and virulent discrimination from the rural South to the industrialized North, added to this dramatic change in the face of America. These newly arrived people not only formed and reformed the demographic landscape of the United States but also helped form the intellectual and cultural texture of American life.

One of the missing elements in this story are the ethnic contributions to American sport. Indeed, sport in our country cannot be considered anything but ethnic-based. Among the many social and cultural institutions, sport assumed a unique, though often misconstrued, role of uniting, integrating, and socializing these newcomers into mainstream America. How successful sport has been in accomplishing this task is still the subject of debate. Yet, with all this interest, sport has remained one of the most sparsely charted territories of this epoch. This book relates ethnic experiences in sport during the years from 1840 to 1990 in the United States and Canada. More specifically, it chronicles sport as a social and cultural institution through which various ethnic and racial groups attempted to gain social and psychological acceptance and cultural integration. The fact that this mechanism almost totally failed to remedy social inequality, as well as institutionalized racism, sexism, and discrimination, should not detract from its perceived role as an "assimilatory" agent. In addition to utilizing sports as a means for socialization, sports participation also provided ethnic communities with the belief in social mobility, self-esteem, and community pride.

North America is, and always has been, an ethnically diverse society. Yet this cultural diversity along religious, ethnic, and national lines had been tolerated only in a limited degree, and even then only on the dominant Anglo-Saxon elite's terms. Thus newly arriving immigrant or migrant communities could nurture, alongside a quest for assimilation, their cultural and religious differences until it did not interfere with mainstream values. An understanding of religion is relatively easy. A definition of ethnicity, on the other hand, is much more complex since in some groups an overlap between nationality, ethnicity, religion, and even skin color can muddle our efforts. We can argue, for example, that Irish Catholics differed from Irish Protestants just as German Catholics held values different from their Protestant compatriots. Even seemingly homogeneous groups such as Italians were distinguishable culturally along north-south geographic lines. If we consider a distinct cultural conflict between German and Russian Jews and Blacks along the lightness or darkness of their skin, it is easy to see that intra-ethnic or racial harmony as such is just a myth.

A definition of race might rely on an outward manifestation such as color or some other physiological sign. Race and ethnicity (and to some degree nationality) also imply a shared socio-cultural heritage and belief system. Finally, race and ethnicity harbor a psychological *self-identification*. Indeed, this last factor is perhaps the most important in defining the identity of an "ethnic" or "racial" individual. It implies a conscious desire on the part of a person to belong to an aggregate of people, which possesses unique cultural characteristics, rituals, and manners and a unique value system.

North American society provided neither full nor unqualified opportunities for immigrant ethnic and national groups in expanding their economic, human, and intellectual potentials. Thus education, occupation, housing, and other opportunities served this new influx of people on various levels and to differing degrees. Sport was one of the chief social institutions in which individual and communal energies could be marshaled in the newly established ethnic communities. This seems natural. Among the many thorny issues sport had to face, there were few more emotionally charged than the relationship between ethnicity, race, and sport. What makes a given individual dominant in certain human undertakings, in this case sport, is one of the least understood yet most controversial issues. Physical superiority of a racial or ethnic group brings into question the most elementary measure of humanity—our physical worth.

Dominance of ethnic or racial groups in sport is neither a new nor unexpected phenomenon. It is a mere reflection of a process called "ethnic succession"—a historical pattern of one group replacing another in such diverse social and cultural variables as crime, housing, education, employment, and, of course, sports. The history of modern boxing provides a good example of this evolutionary process. While the "fighting" Irish became the first boxers, they were soon replaced by Jews and Italians. Black boxers, in turn, dethroned the Italians in the 1940s and 1950s. As the socioeconomic status of ethnic groups changed, so did their sport habits.

Ethnic succession in sports does not end here. This relatively predictable evolution of ethnic and immigrant communities in boxing spilled over to later career choices. While Irish boxers were managed by old-stock Americans, Irish promoters watched over Jewish fighters, and later Jews did the same thing in promoting Italian sluggers. It is a logical process. Today, not surprisingly, Don King is perhaps the most prominent figure in modern boxing. Historically, blacks have perhaps reigned the longest in the history of the ring. Glory, alas, is a fleeting commodity. They are already being challenged, especially in the lighter weights, by Latino fighters. This same process is more or less applicable to sport participation in general. Yet how long an ethnic group remains dominant or participates at all in a particular sport depends only partly on limitations placed on its access to socioeconomic opportunities or resources.

There are intangible factors that social scientists routinely tend to gloss over. For example, often the mainspring of ethnic involvement in sport is a quest for psychological acceptance. This quest is based on the idea that instead of being a passive entity, forced into sport participation by the power elite and economic necessities, an ethnic community actively promotes its own social, cultural, and psychological integration through sports. It is true not only in America but in every country where society itself places heavy emphasis on sport. The dominance of Jews in Olympic fencing through the first half of the twentieth century well documents this rule. However, it is another question of how long, durable, and indeed effective this "psychological acceptance" is in the face of well-entrenched prejudices.

Another common line that runs through the historical development of all ethnic communities is discrimination. While some progressive segments envisaged sport as an "inclusionary" or integrating device into mainstream culture, prevalent discriminatory practices in effect excluded a large majority of the newcomers. Based on their socioeconomic level, ethnic communities made efforts to counteract discriminatory practices by establishing their own sport organizations. The Negro Leagues, the Young Men's Hebrew Associations, and various ethnic country clubs were set up as "parallel institutions." They were established along "mainstream" lines. Again, we can argue that these institutions were at least as much a psychological remedy for the well-being of an ethnic-racial community, in a climate of intolerance and prejudice, as genuine opportunities for the physical expression of a subculture.

On the other hand, the question of how society attempted to use sport in molding these people with diverse ethnic and racial backgrounds into a coherent national and social entity, and how these immigrants and migrants responded to these attempts of acculturation, is also intriguing. Still, social and cultural values held by an ethnic or racial group are a dominant factor. Many social scientists now accept the notion that there is such a thing as "ethnic psyche" or "national psyche." Differences among the value systems of diverse social classes and various ethnic, national, or religious groups have been documented extensively. A recent study of California Olympians found, for example, that a large percentage of past Olympic participants came from Protestant religious backgrounds. Curiously enough, research by West German scientists, where the population is almost equally divided between Catholics and Protestants, showed similar trends not only in sports but also in music, literature, and the sciences.

Obviously, then, the issue of the hierarchy of values is relevant to sports participation. Thus ethnic group values frequently differed, in various degrees, from those adhered to by society. Simultaneously, they differed from each other to a much larger extent. To exemplify these differences, I quote three ethnic authors from among the multitude of voices. Gay Talesa wrote in his gripping childhood memoirs about an uncle who spoke in the fierce accents of southern Italy, quoting an old village aphorism: "never educate your children beyond yourself." The poignant words of the Irish novelist John McGahern that "Irish fathers simmer with envy of their children . . . of their opportunities, their schooling, their unblemished bodies and minds" might be too strong with which to characterize the Irish family. Nevertheless, they describe nicely Irish family dynamics. The Jewish view of the world painted a different picture in stating that "the Irish boys want to be boxers and the Jews—debaters."

In recent years there has been a debate on the question of whether blacks hold physical excellence in higher esteem than whites. The Reverend Jesse Jackson reflected one of the themes of the debate by admonishing black youth that if they would spend as much time and energy over their books as they do on their athletic activities, there would be more black lawyers, doctors, and engineers. At face value, his rationale is sound. But to reach high competitive levels, any athlete, regardless of race or color, must practice a minimum of six to eight hours per day. Mary-Lou Retton, Janet Evans, or Michael Jordan can testify to that requirement.

A sketch of women's lives, a course of their history and involvement in various societal institutions (such as religion, education, housing, sports) within contemporary ethnic communities follows even more complex lines. These lines create two concentric circles that surrounded women. On the one hand, immigrant women encountered an advanced industrial society with a strong attachment to Protestant religious ideas. They were obviously influenced by the host country's dominant norms and values. On the other hand, as ethnic individuals, their role in society, community, and the family was also defined by their group's religious, cultural, and political value system. How fast and far a woman advanced within the new environment depended at least as much on the latter as on the former. Thus Jeanne Nobel's opinion about the status of black women in history is perhaps also characteristic of women of all ethnic groups. She noted that they "labored under the double handicap of race and sex—a Negroid in a white world and a female in a male world."

The purpose of this anthology is to provide an overview of ethnic contribution to sport and, conversely, examine the impact of sport on ethnic culture. The term "ethnic" was used, purposefully, in the widest sense of the word. It connotes both national/ethnic as well as racial groups with identifiable cultural differences. We must come to grips with the realization that in America, in one way or another, we are all ethnics. Thus the book encompasses both the views of a dominant elite about indigenous games and sports, and how these ethnic sports were and are used as means for social maintenance and ethnic identity in a heterogeneous world. It addresses the question of how dominant segments of American society attempted to socialize diverse ethnic groups into "mainstream" North American culture through sports. Simultaneously, it also records the responses of ethnic groups to discrimination in sport and through sport. The idea of how sport can change a group or how a given group assimilates sport into its own subculture is, after all, consistent with how every ethnic community absorbs a social or cultural institution on its own terms. Finally, the complex issue of ethnic women's participation, their struggles and triumphs in the field of sports, is also the focus of this book.

This anthology deliberately includes essays on both the United States and Canada. While there are obvious similarities between the evolution of ethnic communities in the United States and Canada, there are also significant differences. One of the added benefits of this book is to provide a glimpse of these differences. By its nature, this anthology also provides a historical as well as contemporary overview. The chronological arrangement of the chapters coincides with the historical and social development of each ethnic group as it arrived or as it migrated around the continent. We believe this method gives the reader a better spatial and temporal framework. However, revealing our own commitment to an interdisciplinary approach toward this subject, the selected works in this anthology also incorporate techniques from other branches of the social sciences and humanities.

Thus this book is aimed at a diverse audience: those studying the history, sociology, anthropology, and philosophy of sport. While reading many of these chapters one can see that sport is an excellent medium for studying the evolution of a rapidly changing society. Sport and recreational pursuits of ethnic and racial groups represent a slice of life that reflected all the sorrows, happiness, and struggles of their lives. They also provide a glimpse of the changing world of ethnic cultures as well as the evolution of a multicultural society. This anthology, then, should be viewed as an initial step in discovering a never explored piece of our cultural heritage. It is unfortunate that, due to space limitations, we could not include the sport experiences of all ethnic communities and nationalities. Yet it seems reasonable to assume that this book encompasses some generalities that may be applicable to other ethnic experiences as well.

A comparison is obviously needed. It might demystify the sporting life of immigrants and migrants in a turbulent yet exciting epoch of history. This comparison is important because it points toward a certain predictability in the historical evolution of a multicultural and pluralistic society such as North America. Society, and many of the ethnic communities, created opportunities for sports and recreation because of an unshakable belief in social engineering, as well as in the power of sport as a socializing, acculturating, and physical-mental health agent. This was rooted in the belief that assimilation is a matter of time—accomplished in the course of three generations. Thus social engineers of the time were single-minded in their quest to create new citizens through sports. The immigrants and migrants, on the other hand, were no less rational, deliberate, and proactive in using sport as a means of social integration and psychological acceptance.

The question of how successful these social engineers were is a pertinent one. Recent scholarship shows that many established beliefs in the power of sport as an agent of assimilation were based on crucial errors. On the one hand, the concept that sport is an agent of social mobility is seriously challenged on many fronts. On the other, the proponents of the "melting pot" theory, and an inevitability of assimilation, failed to understand certain ethnic and racial groups—Latinos and blacks. They passed over the tenacity of culture while greatly underestimating the importance of race. Thus the continual isolation of different racial groups, engendered by racism, is perhaps the most potent factor for the maintenance of ethnic and racial separateness in sport across several generations.

Ethnicity and Sport in North American History and Culture

1

Early European Attitudes toward Native American Sports and Pastimes

George Eisen

Encounters between the early travelers and the original inhabitants of North America, sporadic as they were, formed the first impressions concerning the customs and manners of many Native-American tribes. Yet their depictions, often misconstrued, were scanty and sketchy by nature. For a more complete and detailed picture of Indian life, we must turn to missionaries and permanent settlers. All European chroniclers of America devoted some efforts to describe Indian customs, manners, and diversions. Opinions nevertheless differed. "I have observed," wrote the Jesuit missionary Paul Le Jeune at Quebec in 1633, "that after seeing two or three Savages do the same thing, it is at once reported to be a custom of the whole Tribe." He further remarked that "there are many tribes in these countries who agree in a number of things and differ in many others; so that when it is said that certain practices are common to the Savages, it may be true of one tribe and not true of another."[1]

The sage advice of this noted Jesuit obviously did not impress many of his contemporaries. The notion of the native as an unspoiled child of nature, on the one hand, and the violent heathen, on the other, was formulated alternately with much fervor. Nevertheless, the historical accounts differed mightily according to the imported national attitudes and religious beliefs of the observers. The historian Evelyn Page was correct in asserting that a historian "edges over into distortions, and into condemnation or praise on social, moral, or religious grounds, the measurements of which he has brought with him." Adventurers, missionaries, colonial administrators, and others were constrained to describe Indians in the terms of their own cultures. Judgments such as those of Lahontan, Wassenaer, de Vries, Penn, and many others have nurtured the concept, reaching its full exaltation by Rousseau, of the Noble Savage. One source wrote: "There is little authority among these nations.

They live almost all equally another's." Despite the obvious shortcomings and vices among the Indians, their society was, according to de Vries, morally superior to European society. In comparing the two cultures, he remarked without hesitation: "Although they are cruel, and live without any punishment of evil doers, there is not one-fourth as much roguery and murder among them as there is among Christians."[2]

This study places a focus on early European impressions of Indian cultures through the medium of play and sporting customs. It looks into how the religious and national differences of the early settlers and missionaries distorted, or at least colored, their views of the indigenous people. Indeed, this study will dispel our notion of a united, monolithic European culture. It was, and is, simply a myth. European societies were just as fragmented, just as tribal as the Native Americans whom they observed. However, we also are able to glean from the surviving narratives a yet uncorrupted sporting life, and associated cultural beliefs, of the native tribes. Indeed, we must go directly to the earliest records for a balanced and complete picture of Indian civilizations. Among the most interesting source materials are the *Jesuit Relations.* Written by missionaries in the early years of the seventeenth century, these fascinating narratives offer many perceptive and humorous comments on the social customs and sporting habits of the Indians of Lower Canada, the Great Lakes, and Louisiana. On the Protestant side, the writings of clergymen and civic leaders shed some light on Indian pastimes and white attitudes toward them. The quality of their writings is obviously inferior to that of the highly educated Catholic missionaries, but both sets of sources reveal how early observers related to and formulated opinions about Indian sporting diversions, games, and gambling. They also provide an understanding of how their descriptions created a curious image of the Indian as both the "unspoiled child of nature" and a "despised heathen." And finally, the opinions expressed in these narratives show how a Protestant "sporting ethic" cast a long-lasting shadow upon the leisure attitudes of this society up to modern times.[3]

The early narratives were unanimous in their opinion about the physical characteristics of the local inhabitants. What emerges from the contemporary accounts is clearly flattering to the Indian. The first English work relating to New England, *Brereton's Relation* (1602), characterized the natives of the area as of "tall stature, broad and grim visage, of a blacke swart complexion." The Hurons were similarly praised: they "are of a Sanguine Constitution" and without any bodily deformity. Louis Hennepin, a Recollect father, could not refrain from drawing a brief comparison between the original people and the Europeans, undoubtedly to the benefit of the former: "The Indians are very robust; men, women and even children are extremely vigorous ... they escape maladies which beset most of our Europeans for want of exercise." The perplexed observer of the New Netherlands, noted that: "It is somewhat strange that among these most barbarous people, there are a few or none cross-eyed, blind, crippled, lame, hunchbacked, or limping men; all are well fashioned people, strong and sound body, well fed, without blemish."[4]

If the Indians' appearance gave any hint as to their mental or spiritual qualities, the French observers were elated at what they saw. The natives appeared not only more pleasing to the eyes than Europeans, but also healthier. Lahontan, for example, could say that: "They are neither strong nor as vigorous as most of the French are in raising of Weights with their Arms, or carrying of Burden on their Backs; but to make Amends for that, they are indefatigable and inured to Hardship . . . their whole Time being spent in the Way of Exercise, whether in running up and down at Hunting and fishing, or in Danceing and playing at Football, or such Games as require the Motion of the Legs."[5] As part of the European view of local customs and habits, an interesting reaction to the mode of native sport participation has unfolded through the first centuries of White presence in the New World. A difference between the European and New World style of sporting was readily emphasized by all observers. Sports and games were vigorous and violent affairs among the Indians as well as among the English. Nevertheless, English sports, not yet "corrupted" by the concept of fair play, were often rough and tumble pastimes in which a wide range of activities bordering on unbridled violence were permitted. Contests of the Indians were conducted in an atmosphere of correctness and mutual respect. Cheating was almost unknown among them. One may compare the contemporary English and French sporting scene with the observation of the Jesuit father Lalemant. In witnessing a Huron feast, the Jesuit wrote that, "everything was done with such moderation and reserve that—at least, in watching them—one could never have thought that he was in the midst of an assemblage of Barbarians—so much respect did they pay to one another, even while contending for victory."[6]

For English spectators, football played by a multitude of tribes was perhaps the most familiar pursuit. The chroniclers repeatedly bemoaned the fact that the English version of the game was violent and often uncontrollable. This caught the eye of a number of contemporaries from a diverse background, such as Henry Spelman, William Strachey, and the Reverend Roger Williams. Spelman, a member of Captain Smith's expedition to Powhaton's country, wrote that the Indians "never fight nor pull one another doune." Strachey, the first Secretary of Virginia, also presented a curious comparison between the American and European codes of conduct in the course of the game: "they never strike up one another's heeles, as we do, not accompting that praiseworthie to purchase a goale by such an advantage." In 1686 John Dunton observed a football game in Agawam, Massachusetts. He, too, was struck by the difference: "Neither were they to apt to trip one another heels and quarrel, as I have seen em in England." To round out the circle of witnesses, a contemporary of these writers, William Wood, should be quoted. A Puritan gentleman, he made valuable observations on football as played by the Indians of Massachusetts. His work, *New Englands Prospects*, is an account of Indian life as the author saw it between 1629 and 1633. His comments on their sporting life, and a comparison with the English one, are revealing: "It is most delight to see them play, in smalle companies, when men may view their swift footemanship, their curious tossings of their Ball, their flouncing into the water, their lubberlike wrestling, having no cunning at all in that kind, one English being able to beate ten Indians at footeball." For our purposes, it is more interesting to read his comment on Indian sportsmanship. "Before they come to this sport [football]," the observant Puritan wrote, "they paint themselves, even as when they goe to warre, in pollicie to prevent future mischiefe, because no man should know him that moved his patience or accidentally hurt his person, taking away the occasion of studying revenge."[7]

Wood's last statement is a fine example of the superficial knowledge so characteristic of many Puritans who were willing to provide impromptu interpretations of their neighbors' customs. The painting of the face and body, in fact, had religious overtones; the game itself carried religious, magical, and medicinal significance in Indian cultures. Of course, it also served often enough as a substitute for war. However, the important thing to note is that Indian football, vigorous as it may have been, was much more moderate than that of the English. Also, Wood was right in assuming—and other chroniclers also support this—that taking revenge for an injury sustained in the course of the contest was almost unknown among the tribes. Roger Williams, the Puritan minister who established the colony of Providence, Rhode Island, made some references to football in this vein. He noticed that during football "they have great stakings, but seldome quarell."[8]

By their nature, many of the native pastimes were violent sporting affairs. The game of lacrosse, for example, was thus characterized by an early traveler: "In fine this Game is so violent that they tear their Skins, and break their Legs very often in striving to raise the Ball." Yet some semblance of sportsmanlike conduct must have existed. Injuries received as a consequence of sport participation were normally attributed to unlucky circumstances rather than to vengeful behavior. This notion of fair play was further exemplified by the fact that any outside interference was traditionally deplored. Nicholas Perrot, whose description of lacrosse was perhaps the most detailed among seventeenth-century works, explained this state of affairs: "However, if any person who does not belong to the party, or who has not made any bet, should drive the ball to the advantage of one of the two parties, one of the players whom the blow does not favor would attack this man, demanding of him whether this were any of his business, and why he was meddling in it." It is conceivable that in the excitement of a heated contest some hot-headed spectators, especially if they bet heavily on one of the teams, lost control over their emotions. It is also likely that encounters such as that described above often resulted in blows along the sidelines. Nevertheless, these incidents were resolved amicably, and the teams began the games anew.[9]

Early authorities rarely accused Native Americans with blatant cheating on or off the ball field, contrary to the hellish scenes of contemporary French or English taverns. A modicum of honesty was recognized by them even in the natives' games of chance. Perrot emphatically stated that the Hurons very often cheated in playing their game of straws, but he also admitted that the cheater was shunned by the community. This was even mentioned by many of the Jesuits who pointed out that the Hurons were frequently given to thievery.

In discussing early European thought about the sporting diversions and gaming habits of the Native Americans, we have to contend with a variety of opinions. The earliest reports belonged to a narrow band of adventurers who by their training could not make more than cursory and scientifically negligible observations. The most substantial reports about these subjects were provided by Catholic missionaries and Protestant clergymen. The difference in their attitudes is sharply illustrated by contrasting approaches toward Indian civilization in general. "The Catholic imperative for converting and including the heathen," Francis Jennings perceptively noted, "compelled Catholics to learn something about them in order to do the holy work effectively, while the Protestant principle of elitism worked out in practice to exclusionism and indifference."[10]

Of course, we might also take into account the fact that beyond these religious differences there was also a cultural rift between the more flexible French and the rigidly dogmatic British and Dutch. But, for a moment, let's consider these two major religious philosophies and their own internal differences: Jesuits, Dominicans, Franciscans, and Recollects on the Catholic side, and various branches of Puritanism and Quakers on the Protestant side. While the Jesuit and Franciscan descriptions of Indian pastimes derived from their residence among the various tribes, the Puritans' and Quakers' views were shaped by occasional visits to their neighbors. The Protestants' sense of mission, coupled with an assumed holiness and intellectual arrogance, prevented their descent to the level of the "Savages." This moral bigotry inevitably precluded the cultural relativism that was the cornerstone of the Jesuit and Franciscan approach to the Indians.[11]

Jesuits and Franciscan friars had arrived in Canada in 1615, at the request of the French explorer Samuel de Champlain. Both orders have been noted for their devotion to learning and their special approach to native cultures. They both adopted a policy of transforming Indian life from within, adapting "themselves and their morality to local customs in order to establish the broadest rapport with the Indians." The colonial historian Michael Kammen went one step further in stating that "cassocked conquistadors tended to permit the heathens great latitude in the sphere of natural conduct." These missionaries' deep excursions into Huron country, the Mississippi Valley, and Louisiana provided them valuable experience concerning indigenous cultures. Prototypes of later anthropological approaches, their writings often reflected an approach toward tribal habits and customs without moral judgment. "Men are men everywhere," Jerome Lalemant observed with a characteristically Gallic tolerance, "this new world has the same nature as the old; it has its virtues and vices just like Europe." A contemporary of these Jesuits, Father Membre, reveals in his narrative neither disapproval of nor objections to Indian diversions. He simply recorded that "they are, besides, much given to play, like all Indians in America, that I am able to know." Gabriel Sagard, another Recollect father, did not forget to add that the Hurons passed their time "in idleness, gambling, sleeping, singing, dancing, smoking or going to feasts."[12]

There is not a trace of reproach from these friars. This tolerance and understanding went so far as to discard superstitions, associated with games and gambling as mere "fooleries" and nothing more. In 1637 Le Mercier remarked, although with some consternation, that "this hunchback [sorcerer] declared that the whole country was sick and had prescribed a remedy, namely, a game of crosse, for its recovery." Curiously enough, even this criticism was not directed toward the game itself but rather the superstitious use of lacrosse. The other discernible objection voiced by the Jesuits was the disproportionate amount of time devoted to sport activities and games, which interfered with religious instruction. Le Jeune, more resignedly than deploringly, noted: "We give the Instruction of Cathecism in our cabin, for we had as yet no other suitable Church. This is often the most we can do: for their feasts, dances, and games so occupy them that we cannot get them together as we would like."[13]

A markedly different picture of the Native Americans emerges from contemporary Protestant sources. Contrary to a commonly held belief in a degree of uniformity between various Protestant denominations, there were major dividing lines starkly visible as to their views on the American Indians. It would perhaps be unfair and misleading to assert that the Puritans, the Dutch

Reformed Church, or the Quakers opposed every form of leisure pursuit and diversion among themselves or among their neighbors, the Indians. It seems that an evolutionary development did take place toward the acceptance of amusements and games, particularly in the second and subsequent generations of colonists. Nothing can illustrate this more eloquently than the comments of a Dutch visitor. Jasper Danckaerts noted in 1679 that "you discover little difference between this and other places [Boston]. Drinking and fighting occur there no less than elsewhere; and as to the truth and true godliness, you must not expect more of them than of others."[14]

Early references all agreed about the harmful effects of misusing time in the service of recreational activities either in Protestant or Indian societies. Indeed, the concept of time had a special meaning in the early Protestant religious ethic. Max Weber's remark that "waste of time was the first and in principle the deadliest of sins" is not an exaggeration. In commenting on the relationship of time and recreation, Oberholzer applied this same reasoning to "the Puritan attitude towards amusements and recreation," which "was closely related to their view of the proper use of time." Increase Mather, a fiery minister of the seventeenth century, emphasized in his sermons that time is a gift of God and its misuse will precipitate divine retribution. This attitude was pertinent to indigenous recreation as well.

The various Protestant denominations did not deplore native sporting diversions per se, but rather for the "valuable" time that was spent on "gaming and lazing." Roger Williams' lamentation about lost time was reminiscent of this concern. "How many vaine inventions and foolish pastimes have the sonnes of men in all parts of the world found out," the pastor mused over Indian diversions and time, "to pass time & post over this short minute of life." Besides violating the sanctity of time, the Indians' violation of the Protestant work ethic was also offensive to the New Englanders. Natives who "rather starve than worke, following no employements," induced William Wood to advise giving up the life of "more pleasures and profit than paines or care." He piously proclaimed his hope that "good example, and good instructions may bring them to a more industrious and provident course of life."[15] The small detail that the Indians were happy and content in their present state apparently could not filter through the thick curtain of moral bigotry.

Indeed, gambling was more offensive to Protestant sensibilities than any other form of recreation. It was not a simple issue of time anymore. We can imagine that the ministers in New England were genuinely alarmed by the prevalence of gambling because it often resulted in financial disaster. But at the same time they did not neglect the corrosive effects of gaming on the spiritual well-being of the colonists. Max Weber's comment that "impulsive enjoyment of life, which leads away both from work in calling and from religion, was as such the enemy of rational asceticism" well documents this aversion to the "irrational gambling instinct."[16]

We should be somewhat cautious in interpreting contemporary Puritan sources since there was a wide gap between religious prescriptions and actual practice. The majority of the surviving documents represent the ecclesiastical and official position of a theocratic ruling elite. Gambling among settlers, as Nancy Struna found, "was more popular and widespread than the General Court would have liked to have believed." There was no better proof of this state of affairs than the notion that the two cultures' experience, English and Indian, was to be the cautionary example for both. The Eternal Judgment was to be on the scale—their salvation. "This life is a short minute," warned Roger Williams, and "eternitie followes . . . our English Gamesters scorne to stake Their clothes as Indians do. Nor yet themselves, alas, yet both Stake soules and lose them to." From this and other remarks it is evident that these English colonizers never adopted in any form the conception of the Noble Savage.[17]

Again, it would be a mistake to assume that there has ever been a unity of opinion among the various Protestant denominations. The Dutch in New Amsterdam, for example, made no concerted efforts during the initial phase of colonization to study the tribal societies in depth, much less to convert them. This ecclesiastical neglect can perhaps be attributed to the sad state prevailing within the Dutch Reformed Church. Kiliaen van Rensselaer had to confess that matters were "in such state, that hardly any semblance of godliness and righteousness" remained in New Netherlands. The most prevalent crimes in the Dutch colonies were dishonesty, licentiousness, and drunkenness. More sadly, the spread of liquor and wine among the natives was also blamed on the Dutch merchants. In comparison, a visitor to New Plymouth in 1627 could not fail to notice that stringent laws and ordinances to censure the spread of immorality were enforced not only within the city limits but even among the neighboring tribes. One of the major differences between the Dutch and the English Puritans of New England was the Dutch's portrayal of the Indians. Van der Donck's observations were quite characteristic of his Dutch contemporaries: "They [Indians] are all free by nature, and will not bear any domineering or lording over them; they will not bear any insult, unless they have done wrong, and they will bear chastisement without resentment." Of course, he could not fail to notice also that "to heavy slavish labour the men have a particular aversion, and they manage their affairs accordingly, so that they need not labour much." Indeed, his comments were rather praising than chastising, tinged with a trace of envy. In general, the Dutch settlers believed in the principle of "live and let live," benefiting both races.[18]

The examination of early Quaker philosophy also reveals marked deviation from the rigid New England orthodoxy. Quakers, often a persecuted minority themselves, disapproved of all excesses in luxury, pleasure, and wanton pastimes. Indeed, the Protestant concern with the proper use of time also prevailed among them. Thus William Penn's opinion that idleness and preoccupation with useless pastimes would promote misuse of time and immorality among the Friends was well within the framework of Protestant ethics. "We are commanded to Redeem the Time, because the Days are Evil; but these People [Gamesters] chuse rather to Lose their Time, and fall into the Evil, they should avoid."[19] But any affinity with contemporary religious philosophies prescribed by the New Englanders ended here. The attitudes of the Quakers toward Native Americans were dramatically different. They did not impose their strict moral code and religious convictions upon non-Quakers in general, and much less upon the neighboring Indians. The early Friends might often seemed to be the extremists among the various Puritan movements, yet the most striking aspect of their life in the seventeenth century was their good relations with neighboring groups. They regarded the natives as children of God deserving respect. William Penn was instrumental in establishing harmonious ties between the two races. Whenever the opportunity arose, he participated in the Indians' games of skill. The prominent statesman saw the local inhabitants as the "most merry creatures that live, Feast and Dance almost perpetually; they never have much, nor want much." "We sweat and toil to live," Penn pondered, "their pleasure feeds them, I mean, their Hunting, Fishing and Fowling."[20]

A comparison between contemporary religious philosophies concerning Indian gambling is also somewhat instructive on their views of Indian culture. Based on the many injunctions against gambling in general, we might assume that the Quakers scorned this vice among the tribes as well. However, both official Quaker records and contemporary narratives are surprisingly mute on this question. The Puritans of New England, on the other hand, left no doubt about their objections against gambling even among the local tribes. One of the Pilgrim fathers, Edward Winslow, in visiting the Massassoit chief, witnessed a gambling-related murder. "It happened," the sober settler noted, "that two of their men fell out as they were in game (for they use gaming as much as any where, and will play away all, even their skin from their backs, yea their wives' skins also, though it may be they are miles distant from them, as myself have seen) and growing to great heat, the one killed the other." Another condemnation of this "unlawful" recreation came from William Wood, a clergyman in the Bay Colony. His thundering oration warned about the harmful and evil consequences of gambling for both body and soul: "This

Pompey can endure no equall, till one dayes adverse lotterie at their game
(called Puimme) metamorphize him into a Codrus, robbing him of his con-
ceited wealth, leaving him in minde and riches equall with his naked atten-
dants." The writings of the French Jesuits were not less preoccupied with gambling related disorders. Curiously enough, however, they limited their
disapproval to the excesses, for example, murder. De Brebeuf, whose narrative was liberally spiced with valuable anthropological observations and
humorous comments on Indian customs, was philosophical. He exhorted that
"gambling never leads to anything good; in fact, the Savages themselves
remark that it is almost the sole cause of assaults and murders."[21]

We must remember that gambling in Indian cultures was both a pastime in
itself as well as an activity that accompanied all sport events. Indeed, gambling
was intertwined with every facet of their life. De Brebeuf pointed out how
much significance was placed on games of chance in Huron medicine. "The
sick man is brought in a blanket," the father wrote, "and that man of the
Village who is to shake the dish (for there is only one on each side set apart for
the purpose), he, I say, walkes behind, his head and face wrapped in his gar-
ment. They bet heavily on both sides." Whether or not the sick man in any of
these cases was restored to his normal health remains a mystery. However, to
ensure every available divine intervention, the Indians also requested the
presence of missionaries at games for the health of a patient. This was, a
French traveler sarcastically remarked, "from a persuasion that their tutelar
genii are more powerful than all others." During football, lacrosse, and other
contests, the natives also bet extensively. Thus Daniel Gookin, whose colonial
adventures brought him into contact with the inhabitants of Virginia as well as
of New England, could observe that "they are addicted to gaming; and will in
that vein, play away all they have." Nothing so completely revealed this ardor
for gambling during sport events than a perceptive remark of Isaack de
Rasieres: "and they win from each other all that they possess, even to the lap-
pet with which they cover their private parts . . . and so they separate from each
other quite naked."[22]

Another troubling aspect of this Indian predilection for gambling was that
the stakes encompassed not only all the possessions one may have had, but
often included sexual favors or personal liberty. The French explorer Marc
Lescarbot's testimony grimly illustrated this passion for gambling among the
Iroquois, who "stake all that they have even to their wives." As for the attitudes of the wives involved, he humorously added: "True it is as to women lost
at play that to hand them over is full hard, for often they make mock of the
gambler and point the finger of scorn at him." The Jesuit father Lalemant
often pondered on the similarities between French and Indian gambling. He

concluded that it "is strong in our France, as well as in yours. I have seen a Savage woman who, having lost all she had, staked herself,—not her honor, but indeed her services,—that is to say, she would have been as a slave or servant of the winner, if she had lost." He softened his harsh judgment by adding that, in contrast to European customs, the "Savages cannot exercise severity, nor harshly exact a service from their Countrymen." That this penchant for gambling was universal in the New World can be inferred from the words of John Lawson, a contemporary of the Jesuit missionaries, who described his experiences in Carolina: "I have known several of them play themselves away, so that they have remained the winners Servants, till their Relations or themselves could pay the Money to redeem them."[23]

The difference between the Jesuits and the Puritans was manifested also in their attempt to alter or influence these activities. The obvious criticism of the Jesuits was directed toward the social implications of reckless gaming among the natives. Yet they always exercised a large degree of understanding in these matters. The Puritans, on the other hand, were outspoken to a fault, directing their attention toward the treat of "Eternal Damnation" which would be the inescapable result of this vice. Nothing could be a more enlightening illustration for that point of view than Roger Williams' lamentations: "I have often told them in their gamings, and in their great losings (when they have staked and lost their money, clothes, house, corne, and themselves, if single persons) they will confesse it, like many an English man: an Emblem of the horrour of conscience, which all poore sinners walk in at last, when they see what wofull games they have played in their life, and now find themselves eternall Beggars." The minister was a frequent guest of the Narrangensetts, yet his comments show how little he knew about them and their culture. During one of his excursions, he was decently shocked upon an invitation to attend one of their gambling sessions. He refused by claiming "that I might not countenance and partake of their folly, after once I saw the evill of them."[24]

In New England the clash of the two diverse cultures was particularly forceful. A cursory comment by Thomas Shepard, another minister, about already converted Indians shed some light on the ethical and legal ramifications of gambling.

One great case that hath come severall times to mee, is about such debts as they owe by gaming, for they have been great gamesters, but have moved questions about it, and are informed of the unlawfulnesse of it, and have there upon wholly given over gaming for any wagers, and all games wherein is a lot, onely use lawfull recreations, and have a Law against unlawfull gaming; but other Indians that are of another mind, come and challenge their old debts, and now they refuse to pay, because it was a sinne so to game.[25]

The sincerity of these new converts, of course, may raise some questions. It hard to believe that the good minister did not see through the ruse of his newly converted flock. Nevertheless, he appealed to the unrepentant creditors and succeeded in reducing the debt of the pious ones by half. Sometimes even a good Puritan had to compromise.

It is interesting to examine the attitudes of the Indians themselves about their gambling habits. Again, the scientifically inclined friars provide a wealth of information on this point. Chrestien Le Clercq noticed, for example, that the natives "are very faithful in paying whatever they have lost at the game, without quarrelling or expressing the least word of impatience." Following his inquiry about the calm acceptance of the outcome of the game, he was reassured that "they play only for diversion, and to enjoy themselves with their friends." This notion was in complete contrast to contemporary European mores. Often the material gain itself was of secondary value for the Indian—another strange concept to the European mind. It was bewildering to see that "they wager a new gun against an old one which is not worth anything, as readily as if it were good, and they give as a reason that if they are going to win they will win as well against a bad article as against an old one which is not worth anything, and that they would rather bet against something than not bet at all."[26]

With all their enlightened and patient approach toward North America's original residents, the fact that the participants enjoyed gambling, whether losing or winning, was perhaps the most astounding revelation for the Jesuits and the Franciscan missionaries. Although murders might occur as a consequence of heated gambling, as we have seen, this might have been more the exception than the rule. The general consensus among the Catholic clergy was that the Indians accepted the outcome of long gambling bouts with stoic calm. Paul Du Ru, a Franciscan friar, studied the inhabitants with a particular interest in their character. Having spent considerable time in their midst, his observations of the Chitimacha were especially unique. These gamblers were masters of their emotions even in the course of the most heated gambling. "It is astonishing how calmly they gamble," he wrote in the mid-seventeenth century. "Apparently winning or losing is alike to them. I have enjoyed watching them to notice how impossible it would be to judge the course of the play by their expression, particularly in the games that call for little movement." This was a deviation from the customary code of behavior associated with European gambling. Lalemant's perceptive remark epitomized this difference between the two civilizations: "Savages, although passionately fond of gambling, show themselves superior to our Europeans. They hardly ever evince either joy in winning or sadness in losing, playing with most remarkable external tranquility."[27]

The perceptions of Indian sporting diversions and gambling habits by European observers constitute only part of the larger issue of human relations between two drastically different civilizations. We cannot discard the possibility that differences of opinion existed along national-cultural lines, such as French, Dutch, and English. However, it is equally true that differences in attitude were more distinguishable by contrasting views on Indian life among various religious groups. The two extremes in evaluating native culture can be placed within the French Catholic and English Puritan religious philosophies. Mentioning only these two is certainly not representative of native-settler relations as a whole. Nevertheless, these two ethical systems made the strongest impact on the fate of the Indians. The answer to the question as to the degree of the impact of European mores and attitudes upon them is, at best, ambiguous. We know that Catholic missionaries were bent on converting the Indians by accommodating their religious doctrines to the local customs. Jesuit scholasticism attempted to arrive at a realistic picture of tribal societies, as far as possible, emphasizing that their recorded experience was confined to the tribes visited. "Ordinarily, the secular concerns of the priests," a historian aptly noted, "did not conflict with their spiritual interests; they remained subordinate."

Puritans, on the other hand, tended to overgeneralize tribal mores, customs, and attitudes. Indian culture was, in the eyes of the Puritan settlers, inferior in every respect to that of the chosen people, themselves. Even the Quakers were only tolerant of, but mildly disinterested in, some customs which might have been beneficial. This total rejection of tribal culture resulted in a misconstrued and distorted perception of the Indian. Thus the image of the "Noble Savage" could not have been the product of Protestant minds. In order to understand the local civilization, both Jesuits and Franciscans were willing to experiment with various aspects of Savage life. It was especially true for Indian medicine. In contrast, New England's Puritan missionaries had, according to Jennings, so "closed their minds that after nearly three decades at their task they knew nothing of Indian medicine."[28]

Attitudes prevailing among the two religious philosophies relating to Indian pastimes were similar in every respect to their approaches to tribal culture in general. Both the missionaries and the settlers that followed them in New France adopted many local customs related to sporting diversions. As these missionaries and fur traders roamed over the North, they freely borrowed many practices from the original inhabitants. Lacrosse is the most familiar sport activity embraced by Canadians, but the use of canoes, toboggans, sledges, snowshoes, and other pastimes can also be mentioned. The settlers willingly participated even in the "gambling games in which Indians delighted, as well as wrestling, and running, and other games." One should perhaps add to this list the healthful custom of sweat-bathing. Nicolas Denys, after experiencing the beneficial effects of sweat-bathing, highly recommended this practice to Europeans. However, this was embraced readily only by the French.[29]

With a few exceptions, Protestants were not particularly interested in Indian customs, much less in adopting their "wanton" pastimes. Imbued with a sense of the superiority of the "White Man," if the Puritans participated in native pastimes at all, they did it only on their own terms. During a game, for example, a tribe in close proximity to the Bay Colony invited Edward Winslow and his companion Stephen Hopkins to participate in their revelry. They invited the visiting Pilgrims to shoot with them at a mark for skins. Seeing that their offer was politely declined, the whites then were requested to demonstrate their shooting ability without wager. Even when the Pilgrim fathers admitted Indian superiority in some skills—such as their swimming style— over that of the English, they chose not to adopt them anyway. It is curious to note that at the time when very few English sailors knew the art of swimming, Indians were praised for their ability "to swim in the water as a goose." Beyond the utility of knowing how to swim, the Indians practiced it diligently, as Lionel Wafer rightly interpreted, because it "is a great Exercise even for the small Boys and Girls; and the Parents also use that Refreshment."[30]

To further demonstrate this Puritan reluctance, one might recall that few medical-recreational practices were so universal among the natives as the sweat-bath. Travelers reported its existence from New France all the way to Florida. The sweat-huts were always situated near fresh water, and a thorough sweating was accompanied by a "run towards the stream into the cold water being agile to swim." William Penn had an opportunity to witness how an Indian chief, Tenoughan, recovered from high fever by sweating profoundly in a "Bagnio" and later, "stark naked (his Breech-Clout only excepted) he ran to the River, which was about twenty Paces, and duck'd himself twice or thrice therein." Even Penn understood that the frequent visits to the sweat-baths were grounded in sound medical reasons. Charles Wolley provided an interesting dialogue between himself and an old Indian medicine man concerning the healing properties of sweat-baths:

I discussed with one of their Me-ta-ows, and told him of the European way of Sweating in Beds, and rubbing our bodies with warm cloth; to which he answered he thought theirs the more effectual was: because the water does immediately stop all passages (as he called the Pores) and at the same time wash off the excrementitious remainder of the Sweat, which he thought could not be so clearly done by frictions.[31]

In retrospect, the reasoning of the old medicine man seems quite modern and scientific, especially in comparison with an almost primitive European medicine. Of course, he could also be vindicated by the fact, attested by contemporary opinions, that common cold and flu were rare phenomena among the natives. Yet neither William Penn, as enlightened as he was, nor other persons from the Protestant religious movements had ever contemplated adopting this beneficial pastime.

As a concluding thought, we might bemoan the fact that Puritan and Quaker observers of the seventeenth century had little or no flair for anthropology. Their brief and religiously prescribed accounts are indeed meager and pale in comparison with the rich ethnographic notes of the scientifically trained Jesuits and Franciscan fathers. Yet the views of both sides are important. They enable the scholar as well as the interested reader to understand a lost cultural and sporting heritage which is just as much a part of American history as that of the white men. Indeed, we should not overlook the fact that Native Americans played their part in shaping a new society on the new continent.

This study has examined some aspects of the white-Indian relationship through Native American pastimes and sports as reflected in the opinions of early observers. The fact that these observers' views were often jaundiced supports the idea that religious philosophies have always been detrimental to understanding and formulating ideas about the role and functioning of every people. The issue as to whether the alternating images of the "Noble Savage" and the "Savage Heathen" have their roots in reality is of only secondary importance here. The metaphor of the "Noble Savage," it seems, was created by the French as a consequence of an intellectual disappointment in and the moral rejection of the mores and behavior of contemporary societies. In an age of absolutism and religious intolerance, the picture of the Indian, free, independent, equal, and master of his own destiny—was to serve as a symbolic guiding light for the disillusioned.

In many ways, the Puritans were also rejecting European culture. Their answer rested on the building of an exclusive "City upon the Hill." Their approach toward Indian culture and recreation, biased as it was, indicated their general attitude toward man, God, and society. It should not come as a surprise that these early Pilgrims in some ways predetermined modern American attitudes toward sports and specifically ethnic sports. Just as the Puritan philosophy excluded the notion of the Indian as a guiding example for a better earthly society, so it discarded many other ethnic and cultural subcultures in more recent times. For them earthly existence served merely to obtain the world to come, and for that the Saints needed neither the Indian example nor, sadly enough, the Indians themselves. The remarkable vision of an early seventeenth-century historian, Adrien van der Donck, serves as an eerie reminder that in the Puritan world view the whole Native American existence was a transitory affair and must be recorded for posterity as a novelty: "Having briefly remarked on the situation and advantages of the country, we deem it worth our attention to treat concerning the nature of the original native inhabitants of the land; that after the Christians have multiplied and the natives have disappeared and melted away, a memorial of them may be preserved."[32]

NOTES

1. Reuben G. Thwaites, ed., *The Jesuit Relations and Allied Documents: Travels and Explorations of the Jesuit Missionaries in New France,* 73 vols. (Cleveland: Burrow Bros., 1896–1901), vol. 1, p. 27.

2. Evelyn Page, *American Genesis* (Boston: Gambit, 1973), p. 216; Baron de Lahontan, *New Voyages to North America,* 2 vols. (London: Bonwicke, 1703), vol. 1, p. 420; David Pietersz de Vries, *Voyages from Holland to America* (Brekegeest: Hoorn, 1655), p. 155.

3. James Axtell, *Beyond 1492: Encounters in Colonial North America* (New York: Oxford University Press, 1992).

4. Louis Hennepin, *A Description of Louisiana,* trans. John G. Shea (New York: John G. Shea, 1880), pp. 280–81; see also John Brereton, *Briefe and True Relation of the Discoverie of the North Part of Virginia in 1602,* ed. H. S. Burrage (New York: Charles Scribner's Sons, 1903), p. 330; Lahontan, *New Voyages to North America,* vol. 1, p. 515; Nicolaes van Wassenaer, *Historisch Verhael,* in *Narratives of New Netherlands,* ed. F. J. Jameson (New York: Charles Scribner's Sons, 1909), p. 72; Adrien van der Donck, *A Description of the New Netherlands,* ed. T. F. O'donnell (Syracuse: Syracuse University Press, 1968), p. 72; Thwaites, *The Jesuit Relations,* vol. 3, p. 74.

5. Lahontan, *New Voyages to North America,* vol. 1, pp. 415–16.

6. Thwaites, *The Jesuit Relations,* vol. 23, pp. 221–23.

7. Henry Spelman, *Relation of Virginiea* (London: Jas. F. Hunnerwell, 1872), p. 114; William Strachey, *The Historie of Travalile into Virginia Brittania* (London: Hakluyt Society, 1849), p. 84; John Dunton, *Letters from New England* (repr. New York: Burt Franklin, 1966), p. 285; William Wood, *New Englands Prospect* (Boston: Prince Society, 1865), p. 96.

8. Roger Williams, *A Key into the Language of America* (Detroit: Wayne State University Press, 1973), p. 230.

9. Nicholas Perrot, *Memoirs of the Manners, Customs, and Religion of the Savages of North America,* ed. Emma H. Blair (Cleveland: Arthur H. Clark, 1911), p. 96.

10. Francis Jennings, *The Invasion of America* (Chapel Hill: University of North Carolina, 1975), p. 57; John H. Kennedy, *Jesuit and Savage in New France* (New Haven: Yale University Press, 1950), p. 109.

11. James T. Adams, *The Founding of New England* (Boston: Atlantic Monthly Press, 1921), p. 345.

12. Kennedy, *Jesuit and Savage*, p. 60; Michael Kammen, *People of Paradox* (New York: Random House, 1973), p. 105; Thwaites, *The Jesuit Relations*, vol. 31, p. 190; Zenobins Membre, *Narrative of 1680-1681* (in the Historical Collection of Louisiana, 1852), p. 151; Gabriel Sagard, *The Long Journey to the Country of the Hurons*, trans. H. H. Laughton (Toronto: Champlain Society, 1939), p. 96. See also *Relation de la Louisianne*, trans. John R. Swanton (American Anthropological Association, 1918), p. 66.

13. Thwaites, *The Jesuit Relations*, vol. 13, p. 131; vol. 8, p. 143; vol. 10, p. 15.

14. Jasper Danckaerts, *Journal*, ed. B. B. Jones and F. J. Jameson (New York: Barnes & Noble, 1913), p. 274.

15. Max Weber, *The Protestant Ethic and the Spirit of Capitalism* (New York: Charles Scribner's Sons, 1958), p. 157; Emil Oberholzer, *Delinquent Saints* (New York: Columbia University Press, 1956), p. 259; Roger Williams, *A Key into the Language of America*, p. 231. See also Winton U. Solberg, *Redeem the Time: The Puritan Sabbath in Early America* (Cambridge, Mass.: Harvard University Press, 1977); George Eisen, "The Concept of Time, Play, and Leisure in Early Protestant Religious Ethic," *Play & Culture* 4 (August 1991): 223-36.

16. Wood, *New Englands Prospect*, p. 88; Weber, *The Protestant Ethic*, p. 167.

17. Nancy Struna, "Puritans and Sport: The Irretrievable Tide of Change" (paper delivered at the Fourth Annual NASSH Convention, Oregon, 1976), p. 13; Williams, *A Key into the Language of America*, p. 23.

18. K. van Rensselaer, *Letters* (Albany: n.p., 1908), pp. 686-88 and 694-95; "Letter of Isaack de Rasieres to Samuel Blommaert," in *Narratives of New Netherlands*, ed. F. J. Jameson (New York: Charles Scribner's Sons, 1909), p. 112; van der Donck, *Description of the New Netherlands*, p. 94.

19. William Penn, *The Frame of the Government of Pennsilvania* (London: n.p. 1682), p. 11; William Penn, *Works*, 2 vols. (London: J. Sowle, 1726), vol. 1, p. 729.

20. Margaret Bacon, *The Quiet Rebel* (New York: Basic Books, 1969), p. 47; William Penn, *A Letter from William Penn* (London: Andrew Sowle, 1683), p. 6.

21. Edward Winslow, *Relation*, in *Chronicles of the Pilgrim Fathers of the Colony of Plymouth*, ed. Alexander Young (Boston: Charles C. Little and James Brown, 1841), pp. 307-8; Wood, *New Englands Prospect*, p. 74; Thwaites, *The Jesuit Relations*, vol. 10, p. 81.

22. Thwaites, *The Jesuit Relations*, vol. 10, p. 187; see also vol. 14, p. 81 and vol. 17, p. 201; Pierre de Charlevoix, *Journal of a Voyage to North America*, 2 vols. (London: Printed for R & J Dodsley, 1761), vol. 2, p. 15-16; Daniel Gookin, *Historical Collections of the Indians of New England* (Boston: collection of the Massachusetts Historical Society, 1792), p. 153; de Rasieres, in *Narratives of New Netherlands*, p. 116.

23. Marc Lescarbot, *The History of New France*, trans. H. P. Biggar, 3 vols. (Toronto: Champlain Society, 1907), vol. 3, p. 197; Thwaites, *The Jesuit Relations*, vol. 16, p. 199; John Lawson, *A New Voyage to Carolina*, ed. H. T. Lefler (Chapel Hill: University of North Carolina Press, 1967), p. 178.

24. Williams, *A Key into the Language of America*, pp. 229-30.

25. Thomas Shepard, *The Clear Sun-shine of the Gospel Breaking Forth upon the Indians in New England* (London: Cotes, 1648), pp. 27-28.

26. Father Chrestien Le Clercq, *New Relation of Gaspesia,* trans. W. P. Ganong (New York: Greenwood Press, 1968), pp. 294–95; *Relation de la Louisianne,* trans. Swanton, p. 65; Sagard, *The Long Journey,* p. 97.

27. Paul Du Ru, *Journal,* trans. R. L. Butler (Chicago: Caxton Club, 1934), p. 52; Thwaites, *The Jesuit Relations,* vol. 16, p. 201.

28. Jennings, *The Invasion of America,* p. 57; see also Kennedy, *Jesuit and Savage,* p. 93.

29. Nancy Howell, "Sports and Games in Canadian Life Prior to Confederation," *Proceedings of the 1st International Seminar on the History of Physical Education and Sport* (Wingate Institute, Israel, 1968), no. 17; Nicolas Denys, in *Description of the New Netherlands,* pp. 416–17.

30. Winslow, *Relation,* p. 46; Peter Lindström, *Geographia Americae with An Account of the Delaware Indians* (Philadelphia: Swedish Colonial Society, 1928), p. 258; Lionel Wafer, *A New Voyage & Description of the Isthmus of America* (Cleveland: Burrows Bros., 1903), p. 152.

31. Lindström, *Geographia Americae,* p. 258; William Penn, *Account of the Leni Lenape or Delaware Indians,* ed. A. C. Myers (Somerset, N.J.: Middle Atlantic Press, 1970), p. 49; Charles Wolley, *A Two Years' Journal in New York* (Cleveland: Burrows Bros., 1902), p. 54.

32. Van der Donck, *Description of the New Netherlands,* pp. 71–72.

2

Forty-Eighters and the Rise of the Turnverein Movement in America

Robert Knight Barney

One of the most fascinating aspects of American culture is a societal penchant for sport and physical exercise, a preoccupation that has grown enormously in the twentieth century. The resulting national exercise craze is one that reflects versatility, which is in harmony with a cultural identity often said to have evolved in "melting pot" fashion. The initiatives from which the phenomenon of organized physical activity evolved were enacted largely in nineteenth-century American history. Among the most important of those early American exercise initiatives was the German-American *turnverein* experience.[1] In fact, aside from the sports and games movement during the latter part of the nineteenth-century, few developments rivaled the contributions made by Turners to nineteenth-century physical education and exercise programs, contributions that demonstrated elaborate organization, intense zeal, and rigorous discipline, all cast in the unique spirit of Germanic thoroughness and efficiency.

FORTY-EIGHTERS IN AMERICA

The most intense period of German immigration to America began early in the Antebellum period (1850–1860) and included a group of individuals who were vigorous adherents of the Friedrich Ludwig Jahn-inspired turnverein movement in Germany. In America these immigrants were often referred to as Forty-Eighters. In effect, they were the defeated, exiled, and still inflamed products of the Republican uprisings in Germany during the years 1848 and 1849. When Forty-Eighters immigrated to America, they carried with them, as part of their "cultural baggage," a distinct penchant for physical fitness gained through exercise based on Jahn's gymnastics principles. Their enthusiasm for physical fitness was complemented by energetic political pursuit of the undeniable rights of the common man and strong Republican-type government supporting the ideals of democracy.

Though the German verb *turnen* was known in America prior to the arrival of the first Forty-Eighters, the word *turnverein* (literally, "to do gymnastic exercise") was missing from the glossary of words denoting German social institutions found in the United States before 1848. German gymnastics had been present in embryo form in America since the early 1820s following the arrival in the United States of Charles Beck and Charles Follen, each of whom had been a disciple of Jahn. However, it was not until organizational efforts by Forty-Eighters were initiated that the uniquely German organizations called turnvereins were spawned in the United States. The evolution of the turnverein phenomenon in America exactly and methodically paralleled the emigration of Forty-Eighter Turner refugees from Germany, some of whom arrived in America as early as 1848 and 1849, but most of whom immigrated after 1850.[2]

The first turnverein established in America is generally considered to have been the Cincinnati Turnverein, formed in November 1848 by a group of that city's Forty-Eighter German immigrants. They were inspired and organized by Friedrich Hecker, adored patriot leader of revolutionary forces defeated at Baden in South Germany earlier that same year. Following initial turnverein organization experiments in the American Midwest, the movement spread rapidly to areas of the country wherever Forty-Eighters settled. The increase in the number of turnvereins established in America before the Civil War correlated closely with the increase in the numbers of Forty-Eighters who immigrated to the United States. Between 1848 and 1851, for example, twenty-two individual turnvereins were organized, and a National Turnerbund concept developed. By 1853 the number of turnvereins in America had increased to seventy. By the end of the decade, at which time Forty-Eighter immigration had all but ceased, there were 157 turnvereins in existence, embracing a membership of roughly 10,000 Turners.[3]

Not all Forty-Eighters were Turners; neither were all turnverein members Forty-Eighters. But the record clearly indicates that the nation's first turnvereins were products of Forty-Eighter organizational energy. For instance, a quantitative analysis of 300 abbreviated biographies of Forty-Eighter immigrants published by A. E. Zucker shows that eastern turnvereins located in the cities of Boston, New York, Philadelphia, Baltimore, Washington, and Pittsburgh were organized by Forty-Eighters. West of the Alleghany-Appalachian Mountains, in the so-called bastion of Forty-Eighter influence, turnvereins in the cities of Cleveland, Columbus, Detroit, Milwaukee, Davenport, Chicago, St. Louis, Cincinnati, Louisville, and New Orleans were formed by Forty-Eighter arrivals from Germany. Their influence was significant in the extension of the movement to rural areas of the American West.

When one considers the total number of Forty-Eighters who immigrated to the United States between 1848 and 1860, especially when that figure is measured against the total German immigration for the same period, it is remarkable that such a small group played such a major role in establishing and/or perpetuating German cultural traditions in America. But this was most certainly the case. Of slightly more than 1,000,000 Germans who immigrated to America between 1848 and 1860, a total of 10,000, at best, may have been Forty-Eighters.[4]

Although some Forty-Eighters settled in the large port cities of the northeastern United States—Boston, New York, Philadelphia, and Baltimore—the larger percentage of them pushed westward in company with thousands of German immigrants seeking land for farming, in fact, those whose emigration from the Fatherland was motivated by economic factors rather than political disenchantment or persecution. After initial experiments at farming, for which they had little experience or proclivity, Forty-Eighters settled at last in villages, towns, and developing cities along the length and breadth of the Ohio-Missouri-Mississippi River valleys, from Wisconsin and Minnesota in the north to Louisiana and Texas on the Gulf Coast of the Deep South.

FORTY-EIGHTER TURNERS AND
SOCIO-POLITICAL IDEOLOGY

Various investigators of the German element in the United States have described the Forty-Eighter as male, in his twenties, unmarried, in excellent physical condition through training in gymnastics, classically educated, politically enlightened and motivated, not without a modicum of financial means and, quite likely, desirous of returning to Germany as soon as possible in order to join once again the forces of revolution against the hated German princes and the influence of their corrupt power. In their newly adopted country, Forty-Eighters were active in the establishment of German culture and in the continued cultivation of those German social institutions already in place. Through journalistic expression in German-language newspapers, many of which they themselves established, Forty-Eighters created an effective forum for expression of their liberal views. The turnverein, on the other hand, offered Forty-Eighters an organizational center for espousing the social and political causes in which they believed so strongly. A consistent theme of purpose pervaded the declarations of Forty-Eighter Turners who commented on the purposes of the turnverein. Wilhelm Rapp, writing in the *Turn-Zeitung*, the national Turner newspaper, declared that the objective of the turnverein should be a quest for political, social, and religious reform. To the noble Friedrich Hecker, the turnverein was "the carrier, developer and apostle of the free spirit." August Willich, whom Karl Marx described as "a Communist with a heart," believed the purpose of the turnverein was "to carry the red flag of socialism." It is evident that early German-American turnverein objectives were focused primarily on social and political reform, and secondarily on gymnastics development. Thus America's first turnvereins became forums for Forty-Eighter espousal and demonstration of a liberal and sometimes radical social and political creed, often at odds with conservative customs and values held by native and foreign-born Americans alike, including older, well-established German Americans who were products of earlier immigration patterns.[5]

As is often the case in history, the human element responsible for change in society is that element which has had the benefit of an education. The Forty-Eighters in America fitted such a pattern. Their educational background in Germany, together with their chosen occupations in the United States, fitted them well for idealistic quests in America. Almost all Forty-Eighter immigrants were casualties of the political turmoil of 1848 and 1849 in Germany, during which time most were students in German universities. Upon arrival in America many sought job-related activities that might reasonably expect to exert influence on German-American thought and practice. Zucker's biographies again provide insight into Forty-Eighter occupations in America. Roughly two-thirds of the sample had direct association with professions described by the words journalist, physician, teacher, Turner, lawyer, businessman, and author.[6]

Through editorials written in German-language newspapers, discussions, debates, public and semiprivate addresses to German Americans, and "plans for action" fomented in turnvereins, Forty-Eighters attempted to rally the type of support which they hoped, in some cases, would bring about change and, in other cases, preserve the status quo. Five areas of Forty-Eighter "cause" and "identity" deserve attention at this point. They are: (1) Nativism, (2) slavery, (3) the Civil War, (4) temperance, and (5) the turnverein and German-American community life. For each of these considerations, Forty-Eighter Turners embraced definite stances. Using their influence in the German-language press and their turnvereins as launching pads for action, zealous and effective crusades were undertaken.

Nativism

The feature of America held in highest esteem by Germans in general, and by Forty-Eighter Turners in particular, was the United States Constitution's Bill of Rights, a document that guarantees a variety of freedoms, of which freedom of speech and freedom of the press were most important to the politically disposed former revolutionaries. The key to preservation and/or modification of the Bill of Rights, in all of its ramifications, lay in the power of the ballot. A voting franchise for Germans in America had to be preserved beyond any other consideration. The credo of the American Nativist movement alarmed Germans in America, particularly with regard to the issue of voting rights for foreign-born immigrants. The concept of "America for native-born Americans" had long been present, in fact, since the first generations of British colonists had arrived in the New World. A strong Puritan influence in American life, promulgated by the pious tenets of Calvinsim, made many an American ever sensitive to the biblical prophecy of Ezekial: "I will bring strangers upon thee, the terrible of the nations, and they will draw their swords against the beauty of thy wisdom, and they shall defile thy brightness." In short, Roman Catholicism (of which there was a sizeable German representation in the United States by the 1850s), atheism (of which Forty-Eighters in particular were often accused), burdens on the American economy (which most immigrants were held as being), and social misfits in the form of "foreign anarchists" (which many Americans viewed the outspoken Forty-Eighters as being) were foremost among those concerns documenting a lengthy list of grievances held by Nativists against immigrants in general.

Though spurious and semisecret in organizational form and action prior to the 1830s, Nativism gathered momentum in the 1840s and 1850s, bursting forth on the American political scene in 1854 with the formation of the American Party. Often called Know-Nothings, candidates of the American Party gathered strong support in the industrial centers of the northeastern United States where the economic impact of immigration was felt most keenly, as well as in the South where plantation owners viewed European immigration as an unwelcome challenge to the use of a cheap, well-entrenched, time-tested, and reasonably efficient black slave labor force. Thus Nativists attempted to limit the economic and political attractiveness of America to immigrants. Their platform, undertaken with missionary zeal, was aimed at ostracizing immigrants already in America and placing American citizenship, and therefore American voting rights, beyond the reach of all but those willing to endure a lengthy, franchiseless residency period.

If the American Party had been successful in its quest, then the status of immigrants in America might well have reverted to that experienced by most Germans in their Fatherland before the political upheaval of the second half of the nineteenth century, a state of affairs that had prompted Forty-Eighters to speak out forcefully, take up arms, and, in many cases, to sacrifice life, be imprisoned, or be sent fleeing from the country of their birth and heritage.

Oddly, recently arrived Forty-Eighters could expect little help from those politically unenlightened and woefully disorganized older Germans already resident in the United States. Forty-Eighters referred to them by the term "Grays." Though certainly not oblivious to the full portent of the Nativist creed, Grays, for the most part, were stymied as to how the Nativist problem might be addressed.

Public protests against Nativism prompted by Germans rose in Milwaukee in 1843 and in Chicago a year later. Their effort was negligible. It remained for the politically conscious, action-oriented Forty-Eighters to organize and implement effective and sustained reaction. Using the German-language press, Forty-Eighters spoke out strongly against the dangers of the Know-Nothing Order and its attempted subversion of American freedom and equality for immigrant Germans. Forty-Eighters did more than combat Nativism through verbal and literary expression. They translated fiery journalism and oratory into deed. Using the turnvereins as training centers for physical fitness and military preparation, Forty-Eighters protected life and property, as well as creed, in armed confrontation with Know-Nothing factions in New York (1850), Hoboken, New Jersey (1851), St. Louis (1852), New Orleans (1853), Louisville (1855), Covington, Kentucky (1856), and Baltimore (1858).

Although Forty-Eighter action failed to eradicate anti-immigrant feelings from American political, economic, and social thought and action during the Antebellum period, it was successful in neutralizing Nativism to the point where it was effectively drowned in the welter of larger and more critical issues associated with the Civil War. After the war, reconstruction of a fractured country occupied the efforts of politicians. There was little energy and small resource for impassioned Nativism in the scheme of post-war regional and national priorities.

Slavery

The issue of slavery was second in importance to the problem of Nativism; indeed, the slavery controversy became the foremost barrier against American sectional unity during the Antebellum period. And German Americans, largely due to Forty-Eighter Turner zeal, were drawn into the controversy even though most of them would have preferred to remain neutral on the subject. Most Germans who immigrated to America for economic reasons, particularly the greater number of them who settled in the urban centers of the northeastern United States, were not aroused by the morality of slavery, which they viewed as a states' rights issue. The urban German immigrant's apathy toward the abolition of slavery rested on a fundamental economic question of concern to all immigrants, regardless of ethnic origin. The all too ominous specter of abolition was the release of thousands of freed black slaves into an already saturated immigrant labor market.

But German immigrants to the American West feared a different set of circumstances. The quest for farms and free homesteads in the West made it important that the extension of slavery from the South to the western states and territories be denied. If slavery was extended to the West, then German opportunity for landholding and agricultural jobs would most certainly be compromised in much the same manner as they had been in the South, which was the chief reason why German immigrants generally avoided settling there. Even though faced with this fact, most Germans in the West were slow in reacting to the cause of abolition. As with the threat of Nativism, action by Forty-Eighters, much of it germinating in turnvereins, at last stirred German reaction on the slavery issue.

The Forty-Eighter, opposing slavery on moral conviction rather than on economic grounds, ignored few opportunities to protest the South's "peculiar institution." Forty-Eighter Friedrich Kapp concluded that in the United States "Anglo-Saxons and Germans were destined, after a separation of fifteen-hundred years, to reunite in the common struggle to extend the frontiers of human liberty." In the New York *Abendzeitung*, Kapp editorialized: "The problem of slavery is not the problem of the Negro. It is the eternal conflict between a small privileged class and the great mass of the non-privileged, the eternal struggle between aristocracy and democracy." German-American Turners, exhorted by their Forty-Eighter leadership, repudiated slavery. At their national convention in 1855, Turners inserted a strong antislavery article into the National Turnerbund constitution.[7]

Though Forty-Eighters espoused vigorous abolitionist messages, their impassioned rhetoric was received in cool fashion by many German Americans living in the West. A practical rationale, rather than moral considerations, had to exist in order for most Germans to rally behind the Forty-Eighter passion for abolition. The Kansas-Nebraska Act enacted in Congress in 1874, legislation which opened the two western territories to slavery, imperiled German landholding and farm labor opportunities in the West. This was motivation enough for most Germans in the West to embrace the cause of abolition. Then, too, the controversial act had been passed in Congress mainly because of extreme pressure exerted by southern Democrats. Thus the Democratic Party, long held by most immigrants to be the party of the common man against the political and economic privilege of the rich, became anathema for Forty-Eighters. With the establishment of the Republican Party in 1854, Forty-Eighters discovered a political body which represented beliefs, especially on the slavery issue, in keeping with their own. In eager anticipation, most Forty-Eighters joined the Republican ranks. And, using such rebukes to German Americans as that enunciated by Democratic Senator Butler of South Carolina in his successful attempt to rally support for the Kansas-Nebraska Act: "The intelligent and judicious master, having his slaves around him in Missouri and Nebraska would be as acceptable a neighbor to me . . . as one of those new immigrants . . . those from the land of the Kraut," Forty-Eighters strove to convert as many German Americans as possible from the standard of the Democrats to that of the Republicans. Concentrating their efforts in the West, Forty-Eighters achieved modest success in Minnesota, Wisconsin, Iowa, Michigan, Illinois, and Missouri, the collective result of which helped to catapult the Republicans into the national political limelight. Together with other support groups, the Forty-Eighters' prodding of German Americans toward the Republicans helped in the 1860 election of Abraham Lincoln to the presidency of the United States.[8]

The Civil War

The election of Lincoln and the Republican Party's commitment to the abolition of slavery were inspiration enough for Forty-Eighters to be among the first to enlist in the Union Army. Their volunteering was followed by the enlistment of German Americans in general. For a portrayal of German-American participation in the Civil War on the side of the Union forces, one must rely on the thorough statistical inquiry of Benjamin Gould, whose post–Civil War study was completed in 1869. Gould placed German-American enlistment at 176,817, by far the largest representation of foreign-born soldiers in the Union Army.[9]

Gould further demonstrated that German-American response toward joining the army was particularly strong in the West, most notably in Wisconsin, Illinois, Ohio, and Missouri. An obvious conclusion is that Forty-Eighters, in the area of their largest concentration and influence, once again used the German-language press to inspire and the turnverein to exhort German Americans to follow them in a crusade against slavery.

One historian of the turnverein movement in America has stated that Turners were among the very first to join the Union cause in the war between the states. In cities where turnverein membership was large enough, entire companies of Turner volunteers were organized. In smaller communities and in rural areas, Turners often became members of local military units. In 1861 the National Turnerbund executive reported that almost 6,000 Turners, of a total national membership of approximately 10,000, had joined the ranks of the Union Army. Numerous authors have pointed out that Forty-Eighters in general, and Turners in particular, contributed a significant number of officers to the Union forces, including three major-generals (Franz Sigel, Ludwig Blenker, and Carl Schurz).[10]

The German-American fighting record in the service of the Union Army during the Civil War was exemplary, as noted by several historians, particularly Wittke. Surprising to many, including traditional historians of the German-American turnverein movement, is the fact that most Turners resident in the Confederate States of America (seceders from the Union) fought for the cause of the South. In the case of Turners resident in the states of the Deep South, severe sociopolitical pressure from fellow Southerners, combined with a desire to preserve hard-won economic status, were factors which stimulated southern Turner support for the cause of the Confederacy. German-American and/or Turner companies were founded in Texas, Louisiana, Georgia, South Carolina, North Carolina, and Virginia.[11]

Temperance

If Forty-Eighters found it difficult to muster support in their defense against challenges to a number of traditional German social customs practiced in America, they encountered little resistance from German-American brethren in the quest to preserve their celebration of the Sabbath in a typically European or "continental" manner. All Germans in America, young and old, early and new arrival, men and women, Catholic and Protestant, "Gray" and "Green," were opposed to the Puritan custom of observing Sunday in strictly pious manner, that is, as a day of prayerful reflection, indeed, as "a day of gloom," rather than as a day of celebration, festival, and hearty indulgence in beer drinking. Many German Americans felt compelled to mask their normally robust Sunday activities in order to prevent the wrath and censure of Nativist followers from descending on them. As one German American facetiously remarked: "Six days shalt thou labor in the sweat of thy brow, and on the seventh shalt thou drink lager to thine heart's content, but secretly, and by theft, like the thief in the night."[12]

Political ideology expressed in the National Turnerbund's constitution addressed the problem of temperance. In 1855, at what would become an historically important national Turner convention, an amendment to the constitution was passed by an overwhelming vote: "Turners are opposed to every temperance law because they consider it undemocratic in principle, unjust, and impractical to administer."[13] Thus Turners challenged temperance openly. Retreating to the open countryside in the warm-weather months, and to their exercise halls in the winter, Turners set a German-American example of defiance to the Puritan Sabbath by engaging in merrymaking and light-hearted activity on Sundays. Speeches, parades, athletic activity, gymnastics exercise and exhibitions, banqueting, dancing, target shooting, military drilling, and vigorous beer drinking were all part of a Turner's Sabbath.

The sensitivity of Forty-Eighter Turners for their traditional continental celebration of the Sabbath was confronted time and time again by reactionary elements, especially Nativists and espousers of the temperance movement. But, whereas religious clergy may have simply railed against "the blasphemous German expression of Sunday," Nativists found such German disobedience excuse enough to march in armed protest and confrontation. Hence Turner activity in rifle shooting, military drill, and fitness exercises often bore practical results in their efforts to defend both property and creed.

The Turnverein and German-American Community Life

Few Germans living in midwestern cities during the American Antebellum period could legitimately argue against the fact that the turnverein was a critical agent for the expression of German culture and consciousness. In the turnverein's various facilities and venues, social, intellectual, artistic, and exercise programs were presented, each of pronounced German character. Collectively, such programs included craft exhibitions, parades, poetry readings, oratory and lectures, debates, theater productions, social gatherings and parties, musical concerts and recitals featuring instrumentalists, singers, and dancers, and gymnastics and athletics festivals and instructional programs.

Whereas many Germans may have differed with turnverein members on political matters, most were grateful for the work of the turnverein in matters pertaining to the retention, indeed the extension, of German culture in America. Ludwig Stierlin, patriarch historian of the German element in Louisville, Kentucky, observed that "few Germans saw fit to question, challenge, or be ungrateful for the effort displayed by Turners in preserving and advancing German culture."[14]

FORTY-EIGHTER TURNERS AND PHYSICAL FITNESS

Turner ideals on the subject of gymnastics and fitness exercise were both lofty and pronounced. The literary plea of the ancient Roman writer Juvenal, *Mens sana in corpore sano*, was adopted by Turners as their motto. The turnverein dictum, "Cultivation of rational training, both intellectual and physical for the express purpose of strengthening the national power and of fostering true patriotism," applied directly to Turner lifestyle.[15] Rational training of the intellect was attempted through the constant application of resources and energy to areas of literary and verbal discourse: discussion, debate, argument, and persuasion. Rational training of the physical was achieved through the

organization and implementation of gymnastics instruction and exercise patterned after the time-tested teachings of Father Jahn and his disciples. In the
best of times, during those periods when the energy- and resource-draining
implications of social and political upheaval were absent, gymnastics occupied
the center of attention in turnverein activity. Unhappily for the history of physical education in America, the Antebellum and Civil War periods were not
"the best of times" for turnverein gymnastics. Gymnastics were relegated to a
secondary position in turnverein priorities during the two periods. Further,
gymnastics served as "a means to an end" in Turner philosophy and practice.
The "end," of course, was the realization of desired social and political quests.

Despite the dilemmas posed to Turners during the Antebellum and Civil
War periods, developments materialized in turnverein gymnastics which aided
the cause of exercise and fitness in America. Such developments helped to lay
a foundation for an awareness and concern for personal health, fitness, and
physical education in the curricula of American public schools. As far as gymnastics were concerned, Forty-Eighter Turners applied their energies to four
distinct dimensions of consideration: (1) physical fitness through gymnastics
instruction and practice, (2) organization of a national body (Turnerbund) and
national exercise festivals (turnfests), (3) establishment of a nationally circu-
lated newspaper (*Turn-Zeitung*) as well as other publications for the dissemination of information on gymnastics, and (4) attempts to organize teacher-training courses for future gymnnastics teachers.

Physical Fitness/Gymnastics Instruction/Practice

From the earliest experiences of *turnen* in the Cincinnati and Louisville
turnvereins, to the exercise programs of turnverein organizations subsequently established throughout the United States, gymnastics activity served
as an agent of health and physical fitness, as well as a psychological safety valve
for temperaments often inflamed by political issues. Classes were arranged for
both boys and girls, as well as for adults. Exercises were carried out on various
pieces of apparatus, such as vaulting horses, parallel bars, inclined ladders,
hanging ropes, and balance beams. Free exercises performed with wands,
Indian clubs, and light dumbbells combined with running, jumping, and climbing activities were also present in the program, as were games testing skill, agility, strength, endurance, and courage. Of importance for males were the oblig-
atory exercises of marching and drilling with sword and musket, fencing, and
target shooting, each of which at times stimulated both the curiosity and ani-
mosity of non-German citizens in the community. In Cincinnati, for instance,
prior to the time when an indoor exercise hall was finally constructed, Turners
built a high board fence around their outdoor exercise grounds in an attempt

to prevent a deriding public from disturbing activity which both Nativists and clergymen sometimes termed "outlandish activity," at other times, "expressions of socialistic militarism."[16] There can be little doubt that the measure of fitness that Turners developed through turnverein gymnastics served them well in the demanding campaigns and field life of the Civil War.

The National Turnerbund/Turnfest

Critical on the list of important considerations for Forty-Eighter Turner achievement was the organization of individual turnvereins into one cohesive union, a consolidation inspired in part by appreciation of the proverb "in unity there is strength." Whereas the earliest individual turnverein organization attempts occurred in the West, the impetus for a national organization was spawned in eastern societies. In early July 1850, attempts were undertaken in New York to organize a national turnerbund. Later that same year, in October, the Philadelphia Turnverein convened delegates from other eastern cities and formed the United Turnvereins of North America. In 1851 an invitation was extended to all turnvereins in America to join the national body, an overture which seventy societies had accepted by 1853. By the end of the decade, a total of 150 societies comprised the national organization.

An early order of business for the Bund was the organization of national and/or regional turnfests, at which individual and mass exhibitions, demonstrations, and competitions in gymnastics activity were presented. The historic inaugural of the national turnfest tradition in America, a legacy that continues in modified fashion to this day, occurred in September 1851 in Philadelphia. The first issue of *Turn-Zeitung* reported that almost 700 Turners attended and that the historic fest had been "a complete success."[17]

In order to enhance participation by decreasing the travel burdens imposed on Turners scattered throughout America, the Turnerbund implemented a plan for staging two turnfest celebrations annually, one in the East and one in the West. Subsequently, in September 1852 the eastern edition of Turnfest II was presented in Baltimore, while in the West, Turners from thirty different societies convened in Cincinnati to participate in athletics and gymnastics competition. In 1853 the dual turnfest scheme continued. The New York Turnverein hosted the eastern aspect of Turnfest III, and Louisville provided the site for the western meeting. From the pages of the *Louisville Anzeiger*, one learns firsthand of the flamboyant events surrounding a turnfest celebration. The *Anzeiger* description of formidable welcoming ceremonies, parades, gymnastics and sports competitions, banquets, speeches, and a gala ball renders a graphic picture of the exciting and festive atmosphere prevalent at such meetings. Noting that 1,400 Turners attended the competitions, the *Anzeiger* triumphantly reported the National Bund's wisdom in awarding the festival to Louisville: "The gathering for competitive gymnastics exercises shows the high esteem accorded the Louisville Turners by other societies in the United States."[18]

Despite this kind of regional success, the Turnerbund's annual dual-turnfest scheme was shortlived, being abandoned in 1854 in favor of a formula to stage a single national turnfest each year, hosted alternately by turnvereins in the East and West. Accordingly, succeeding turnfests for the remainder of the decade were held in Philadelphia (1854), Cincinnati (1855), Pittsburgh (1856), Milwaukee (1857), Belleville, Illinois (1858), Baltimore (1859), and St. Louis (1860).

The competitive program of athletic events, organized into three classifications (juniors, actives, and seniors), included a military division featuring target shooting, fencing with sabre and foil, and bayonet thrusting. A so-called "free-turning" classification provided for competitions in wrestling, weightlifting, sprint running, hurdles racing, high jumping, javelin throwing, stone putting, swimming, and stilt walking. However, the "blue ribbon" activities of the turnfest, from the outset of its experience, were competitions in apparatus turning, specifically, rope climbing and work on the horizontal and parallel bars, swinging rings, and vaulting horse.

Turner, turnverein, and National Turnerbund preoccupation with various political agendas prevented vigorous growth in the national turnfest phenomenon during the latter part of the 1850s. And, of course, the Civil War interrupted the great festivals for a period of five years. But the turnfest's honored place in German-American turnverein life was reason enough to give top priority to its reestablishment immediately following the cessation of armed hostilities.

The *Turn-Zeitung* and Gymnastics Literature

Similar to most organizations seeking political and educational impact, the National Turnerbund applied both industry and resources toward establishing a literary organ for the dissemination of news, ideas, and messages of persuasion. The first issue of the *Turn-Zeitung* appeared on November 15, 1851. It featured illustrated text on the theory and practice of gymnastics. The content of early editions of the *Turn-Zeitung* was strongly accented toward material on physical training, especially articles written on the subject by Eduard Mueller, an early Forty-Eighter Turner immigrant to America who taught gymnastics professionally at the New York Turnverein. Mueller, a dedicated Jahn follower who continued to affect in America the peculiar character of the *Turnvater*'s hairstyle and dress, wrote one of the first substantial treatments of

German gymnastics published in America. The circulation and sale of *Das Turnen*, a 350-page, illustrated work which appeared in 1853, was disappointing. At seventy-five cents per copy, only half of an edition of 1,000 copies were sold. In the middle and latter part of the 1850s, focus on gymnastics content in the *Turn-Zeitung* was sacrificed in favor of material aimed at social and political issues of concern to Turners.[19]

Training German Gymnastics Teachers

A serious problem in the early history of German-American turnvereins concerned the lack of trained teachers to teach gymnastics to both young and adult Turners. The larger turnvereins in the United States, such as those in New York and Philadelphia, could afford to employ teachers from Germany who had received formal instruction in turnen. But few smaller societies found the means to provide such a luxury. Initially, the executive of the National Bund attempted to solve the dilemma by circulating illustrated instructional pamphlets to member organizations. Later the Bund published articles and diagrams in the *Turn-Zeitung* and commissioned Mueller to write a gymnastics textbook (*Das Turnen*). Then, too, Louis Winter, an expert Turner from Leipzig, was engaged as a "circulating" teacher of gymnastics. His mission was to visit the smaller, more isolated turnvereins in the nation and carry out instructor-training sessions. None of the Bund's approaches proved particularly successful. The problem festered; demands for qualified teachers of gymnastics increased proportionately with the noted increase in the number of newly organized turnvereins applying for Bund membership. In an attempt to meet the obvious challenge, the Bund enacted legislation at its national convention in Pittsburgh in 1856 which took a tentative step toward providing a solution: "A school shall be set up at the place where the National Executive is located, for the complete mental and physical development of Turn teachers." Unfortunately, the Cincinnati Turners, in whose city the National Committee headquarters were located in 1856–57, reported that "lack of means" prevented them from carrying out such an action. At the Rochester Convention in 1860, the National Executive once again affirmed the need to establish "a central normal school."[20]

Despite rhetoric, apology, and reaffirmation of intention, nothing developed on the issue of gymnastics teacher training until after the Civil War. The commencement of the war between the states in 1861 interrupted the planning and implementation of what might indeed have been America's first teacher-training institution for physical education.

POSTWAR: THE GILDED AGE OF
GERMAN-AMERICAN TURNVEREINS

One month before the Civil War formally ended, the National Turnerbund convened in Washington, D.C., to reestablish the organization's programs interrupted by armed hostilities. With peace restored, the Turnerbund shed its preoccupation with national politics and the issues of slavery and Nativism, favoring instead attention to endeavors less controversial and more in tune with the German-American turnverein movement's educational purposes. Principle considerations were: (1) to reenergize efforts to form a teacher-training institution for prospective instructors of German gymnastics, (2) to establish German gymnastics in America's public schools as the fundamental form of physical education, including action aimed at lobbying for enactment of state laws making the subject mandatory in school curricula, (3) to resubstantiate the national turnfest phenomenon, and (4) to increase opportunities for girls and women in turnverein/turnfest programming.

German Gymnastics Teacher Training

In November 1866 a German gymnastics teacher-training institution (the National Turnerbund Normal School) was opened in New York City, exactly ten years after a proposal for such an initiative had first been raised. The curriculum offered courses of instruction in the history and aims of German turnen, anatomy and aesthetics in their relation to gymnastics, first aid, gymnastic nomenclature, the theory of different systems, and practical instruction with special regard for the training of boys and girls. Later the school was transferred to Chicago (1870), subsequently to Milwaukee (1874), and finally to Indianapolis (1907). In time the school's activities became permanently identified with Indiana University, where it formed the seed from which the School of Physical Education evolved at that institution. By 1883 a succession of over 100 men and women graduates from the Bund's Normal School were employed as gymnastics teachers in turnvereins. They settled in such cities as Kansas City, Chicago, Rochester, Louisville, St. Louis, Milwaukee, Cleveland, Dayton, and Cincinnati, where they were instrumental in helping to introduce German gymnastics instruction into the public schools.[21]

German Gymnastics Curriculum in
American Public Schools

Dr. Edward M. Hartwell, a distinguished nineteenth-century historian of physical education, identified the American Turners as *the* most influential group in bringing about the introduction of gymnastic exercises in the nation's public school system. To aid in such a quest, delegates from the National

Turnerbund regularly attended annual meetings of the fledgling American
Association for the Advancement of Physical Education (established in 1885)
where they promoted German gymnastics as the most comprehensive form of
physical education for the nation's public school children. German-American
Turners, too, were active campaigners for the enactment of local and state
laws for mandatory physical education in school curricula. California was the
first (1863) to put such state laws in place, followed by Ohio, Illinois, Missouri,
and other midwestern states. At the local level, Carl Betz of Kansas City
(Missouri) was the first to be successful in convincing school authorities to
implement German gymnastics in the city's public schools. This occurred in
1885. The success of Betz in Kansas City was followed by identical achievements in Chicago (1886), Cleveland, Ohio and Davenport, Iowa (1887), St.
Louis, Missouri and Sandusky, Ohio (1890), and Columbus, Cincinnati, and
Dayton, Ohio, and Milwaukee, Wisconsin (1892). In the East, similar initiatives were less successful. There German exercise expression rivaled numerous alternative systems of exercise, notably, the Swedish Ling System, Danish
gymnastics, Dioclesian Lewis' system of physical education, Delsarte Gymnastics, military drill, sports and games, etc.[22]

The National Turnfest Phenomenon

Following the Civil War, the National Bund embarked on an energetic
campaign to reestablish the national turnfest phenomenon. In effect, these
colorful ethnic celebrations were the most important and visible propaganda
element of the National Turnerbund. As well, the festivals were an expression
of ethnic pride and solidarity, carefully crafted to underscore Turner allegiance to the United States. And finally, there is little doubt that the turnfests
exhibited traditional German family values, especially the disciplined and
respectful decorum demonstrated by the youthful factions of the festival participants toward their more senior peers. The atmosphere of the turnfests,
though joyous in its celebrative qualities, was also at times a somber but proud
reflection of German ethnic culture and creed. The first post-war turnfest was
celebrated in Cincinnati in early September 1865. The usual opening ceremonies and parade, the various competitions in gymnastics and other sporting
events, and the concluding grand ball and speeches were all especially festive
on that occasion; the Civil War and its grievous toll on American citizens had
ended.

Commensurate with the steady growth in the number of events and participants in the National Turnfest were the demands placed on the turnverein
responsible for hosting the grand spectacle. In time they became so burden-
some that the Bund initiated a plan whereby the celebration would occur on a

biennial basis. The first of such biennial editions of the National Turnfest was celebrated in Baltimore in June 1867. Despite this measure, like the Olympic Games of antiquity (and of the modern era, too), the Turnfest continued to expand its program of events, increase its participation numbers, and in turn be faced with a multiplication of problems associated with organization and funding. All this finally prompted the Turnerbund to abandon the biennial format in favor of a quadrennial scheme.[23] The last of the biennial affairs was held in 1881 in St. Louis; the first of the quadrennial festivals was staged in Newark, New Jersey, in 1885.

By 1870 the Turnerbund's annual turnfest had already assumed many of the characteristics which a quarter century later would be reflective of the modern Olympic Games, including: (1) a varied program of athletic competitions, (2) a model for awarding prizes, (3) a formula for staging the festival at defined periodic intervals, (4) a scheme for making the festival ambulatory across America, and (5) a place for women in the physical activity proceedings (see below). Since 1885 the gala National Turnfests have been organized almost without fail every four years, with the exception of those scheduled for the years encompassing World Wars I and II. The most recent National Turnfest was held in Indianapolis, Indiana, in the summer of 1991; the next is scheduled for Aurora, Illinois, in 1995.

Women in Turnverein/Turnfest Programming

Contrary to a generally held assumption that the German-American turnverein movement was solely a patriarchical phenomenon, members of the fairer sex, from both theoretical and practical perspective, figured prominently in turnverein activity. Beyond the insular environment of the turnverein itself, Turners stood solidly behind the rights of women in greater American society. Bothersome to Turners were such long-standing denials in American society of a woman's right to vote in public elections, her right to hold public office, and her right to be accorded equal opportunities in education.

When German-American turnvereins organized their first youth classes in music, art, literature, history, language, and gymnastics instruction, such opportunities were implemented with respect to *both* boys and girls. However, female participation in gymnastics classes was never equal to their enrollment in the other types of "cultural" courses noted above. Following the Civil War, with political issues largely put to rest, and concentration on gymnastics education for youth in the forefront of their activities, Turners sought to improve the glaringly disparate situation between the number of boys and girls enrolled in the turnverein's gymnastics classes. In April 1865, at its first National Convention since the outbreak of the Civil War, Turners convened in Washington, D.C., where it was reported that a mere fifty girls were receiving instruction in gymnastics; this was a national statistic, and represented twenty-two and twenty-eight girls in the New York and Cincinnati turnverein's classes, respectively. A year later, modest improvement was noted. According to the turnverein's national statistics for the year 1866, 120 girls were taking gymnastics instruction in classes offered by three turnvereins. But the ratio of gymnastics class membership between girls and boys (120 to 3,317) was alarming.[24]

Youths were encouraged to begin gymnastics instruction at six years of age. Boys were eager pupils; girls, less so. Turners were well aware of the fact that in order to convince public school authorities that German gymnastics exercise was a superior form of physical education for *both* boys and girls, improvement in girls' programming had to be achieved in individual turnvereins. "Girls' classes could be (made) far more popular and attractive . . . in order to impress outsiders," stated an annual report submitted at the National Turner Convention of 1870. By 1870 more improvement had been noted, even though the enrollment ratio between boys and girls hardly changed (4,770 boys, 211 girls). More encouraging was the fact that female gymnastics classes were now presented in nine different turnvereins: Boston, Chicago, Milwaukee, Cleveland, New Ulm (Minnesota), Jersey City, Detroit, New York, and Cincinnati. By 1872 the number of girls in exercise instruction classes had almost doubled (394); so, too, had the number of turnvereins offering classes for girls (18). By the late 1880s, the New York Turnverein could boast of ladies' turning classes numbering 150 participants. By 1885 the disparity between boys' and girls' turnverein gymnastics instruction was far less pronounced (12,288 to 4,005). The turnverein's gymnastics class instruction annual enrollment peaked for both boys and girls in 1905, when 18,033 boys and 10,823 girls were recorded.[25]

There is little doubt that turnvereins across the United States, from Boston to San Francisco, from Milwaukee to New Orleans, improved the awareness of, and participation in, girls' physical education in the last quarter of the nineteenth-century. As the century ended, turnverein gymnastics classes for girls and women had blossomed as more professionally trained teachers were graduated from the Bund's teacher-training institution, and as more and better instructional materials and facilities were developed.

Aside from gymnastics instruction classes for girls and young ladies, older women, too, were actively involved in turnverein matters. The right for women to be turners and turnverein members had always been asserted by both the National Bund and its individual organizations. Women organized themselves into what became known as the Turnverein Ladies' (or Women's) Auxiliary. Much of the turnverein's social calendar, for youth and adults alike, rested in the custodianship of the Ladies' Auxiliary. This was also true with respect to both social activities and arrangement matters associated with hosting local, regional, and national turnfest celebrations.

The celebration of national turnfests proved in time to be the most important indicator of female involvement in turnverein gymnastics programs. The showcasing of girls' and ladies' gymnastics at national turnfests was usually the responsibility of the host turnverein, and such a component was usually provided by enlisting the efforts of its own female gymnastics class members. The first record of such involvement, however, appears to have been a slightly different arrangement. At the national turnfest in Indianapolis in 1871, young ladies from one of the Louisville Turnverein's classes, under the direction of Turner Anthos, performed an exhibition of turning.

This girls' exercise exhibition phenomenon became regular fare at national turnfests. In 1893, at Milwaukee, hundreds of girls and women exercised with wands and Indian clubs in mass formations. Four years later, in St. Louis, ladies and girls exhibiting mass exercise techniques numbered more than 1,000. At St. Louis, too, girls and ladies joined with men and boys to form a startling mass exercise formation of over 5,000 individuals.

Girls, young ladies, and women, consistently a steadfast part of the turnfest's mass exercise exhibition dimension, realized a revolutionary development in 1921. At the national turnfest staged in Chicago that year, females, for the first time, were permitted to enter gymnastics and sports competitions for prizes. Women's competition exploded from that date on. In subsequent national turnfests held in Louisville (1926), Buffalo (1930), Cleveland (1936), and Springfield, Massachusetts (1941), women competed in such sports as track and field events, apparatus and free gymnastics, volleyball, swimming, diving, tennis, golf, and fencing.[26]

Turnverein programs in physical education and fitness for females provided a worthy model for emulation by other organizations bent on distaff exercise initiatives. And it is worthy to note here that the participation of females in the great national turnfest celebrations evolved far earlier and far more rapidly than did the same phenomenon in the modern Olympic Games. Both of these considerations are vigorous testimony to the progressive enlightenment of Turners and the German-American turnverein movement.

SUMMARY AMD CONCLUSIONS

It is apparent that the uniquely German institutions called turnvereins, established for the first time in America during the Antebellum period, were distinct products of Forty-Eighter vision and energy. Forty-Eighter immigrants arriving from Germany, inflamed with the revolutionary spirit, encountered in their new land many of the abuses to human liberty and equality against which they had previously raised "sword, musket, pen, and voice." Though gymnastics exercise and training were cornerstone considerations for Forty-Eighter Turners in the planning, implementation, and development of turnvereins, sociopolitical issues of the 1850s rapidly commanded major portions of their energy and resources. Using several means available to them, of which two forums, the German-language press and the turnverein were the most critical, Forty-Eighter Turners were generally successful in securing their aims: (l) neutralization of the Nativist movement and retention of voting rights, (2) support for and election of a Republican president, (3) the ultimate abolition of slavery, (4) maintenance of the right to celebrate the Sabbath in a continental manner, (5) demonstration of their "active commitment to cause" through service in the Civil War armies of both the North and the South, and (6) providing leadership to German Americans toward preserving and extending German culture and customs in the United States.

Forty-Eighter passion for involvement in American socio political issues relegated gymnastics to the background of turnverein activity until the postwar years of nineteenth-century America. Despite its secondary priority in the greater scheme of turnverein activity during the Antebellum and Civil War years, gymnastics experienced modest development. Forty-Eighters were successful in establishing a body of gymnastics literature in the form of pamphlets, diagrams, newspaper articles, and books. Gymnastics classes for male and female youths and adults were organized, along with such military-oriented activities as marching, drilling, fencing, and target shooting. And, finally, preliminary plans were made for the establishment of a gymnastics teacher-training course of study. Though gymnastics were often compromised during the period addressed, the turnverein investment in them paid handsome dividends in the last third of the century.

By the late 1850s the commanding influence of Forty-Eighter Turner membership in America had withered noticeably. The first indication that a cultural transition was under way, that is, that turnverein leadership in the United States would ultimately be assumed by American-born, non–Forty-Eighter elements, appeared in 1858 when the executive committee of the National Bund's Western Association reported that fifteen new turnvereins had been organized in the West by Turners of native-American birth. As the years passed, such a phenomenon became the rule rather than the exception. By 1872 the executive committee of the National Bund (by then known as the North American Gymnastic Union) observed the following: "The Turners of America have nothing in common with the Turners of the old fatherland, except the system of physical training." Such a proclamation made by the Bund at any time during the formative years of the German-American turnverein experience, immersed as it was in the political atmosphere of Antebellum America, would surely have induced cries of heresy from Forty-Eighter Turners.

Even though Forty-Eighter imagination, passion, and action-oriented energy had been diluted from turnverein "thought and practice" by 1872, the memory of their legacy lingered: "Of our endeavors for reform in political, religious, and social fields, of the struggle against corruption and slavery in all forms, the Turners in Germany know nothing, although this *has been* the object and the inspiration of our Turnerbund."[27]

As the nineteenth-century drew to a close, the number of turnvereins and Turners in America had increased in phenomenal fashion. By 1895 the Bund reported 314 individual societies, embracing a collective membership of approximately 40,000 Turners.[28] By 1920 the number of turnvereins in America had decreased to less than 200, and the National Turnerbund membership to less than 33,000. The zenith of the German turnverein movement in America had passed. The history of the German-American turnverein movement can be likened to a human life cycle. The span of years between 1848 and 1860, featuring the Forty-Eighter period of turnverein history can be equated to its infant and adolescent period, featuring many of those less than gracious characteristics of youth: impetuosity, pugnaciousness, inconsideration, impatience, intolerance, temper, and stubbornness. The Forty-Eighters embodied all those qualities. But they also represented many of the more admirable character traits found in youth, such as spontaneity, curiosity, joyfulness, verve, industry, and sense of mission and dedication as yet unaffected by the fatigue and multiplying personal responsibilities of advancing years. The post–Civil War years, the remainder of the nineteenth-century, and the first decade of the twentieth-century before World War I featured the turnverein movement's most robust years of growth and activity. Those years can be likened to a human being's full adulthood and maturity stage, with all the energy and productivity therein expected and usually produced. The years between the two great World Wars, featuring as they did the rapid evolution of a transformation away from deeply rooted Germanic customs and institutions toward rapid American acculturalizaton, obviously portrays the "preretirement" phase of the life cycle, indeed, an abating of all the intensities noted in earlier times. From mid–twentieth-century to the present, the turnverein movement can be seen to be in full retirement; it is certainly there for the viewing, but it is only a shadow of its once prominent presence in days which now seem so long ago. The human life cycle, of course, ends in death. Be that as it may, the turnverein movement in contemporary America is not quite ready for its obituary to be noted. Despite a continuing decline in the number of turnvereins now present in the United States (approximately sixty), despite shrinking membership in the national organization (presently about 14,000), despite national turnfest celebrations that pale in comparison to those of the late nineteenth and early twentieth-centuries, despite an erosion of turnverein activities culturally German in favor of those typically American, despite anti-German feeling expressed against German institutions by many Americans during the periods of two great World Wars, despite an explosion of alternative attractions in sport and exercise for their youth, indeed, despite all, Turners and their turnvereins survive.

NOTES

1. For a survey of the historiography of the turnverein movement in North America, see Robert K. Barney, "The German-American Turnverein Movement: Its Historiography in North America," in *Turnen and Sport*, ed. Roland Naul (Münster/New York: Waxmann Verlag, 1991), pp. 3–20.

2. Erich Geldbach, "The Beginnings of German Gymnastics in the United States," *Journal of Sport History* 3 (Winter 1976): 236–72; Carl Wittke, *Refugees of Revolution* (Philadelphia: University of Pennsylvania Press, 1952), p. 3.

3. See Leonard Koester, "The First Turner Society in America," in *Louisville Turners: A Review of Our First Hundred Years* (Louisville, Kentucky: 1950), pp. 5–9; Robert Knight Barney, "America's First Turnverein: Commentary in Favor of Louisville, Kentucky," *Journal of Sport History* 11 (Spring 1984): 134–37; Henry Metzner, *History of the American Turners*, 3rd rev. ed. (Rochester, N.Y.: National Council of American Turners, 1974), pp. 8–9; Fred Eugene Leonard and George B. Affleck, *The History of Physical Education* (Philadelphia: Lea and Febiger, 1947), p. 295.

4. A. E. Zucker, ed., *The Forty-Eighters* (New York: Columbia University Press, 1950), pp. 269–357; Albert Bernhardt Faust, *The German Element in the United States*, vol. 1 (New York: Steuben Society of America, 1927), p. 582; Lavern J. Rippley, *The German Americans* (Boston: Twayne Publishers, 1976), p. 52. For a more conservative estimate, see Zucker, p. 45.

5. See Joseph Wandel, *The German Dimension in American History* (Chicago: Nelson Hall, 1979), pp. 81–82; Ripley, *German Americans*, pp. 51–52; Zucker, *Forty-Eighters*, pp. 50–51; and Wittke, *Refugees*, pp. 4–5, 92–108; *Turn-Zeitung*, November 15, 1851; *Friedrich Hecker und sein Antheil an der Geschichte Deutschland und Amerikas* (Cincinnati, 1881), pp. 62–71; cited by Wittke, p. 152.

6. See Zucker, *Forty-Eighters*, p. 270.

7. See Herbert Weaver, "Foreigners in Ante-Bellum towns of the Lower South," *Journal of Southern History* 13 (1947): 62–73; Wittke, *Refugees*, p. 191; Lawrence S. Thompson and Frank Braun "The Forty-Eighters in Politics," in Zucker, *Forty-Eighters*, p. 121; *Minutes of the National Turner Convention*, recorded by the National Executive Committee, Buffalo, New York, September 1855. For an analysis of the slavery issue in the internal politics of the National Turnerbund, see Robert Knight Barney, "German Turners in American Domestic Crisis," *Stadion* 4 (1978): 344–57.

8. Richard Connor, *The German-American* (Boston: Little, Brown and Company, 1968), p. 128. For a comprehensive analysis of the influence of the German vote in the West in the election of Lincoln, see W. E. Dodd, "The Fight for the Northwest, 1860," *American Historical Review* 16 (July 1911): 774–88; Donnal V. Smith, "Influence of the Foreign-Born of the Northwest in the Election of 1860," *Mississippi Valley Historical Review* 19 (September 1932): 192–204; and Joseph Schafer, "Who Elected Lincoln?" *American Historical Review* 47 (October 1941): 51–63.

9. Benjamin Apthorp Gould, *Investigations in the Military and Anthropological Statistics of American Soldiers* (New York: United States Sanitary Commission, 1869), p. 27.

10. Metzner, *History*, p. 17. *Minutes of the National Turner Convention*, recorded by the National Executive Committee, Rochester, New York, July 1860. For a well-documented account of German-American officer leadership in the Civil War, see Wittke, *Refugees*, pp. 221–43.

11. J. G. Rosengarten, *The German Soldier in the Wars of the United States* (Philadelphia: J. B. Lippincott, 1886), pp. 76–86. For a description and analysis of the German-American Turners in the Deep South during the late Antebellum and Civil War periods, see Robert Knight Barney, "German-American Turnvereins and Socio-Politico-Economic Realities in the Antebellum and Civil War Upper and Lower South," *Stadion* 10 (1984):135–81. For a specific case study underscoring Turner loyalty to and action for the cause of the Confederacy, see K. B. Wamsley, "Loyal to the Confederacy: Galveston, Texas Turners and National Turnerbund Ideology, 1840–1865" (M. A. thesis, University of Western Ontario, 1987).

12. Quotation cited by Oscar Handlin in *This Was America* (Cambridge, Mass.: 1949), pp. 262–63.

13. *Minutes of the National Turner Convention*, recorded by the National Executive Committee, Buffalo, New York, September 1855.

14. Ludwig Stierlin, *The State of Kentucky and the City of Louisville: With Special Consideration of the German Element, Part I*, unpublished manuscript, Louisville, 1873 (English trans. John J. Weisert in 1976 of Stierlin's original work in German), p. 209.

15. "One Hundred Years of American Turnerism," *Cincinnati Central Turners* (One Hundredth Anniversary Program), 1948, p. 22.

16. Wandel, *The German Dimension*, p. 91.

17. Leonard and Affleck, *Physical Education*, p. 295. In the year of its founding the National Turnerbund was named the *United Turnvereine of North America*. In 1851 its name was changed to *Socialistischer Turnerbund*, in 1865 to *North American Gymnastic Union*, in 1919 to *American Gymnastic Union*, and in 1935 to *American Turners*. *Turn-Zeitung*, November 15, 1851.

18. See Metzner, *History*, p. 10; *Louisville Anzeiger*, May 31, 1853.

19. Zucker, *Forty-Eighters*, p. 321. The first treatment of German gymnastics published in America was, in effect, Charles Beck's translation into English of Jahn's *Treatise on Gymnastics*. Beck's work, *A Treatise on Gymnastics, Taken Chiefly from the German of F. L. Jahn*, was published by Simeon Butler of Northampton, Massachusetts in 1828. Eduard Mueller, *Das Turnen* (New York: Buchdruckerei von John Weber, 1853); Leonard and Affleck, *Physical Education*, p. 297.

20. *Minutes of the National Turner Convention*, recorded by the National Executive Committee, Pittsburgh, Pennsylvania, 1856; Detroit, Michigan, 1857; and Rochester, New York, 1860.

21. See Fred Eugene Leonard, *A Guide to the History of Physical Education* (Philadelphia/New York: Lea & Febiger, 1923), p. 297. For a thorough history of the events detailing the evolution of Indiana University's School of Physical Education from the National Turnerbund's Normal School, see Emil Rinsch, *The History of the Normal College of the American Gymnastic Union of Indiana University, 1866–1966* (Bloomington, Indiana: Indiana University Press, 1966). See also Robert Knight Barney, "German Turners in America: Their Role in Nineteenth Century Exercise Expression and Physical Education Legislation," in *A History of Physical Education and Sport in the United States and Canada*, ed. Earle F. Zeigler (Champaign, Illinois: Stipes Publishing Company, 1975), p. 118.

22. Zucker, *Forty-Eighters,* p.109; Robert Knight Barney, "A Historical Reinterpretation of the Forces Underlying the First State Legislation for Physical Education in the Public Schools of the United States," *Research Quarterly* 44 (October 1973): 346–60, 305.

23. Dr. Edward Hitchcock, "Reports of the Special Committee on Observation," *Twenty-Sixth National Festival of the North American Gymnastic Union* (St. Louis: Executive Board Turnerbund, 1893). For more on this, see Robert K. Barney, "For Such Olympic Games: German-American Turnfests as Preludes to the Modern Olympic Games," in *Sport: The Third Millennium*, ed. F. Landry, M. Landry, and M. Yerles (Quebec: University of Laval Press, 1991), pp. 698–705.

24. *Minutes of the National Turner Convention*, recorded by the National Executive Committee, Washington, D.C., April 1865 and St. Louis, April 1866.

25. *Minutes of the National Turner Convention*, recorded by the National Executive Committee, Pittsburgh, Pennsylvania, May 1870 and Louisville, Kentucky, May 1872; George Brosius, *Fifty Years Devoted to the Cause of Physical Culture, 1864–1914* (Milwaukee: Germania Publishing, 1914), p. 20; Leonard, *Guide,* pp. 296, 306.

26. *Minutes of the National Turner Convention*, recorded by the National Executive Council, Indianapolis, Indiana, 1871; *26th Turnfest of the North American Turnerbund* (Milwaukee: Ring, Fowle, 1893), pp. 47–53; *Illustrated Souvenir of the 27th National Festival of the North American Gymnastic Union* (St. Louis: Western Engraving, 1897), pp. 34–36, 45–47, 50–54, 58–60; *The First Hundred Years, 1848–1948, Cincinnati Central Turners* (Cincinnati: Cincinnati Central Turners, 1948), p. 33; *Official Souvenir and History of the Thirty-third National Turnfest of the American Turnerbund* (Louisville: Standard Printing, 1926); *Program of the Thirty-fourth National Turnfest of the American Turnerbund* (Buffalo: Buffalo Turnverein, 1930); and *American Turners: Thirty-sixth National Turnfest* (Springfield, Mass.: Wisly-Brooks, 1941).

27. *Minutes of the Western Turner Convention*, recorded by the Western Association Executive Committee, Indianapolis, Indiana, 1858; *Minutes of the National Turner Convention*, recorded by the National Executive Committee, 1872. Leonard and Affleck, *Physical Education*, p. 310.

28. Leonard and Affleck, *Physical Education*, p. 310.

3

A Home in the South: The Turners of Galveston, Texas, 1840–65

K. B. Wamsley

In the body of literature describing the nineteenth-century experience of German-American immigrants, particularly the Turners, there are a number of discrepancies surrounding various Antebellum and Civil War issues. Many scholars have emphasized a countrywide pattern of universal thought and action by Turners during this most disruptive period in United States history. More recent studies, however, document a blatant regional disparity in Turner behavior. In light of this dilemma, it is the intent of this study to document the German-American immigrant experience in a southern city through an examination of the social and political initiatives of the Turners. Adaptation to a new home and emergence as an active political and economic force in the community are factors which provide a possible explanation for Turner attitudes toward particular issues of the period.

There is little doubt that German immigrants contributed immensely to the establishment of physical and intellectual traditions in cities across the United States during the nineteenth-century. Through the establishment of social and political clubs, especially the turnverein, newly arrived German Americans secured immigrant political rights, promoted physical fitness, and encouraged an appreciation for education and German culture wherever they settled. Historians of the German-American Turner movement have concluded that political and moral postures of all Turners were universal throughout the United States during the Antebellum and Civil War periods. Such scholars contend that the Turners adhered to National Turnerbund or central governing body principles which included adopting an abolitionist stance on slavery, supporting Abraham Lincoln in the election of 1860, and fighting for the Union Army during the Civil War. Further analysis suggests, however, that the politics of the Turners was mediated by dominant economic structures and relationships fundamental to particular regions of the country.

Through a case study examination of the New Orleans Turnverein, Barney challenged the universality thesis by hypothesizing that conformity to environmental pressure was the greatest influence on the southern Turner. He suggests that, in general, southern Turners responded to various social, political, and economic pressures in selecting their political and military stance during the Antebellum period. To further examine this controversial issue, other Turnvereins in southern locations must be investigated. The Deep South city of Galveston, Texas, was selected for this study, particularly because of its location, large German population, and established turnverein.

Immigrants from the Germanic states, France, Ireland, Spain, and Italy, as well as native-born Americans comprised the cultural make-up of the port city of Galveston. Along with harbor and shipping facilities, the most pervasive commercial enterprises of Galveston were the exporting and importing of commodities to and from European locations and the northern and eastern states of America. Throughout the 1850s millions of dollars worth of goods—cotton, sugar, molasses, hides, wool, wheat, tobacco, and beef—were shipped out of Galveston. As well as the shipping industry and its affiliated companies, a variety of shops, stores, professional services, and businesses belonged to the city's economic community.[1]

A group of wealthy, native–born American families obtaining income from the shipping and transportation industries, plantation productivity, newspaper publishing, and mercantile pursuits maintained a dominant political and economic status in Galveston. The city's political offices rotated consistently among representatives of the leading families. Galveston newspapers echoed the boundaries of political discussion in the South and were utilized to gain votes for candidates in the city, state, and federal elections. The newspapers with the largest circulation in the city were the Galveston *News*, Galveston *Civilian*, and *Die Union*. Other contemporary issues discussed through the newspaper medium were slavery, temperance, foreign affairs, exercise, sport, and cultural activity in the city.

It was estimated that the total population of Galveston during the 1850s was one-third to one-half German. The newspapers reported briefly on the immense flow of German immigrants to Texas throughout the 1840s and 1850s.[2] Hamilton Stuart, editor of the *Civilian*, patronizingly harmonized that the Germans were a respectable contingent in the city: "The German emigrants... are as fine looking people as we wish to see make their homes among us... habits of industry, economy and perseverance... and succeed better as a body in this country, than almost any other class."[3]

Institutions that were established by the Galveston Germans included schools, churches, a variety of social clubs, and a Reading Room. The first German Evangelical Church (Protestant) was founded in 1850 and the German Catholics established St. Joseph's Church in 1859. Also during the 1850s, the German Lutheran Church was established. The German Reading Room contained several hundred volumes and employed a full-time librarian. Originally called the *Zeitung*, the German newspaper in Galveston was purchased in the mid–fifties by Ferdinand Flake who renamed it *Die Union*. Stuart referred to the paper as "one of the best papers published in the German language in the South." German social clubs in Galveston included the German Friendship Society, Casino Association, Tivoli Society, Herman Lodge, and Turners' Association. The Tivoli Society, composed of some sixty German members, was organized to "present amateur theatricals." The Galveston Turnverein was the most prominent of the German clubs during the 1850s in terms of membership, public activity, and newspaper acknowledgment.[4]

It is evident that some German Turners immigrated to Galveston in the late 1830s and early 1840s. These Turners joined fellow Germans who traveled to Texas for economic reasons. In all probability they were not political refugees. However, like Forty-Eighter Turner immigrants arriving later, they were politically oriented intellectuals, concerned with the rights of Germans in Galveston.[5] As early as 1845, a German political society held regular meetings at Beisner's Hotel in Galveston. The society acknowledged that Anglo-Americans exercised control over the country's government. Even so, members pledged a passive cultural resistance, to act as faithful Democrats, not seeking to form a separate German state. In this sense, the turnverein and its members served an integrative function, helping German immigrants adapt to the dominant political and economic structures of the southern states. In a December 1845 meeting, presided over by Turner J. E. Rump, it was resolved by the society to translate the Constitution of Texas into German so that immigrants could understand their rights and duties as citizens.[6] Rump, with the assistance of "leading mercantile members" of the community, persuaded the Texas Supreme Court at Galveston to grant the County Court a right to issue letters of citizenship to immigrants in the city. Thus immigrants obtained the right to vote one year after their arrival in Galveston.

The Galveston Turnverein was established at Theron's Hall in 1851. Through the 1850s the membership grew to 250. The Turners held regular meetings on the first Thursday of each month, but the hall was open daily for the use of its members. The purpose of the club was "to develop the physical and mental faculties." Apparatus gymnastics were taught to active Turners by Turner Jordan, professor of gymnastics.[7] Turner Billig was responsible for poetry and literary works, and the turnverein's leader of music was Turner Behrmann. The National Turnerbund recommended that two evenings per week be devoted to practical turning or apparatus gymnastics. As well as apparatus, free, and nature turning, the Bund suggested that wrestling, running, climbing, throwing, and swimming should comprise the weekly physical activities at all turnvereins. The Galveston Turnverein was equipped with sets of parallel bars, horizontal bars, rings, and vaulting horses. Also included as activities to enhance the Turners' personal discipline and physical constitution were regular military drilling and parading.

In the mid-1850s, at the peak of its membership, the turnverein divided into two clubs for a brief period. To establish better facilities, in 1858 the two turnvereins amalgamated into one organization and erected a new hall for the sum of $6,000. The Galveston Turnverein was a successful enterprise with a large number of members and private, fully equipped facilities. Turnverein membership consisted of men from varied groups in the city. True to F. L. Jahn's ideal of common participation, laborers, carpenters, and brick masons shared club membership with wealthy merchants. The turnverein promoted a certain temporary articulation between groups through shared ideologies and common participation in symbolic cultural traditions. To illustrate some differing characteristics of turnverein members, the following paragraphs consist of brief biographical sketches of Galveston Turners Kleinecke and Kuhn.

Theodore Kleinecke arrived in Galveston in 1846 with his parents. The Kleineckes and other passengers aboard the ship were sponsored by the German Colonization Society for the purpose of settling in Texas. Kleinecke settled in Galveston, married, and successfully operated a business as a butcher for twenty-two years. As well as being a member of the Galveston Turnverein, Kleinecke belonged to the Herman Lodge, German Lutheran Church, and the German Friendship Society.[8]

Dr. J. C. Kuhn was a Turner and a well-respected merchant in Galveston. Kuhn, a "merchant of enlarged and liberal views," was complimented on his contributions to the city in "erecting the first permanent and elegant business."[9] Willard Richardson, editor of the Galveston *News*, referred to Turner Kuhn as an "old citizen held in universal estimation." By 1860 Kuhn had accumulated over $75,000 in personal wealth and property.[10]

Although the Temperance movement was active in Galveston, in the form of parades, lectures, and meetings, Turners ignored its message and followed the tradition of beer drinking. Dinners and formal balls were held regularly at the turnverein. One of the club members, Turner Weidenbach, operated a beer saloon in Galveston. The Galveston Turnverein was a member of the

New Orleans District in the National Turnerbund organization. In 1855 many of the southern turnvereins seceded from the Bund because of its anti-slavery platform. The Galveston Turnverein is not noted in the National Turnerbund membership list between 1855 and 1860. The Galveston Turners adhered to only some of the principles advocated by the National Turnerbund constitution. For example, according to Bund regulations the Turners did indeed practice apparatus gymnastics regularly under the instruction of a Turnleader or Turnward. The National Bund also ordered all Turners in the United States to oppose slavery openly and to be prepared to fight for that stance. There was no evidence in the Galveston *Civilian* or the Galveston *News* to suggest that Galveston Turners publicly opposed slavery. Fornell maintains that the Germans tolerated the institution of slavery and purchased slaves for their own businesses.[11] Both the *News* and *Civilian* supported the institution of slavery throughout the Antebellum period. Richardson, of the *News*, once remarked, "those who denounce slavery as an evil in any sense, are enemies of the South."[12] Flake, editor of *Die Union*, opposed the reopening of the slave trade and drew a great deal of criticism from the other newspapers and from fellow German citizens.[13] It is evident that public denunciation of slavery was a rarity in Galveston. Both Stuart and Richardson were consistently complimentary in their respective newspaper columns toward the social activities and political opinions of Galveston Germans, in general, and Turners, in particular.[14]

Based on a content analysis of all politically oriented newspaper columns written during the election campaigns of the 1850s, it can be asserted that Germans and Turners in Galveston were fragmented in voting stance. Slavery was not the issue that divided German political posture. The Germans were very hesitant in supporting candidates connected in any manner to the Nativist or Know-Nothing party. Nativists sought to restrict the rights of immigrant peoples in America, including of course Germans. For example, a debate among Germans was waged in the newspapers during the state election campaign of 1859 concerning the candidacy of Sam Houston, a former Nativist sympathizer. During the same campaign, Germans expressed their hesitancy in supporting Houston's opponent, Hardin Runnels. Runnels advocated secession from the Union. Some Turners, though extremely vocal about the political freedom offered by the United States, were undecided in preference for secession or union. That fact is illustrated by the following letter to the *News*:

We came here sir, with an intense desire for freedom—we have long sought for the country which guarantees us that full share of political and religious liberty denied to us at home. We found that blessed country in this great Union, and this imposing confederacy of several states, and we will cling to it forever.[15]

The National Turnerbund urged all Turners in the United States to vote for Abraham Lincoln in the federal election of 1860. Lincoln's platform included vehement anti-slavery and pro-Union stances. It is impossible to assess the voting patterns of Germans and Turners in Galveston with regard to support for Lincoln and the Republican Party because neither was represented on the election ballot in Texas. There was no evidence in the Galveston newspapers indicating any support whatsoever for the Republican Party throughout the election campaign. Given the delicacy of the slavery issue in Texas, it is probable that any mention of Republican support would have been highly publicized, and responsible individuals would have consequently been chastised by citizens of Galveston.

After the election of Lincoln as president there were threats of secession and Civil War. When war was declared, Turners across the United States were called upon by the Bund to fight for the Union Army. In the South, however, a measure was passed in August 1861 by the government of the Confederate States of America stating that all individuals, fourteen years of age and older, who did not take the "oath of secession" would be banished from the South. Expulsion was the penalty levied against individuals who did not openly declare allegiance to the South and its institutions and who were not prepared to defend the Confederacy. Vigilance committees were organized throughout the South to ensure that residents complied with the law. As well, a conscription program was implemented in 1862 to strengthen the Confederate Army.

Germans in Galveston were drilled and trained as the Bund requested, but their military efforts ultimately supported the Confederate Army and aided in defense of Galveston from Union attack. The Turner Rifles from Houston also defended the city at the Battle of Galveston in 1862.[16] Many Galveston Turners joined the Confederate Army, engaging in battle in other parts of the South: "and when the war cloud dispersed, the bones of many of them were bleaching on the battle fields of Virginia, Tennessee and Georgia."[17]

In brief summary, evidence suggests that Galveston Turners adhered to National Turnerbund policy in the following respects only: (1) maintenance of physical fitness through apparatus gymnastics, (2) military efficiency through drilling and weapons training, (3) political participation and consciousness, and (4) opposition to Nativism. The Galveston Turners did *not* adhere to the following Turnerbund principles: (1) public opposition to slavery, (2) support of Abraham Lincoln and the Republican Party, and (3) allegiance to the Union Army in the Civil War.

Given the large German population in Galveston and the number and influence of Turners within that group, it is possible that the Turners could have supported Bund principles in total. Since the population of Galveston was almost one-half German during the 1850s, and the Turners were respected as politically knowledgeable intellectuals, a public anti-slavery campaign might have been conducted if the Turners had been so disposed. If Galveston Turners had elected to stand by Bund principles, or remain quiet on political issues, they would ultimately have been forced by the "oath of secession" law in 1862 to leave Galveston. Instead, the Turners, as loyal citizens of Galveston, chose to support the South and its institutions throughout the Antebellum and Civil War periods.

Even though this particular generation of Turners demonstrated pride in the German culture, of which brother and sisterhood with fellow Germans was paramount, it would be ludicrous to expect that the Galveston Turners would adopt the distinctly "Northern disposed" principles of the National Bund. Permanent settlement in the Deep South, establishment of businesses, a tolerance of slavery, and in some cases the ownership of slaves are collectively indicative of at least partial acceptance of the value structure of the South and its economy.

Upon imigrating to Galveston the Turners established businesses, trades, and homes and raised families. As merchants, tradesmen, and laborers, Turners were economically successful. As a result of their economic achievements, the Turners gained a personal "stake" in Galveston. Essentially, the protection of this personal stake or "rootedness" in the community of Galveston was a greater priority to the Turners than membership in and adherence to the National Turnerbund and its principles. An analysis of personal "stake" or "rootedness" in the community illuminates some foundations underscoring Turner attitudes and practices.

Inherent in the concept of community rootedness is a complex system of societal variables, of which marital status, number of children, community participation, involvement with social clubs, business characteristics, wealth, property ownership, and business interactions might be considered. Because of the limited amount of available data, this study utilizes wealth holding and real estate ownership as variables indicative of a personal stake in the community. The argument asserts that Turners accumulated personal wealth, achieved business ownership, and demonstrated social participation in common with other members of the Galveston population. Success in these pursuits rendered them an integral part of the community. An accumulation of real estate and personal wealth, in particular, would indicate that the Turners were successful in business and functioned efficiently in the Galveston economic community. The establishment of a personal stake may explain why the Turners adopted principles which served their best interests as citizens of Galveston.

Assuming that holding real estate and personal wealth is at least partially indicative of community rootedness, it was necessary to examine the wealth holding of Galveston Turners relative to other citizens in the city during the Antebellum period. A list of eighty-two Germans registered as members of the Galveston Turnverein in 1860 was obtained from the *Civilian* newspaper of Saturday, April 20, 1872. A search through the United States Manuscript Census was conducted to gather information on the Turners and the sample group. The criteria for matching the list with the census were last names and first name initials. In cases where the last name matched phonetically and spelling did not, the first name or initials were the determinants (for example, Geo. Schneider = Geo. Snyder). Sixteen names from the Turner list of 1860 were found in the census of 1850. The census provided information including name, age, occupation, value of real estate, and place of birth of adult males, adult females, and children. In order to compare real estate holding by Turners and other citizens of Galveston, an adult male workforce sample of 100 was randomly chosen from the census.[18] Fourteen Turners, those with occupations, were compared to the sample group in a simple data analysis.

A comparison of contingency tables indicates that observed real estate holding was roughly the same as expected values. Thus it was not necessary to determine the significance of the relationship. However, to illustrate that being a Turner and holding real estate were independent of one another, the contingency coefficient was calculated and equaled zero. Being a Turner and holding real estate were not related in 1850. With respect to real estate holding in 1850, the Turners were neither more nor less rooted in the Galveston community than the adult male population represented in the sample.

Utilizing the same methodology and list of Turners as the analysis of 1850, the United States Manuscript Census of 1860 was examined. A total of thirty-one Turners, twenty-nine with occupations, were found in the census. With the same sampling methodology, an adult male workforce sample was obtained from the census. The census of 1860 provided the same categories of information as the previous decade, with the addition of personal wealth. In the analysis of data from 1860, the values of real estate and personal wealth were combined in a figure of total wealth. As well, various wealth categories were established, making the analysis more detailed relative to the "yes–no" tables of wealth holding in 1850 (see Table 3.1).

Analysis of the data indicates that the Turners were more likely to own real estate and personal wealth than citizens represented in the sample group.

Hence the Turners appeared to be very successful in their business and economic pursuits. According to the group studied, not only did the Turners establish permanent businesses, but they also tended to be married with children.[19] These facts, coupled with their respected qualities of community social and political participation, indicate that the Turners were reasonably "rooted" or had a stake in the community.

An attempt was made to conduct a longitudinal survey of the Turners' improvement in wealth holding between 1850 and 1860. The names of only six Turners were found in both the 1850 and 1860 Manuscript Census. Five of those six Turners showed substantial increases in wealth during that particular decade, lending support to the thesis that Turners successfully established themselves in the community during the ten-year period.

Wealth holding is a very simplistic representation of rootedness in a community. In effect, it is only one element in a complicated structure of societal variables. It is possible that the Turners acted in accord with southern principles because they shared southern ideals with other Galvestonians, including the embrace of slavery. Perhaps such ideals became more attractive as the accumulation of property increasingly attached the Turners to the community. Thus it seems reasonable to suspect that Turner support of National Bund principles was eroded or superseded by material interests. The study offers one possible explanation of why the Galveston Turners did not adhere to National Turnerbund policy on some Antebellum and Civil War issues.

The Turners, an important group in the multicultural port city of Galveston, promoted physical fitness, cultural activities, and political awareness. Members of the turnverein played a critical role in securing immigrant rights

Table 3.1
Total Wealth Holding in 1860

Turners n = 29		Adult Males n = 100		
Observed Total Wealth (Real + Personal, in Dollars)				
Categories	0	1–1000	001–5000	5001+	Total
Turners	7	7	11	4	29
Adult Males	53	11	18	18	100
Titak	60	18	29	22	129
Expected Total Wealth (Real + Personal, in Dollars)				
Categories	0	1–1000	001–5000	5001+	Total
Turners	13.5	4	6.5	5	29
Adult Males	46.5	14	22.5	17	100
Total	60	18	29	22	129

and politically educating fellow Germans. Against National Turnerbund constitutional orders, Galveston Turners supported the South through the Antebellum and Civil War periods.

The results of the study support the earlier work of R. K. Barney illustrating that there was an absence of continuity in American Turner policy regarding the political issues of the period. By examining Turner behavior in specific locations and avoiding general conclusions, one may more accurately portray the German-American Turner experience in Antebellum America.

NOTES

1. Horst Ueberhorst, "De Nordamerikanischen Turner and ihr Jahnbild," *Stadion* 4 (1976): 358; Henry Metzner, *History of the American Turners*, 3rd rev. ed. (Rochester, N.Y.: National Council of American Turners, 1974), p. 17; Lawrence J. Rippley, *The German Americans* (Boston: Twayne Publishers, 1976), p. 58; G. S. Brosius, *The Turnvereins, the Turnerbund, and the Establishment of Physical Education in Our Schools: Fifty Years Devoted to the Cause of Physical Culture* (Milwaukee: Germania, 1914), p. 85; Robert Knight Barney, "German-American Turnvereins and Socio-Politico-Economic Realities in the Antebellum and Civil War Upper and Lower South," *Stadion* 10 (1984): 135–81; Galveston *News*, September 14, 1858.

2. E. W. Fornell, *The Galveston Era* (Austin, Texas: University of Texas Press, 1961), pp. 87–89, 129; Galveston *Daily News*, February 29, 1976.

3. *Civilian*, December 16, 1843.

4. Galveston *Daily News*, February 29, 1976. *Galveston City Directory*, 1859–60, p. 47. *Civilian*, March 21, 1856 and May 5, 1857.

5. For detailed accounts of the history of the Forty-Eighter Turners in Germany and the United States, see Robert Knight Barney, "Knights of Cause and Exercise: German Forty-Eighters and Turnvereins in the United States during the Antebellum Period," *Canadian Journal of History of Sport* 13 (December 1982): 62–79; A. E. Zucker, ed., *The Forty-Eighters* (New York: Columbia University Press, 1950); Carl F. Wittke, *Refugees of Revolution* (Philadelphia: University of Pennsylvania Press, 1952); and Hurst Ueberhorst, *Friedrich Ludwig Jahn 1778/1978* (Bonn-Bad, Godesberg: Inter Nationes, 1978). For a description of Turners in the United States and the specific activities of the National Turnerbund, see Robert Knight Barney, "German Turners in American Domestic Crisis: Jahnistic Ideals in Clash with Southern Sentiment during the Antebellum and Civil War Periods," *Stadion* 4 (1978): 344–57, and K. B. Wamsley, "Loyal to the Confederacy: Galveston, Texas Turners and National Turnerbund Ideology, 1840–1865" (M.A. thesis, University of Western Ontario, 1987).

6. *Civilian*, December 10, 1845; ibid., April 20, 1872.

7. *Galveston City Directory*, 1859–60, p. 53; ibid., 1856–57, p. 38.

8. *Manuscript Census*, 1850 and 1860. For a complete listing see Wamsley, "Loyal to the Confederacy," pp. 92 and 94; *History of Texas* (Chicago: Lewis Publishing, 1895), pp. 312–33. (author unknown).

9. *News*, June 8, 1858.

10. Ibid.

11. Fornell, *The Galveston Era,* pp. 132–33, 137–38; *Die Union,* May 15, 1858; *Manuscript Census,* 1860; *Galveston City Directory,* 1856–57, p. 38 (Turner Jordon), 1859–60, p. 53 (Turner Jenny); *Civilian,* April 20, 1872 (Turner Hendel).

12. *News,* March 3, 1857.

13. See *News,* July 19, 1859; July 26, 1859; and August 2, 1859.

14. See *Civilian,* December 13, 1843; *News,* July 8, 1858, July 19, 1859, for examples.

15. *News,* July 19, 1859.

16. W. T. Tenney, ed., *American Annual Cyclopaedia and Register of Important Events for the Years 1861 to 1865* (New York, n. p.: 1866), p. 147; *News,* May 28, 1857; *Civilian,* May 18, 1858; Galveston *Daily News,* February 29, 1976.

17. *Civilian,* April 20, 1872.

18. The sample included males aged fifteen or older with occupations. Numbers from Random Numbers Tables were matched with census page numbers. The location of name chosen from the census page was as follows: (alternating, with one name from each random page) middle of the page, up from the middle, down from the middle, second up from the middle, second down from the middle.

19. Ninety percent of the Turners involved in the analysis were married by 1860. Eighty-nine percent of those Turners had at least one child by 1860.

4

The Shamrock and the Eagle: Irish Americans and Sport in the Nineteenth Century

Ralph C. Wilcox

Since the first Irishman stepped ashore in the New World in 1492, millions of Erin's sons and daughters have crossed the Atlantic Ocean in search of personal freedom and economic opportunity. The United States Census of 1980 revealed that more than 40 million Americans (18 percent) claimed Irish ancestry, third only to those descendants of English and German immigrants (22 percent each). Throughout the Colonial period, the majority of Irish immigrants were Protestant merchants who commonly shared the values and lifestyle of mainstream America. However, as Ireland's population increased and her domestic, small farm economy offered limited opportunity for employment, an unprecedented, nineteenth century Gaelic wave of mostly poor, illiterate, rural Catholics began to arrive on American shores. Further prompted by the clearance of tenants from country estates, to make way for livestock, and a series of famines culminating in the Great Famine of 1845–49, their numbers steadily increased through mid-century.[1]

During the 1820s Irish denizens represented more than one-third of the total immigrants to the United States, rising to almost half by the end of the 1840s and replacing the English as the chief source of aliens by mid-century. Between the years 1841 and 1860, 1.7 million Irish immigrants disembarked at the gateways of the northeast, New York, Boston, and Philadelphia. Limited in mobility, through lack of funds, they commonly clustered in inner-city enclaves. Often employed as longshoremen and factory workers, it has been argued that Irish Americans furnished the cheap labor foundation upon which the nation's industrial success was built. As westward expansion grew, Irishmen joined the ranks of canal and railroad navies ensuring strong Gaelic representation in Chicago, San Francisco, and St. Louis during the post–Civil

War years. Economic hardship was but one of the problems that the Irish immigrants had to endure. While their poor health and high mortality rate was, in part, balanced by their unsurpassed fertility rate, their language, brogue, religious beliefs, and ethnic stereotype became the target of the nation's most serious bigotry. Yet, despite the many hurdles, the story of Irish Americans must generally be considered one of success. They were instrumental in transforming the Roman Catholic Church from a small, often despised sect to the largest organized religion in America. They were active in establishing the American labor movement, in providing such public service as performed by police forces and fire companies, together with pioneering democratic inroads into American urban politics. Above all, the Irish immigrant paved the way for the more speedy acceptance of later immigrant groups to the New World.[2]

It is likely that much of this progress would not have occurred had it not been for the innate clannishness of the Irish immigrant. Founded in 1737, the Charitable Irish Society of Boston became their first fraternal-charitable organization, soon to be followed by the Friendly Sons of St. Patrick, each perceived as social clubs by their wealthy, Irish merchant patrons. Early in Irish-American history, immigrant aid societies, such as the Irish Emmigrant Society of New York (1841), were established to furnish immediate assistance to the hordes of fellow countrymen arriving daily. Fraternal and benevolent societies were set up by lower status Irish workers who were willing to give of their meager earnings to protect against uncertainties. Furthermore, the church was instrumental in establishing numerous socioreligious and temperance groups including the Irish Catholic Benevolent Union and the Catholic Total Abstinence Union. In 1858 the first significant political group was formed by Irish Americans. Viewed as an outgrowth of the native Irish Republican Brotherhood (1858), the Fenian Brotherhood was the forerunner of the more revolutionary and secretive Clan Na Gael association founded in New York City in 1867. The appearance of these and other nationalist organizations was expected in the New World where animosities, born of Cromwell's atrocities in Ireland, were frequently rekindled. The St. Patrick's Day parade came to mean much more than a religious celebration to Irish immigrants. First held in Boston in 1737, and followed by New York City in 1762, it offered citizens of various ethnic affiliations the opportunity to "wear the green" and glory in the sights and sounds of Erin. By 1872 the New York City parade had 50,000 marchers and attracted a throng of 500,000 spectators.[3]

Much has been written of the Irish-American experience.[4] While some scholars have been content with describing the Irishman's lot, others have attempted to explain it in terms of various theses associated with ethnicity and immigration. Today it is most generally agreed that no one theory can effectively explain the story of the Irish immigrant. Utilizing Robert E. Parke's oversimplified view of the "melting pot" process of assimilation, Milton M. Gordon's somewhat refined differentiation between cultural and structural assimilation and Horace M. Kallen's once radical support for cultural pluralism, scholars have struggled to find greater meaning in the Irish-American's fondness for politics and other avocations. The purpose of this chapter is to examine the role that sport played in the life of nineteenth–century Irish immigrants, to identify those factors that determined their sporting opportunities, and to evaluate the contribution of Gaelic Americans to sport history.

Upon departing for the New World in the first half of the nineteenth century, Irish emigrants left behind a sport system very much patterned after England. While field sports such as fishing, shooting, and hunting were popular among the gentry, the great majority of Irish peasants devoted what little leisure time they had to the simple rural sports practiced in the fields and at country fairs. Formal sport, for the most part, was organized and controlled by the Amateur Athletic Association of England, a factor which became the singlemost important determinant in establishing the Gaelic Athletic Association in 1884. In the years that followed, Ireland witnessed a resurgence in popularity for the traditional and ancient Tailtean Games which, evidence suggests, may have predated the athletic festivals of ancient Greece. Included in this late nineteenth-century Gaelic athletic renaissance was increased structure and codification of the traditional team sports of hurling and Gaelic football. This point is important since, contrary to past scholarly opinion, any early attempts to introduce these team sports to America were made informally and without the support of a native governing body. Indeed, rather than carry these games as part and parcel of their cultural baggage, it seems that early Irish immigrants found greater favor with the popular pursuits of the New World, those that had been brought to America by Englishmen.[5]

SPORT AND "THE MELTING POT" PHENOMENON

Fishing, billiards, cockfighting, prizefighting, pedestrianism (later track and field), swimming, rowing, cricket, and eventually baseball not only promised some degree of acceptance by mainstream America, but experience showed that these sports could represent the ladder to the socioeconomic enhancement of which all immigrants dreamed.[6]

More has been written on Irish success in the American prize ring than about any other ethnic group in sport. It is somewhat regrettable that authors have found it necessary to dwell upon the Irish American's pugilistic endeavors at the expense of his other athletic pursuits. It has long been argued that boxing has found greatest appeal to oppressed minorities, promising a rapid escape from poverty and discrimination. The Irish immigrant surely has not disappointed these theorists. The names of Sam O'Rourke, Cornelius Horrigan, John C. "Benecia Boy" Heenan, James "Yankee" Sullivan, and John Morrissey fill the annals of the American ring before the Civil War. Born James Ambrose in Ireland in 1807, "Yankee" Sullivan earned his nickname from the American flag that he wore around his waist while in the ring. In 1853 Sullivan lost his American heavyweight title to John Morrissey, a New York resident who also hailed from the Land of Erin. Morrissey went on to be elected to Congress in 1866 and again in 1868, lending support to the notion that Irish Americans treated boxing and politics as one and the same.[7] In the post–Civil War years, the foremost heavyweight fighters were also of Irish-American stock. Paddy Ryan, Jake Kilrain, John L. Sullivan, and "Gentleman Jim" Corbett each attested to the Gaels' affinity for the sport. Sullivan, better known as "The Boston Strong Boy," was born in "The Hub" in 1858, the son of Irish immigrants. He was the link between the London Prize Ring and Marquess of Queensbury Rules, pioneering the transition from bareknuckle boxing to the gloved era. World Heavyweight Champion from 1882 to 1892, Sullivan has been credited with anywhere between 75 and 200 victories in the ring. "John L." became the first modern sporting superstar. Among the personal entrepreneurial ventures that he used to supplement the purses from prizefighters was a token appointment as sports editor of the New York-based *Illustrated News*, his endorsement of a Lipton Beef Company product, numerous and varied stage roles, and even an attempt to establish his own "John L. Sullivan Motion Picture Company." Having met with royalty, Pope Leo, and every president since James A. Garfield, Sullivan's decision to pursue the favorite Irish pathway to politics was not unexpected. Failing in his bid to win a seat in the Massachusetts House of Representatives in 1895 and losing on the New York City ballot for alderman four years later, he eventually withdrew from a second congressional race in the Bay state. The subject of at least nine autobiographical and biographical works, Sullivan's earnings have been calculated at greater than $1 million. He soon became a cultural hero and a model to which young Irish immigrants might aspire in their search for socioeconomic uplift. Upon his loss to "Gentleman Jim" Corbett, ambassador of San Francisco's "lace curtain" Irish, in 1892, it was the victor who had to answer for the effrontery that he had shown in beating a fellow descendant of Erin.[8]

Pedestrianism also offered poor Irish immigrants the opportunity to fill their pockets with prize money. While Edward Payson Weston is most often lauded as America's nineteenth-century "Champion Pedestrian of the World," the comparable achievements of Daniel O'Leary have frequently gone unnoticed. Born in County Cork, Ireland, in 1846, O'Leary immigrated to New York City at the age of twenty. Moving on to Chicago, his professional career in pedestrianism began with the defeat of Weston in a 200-mile race in October 1874. One year later O'Leary beat Weston in a six-day walking match held in Chicago. Weston's complaints of foul play were largely responsible for a long-awaited rematch at the Agricultural Hall in London, England, beginning on Easter Monday of 1877. Billed as "the greatest athletic feat on record," the $5,000 stake generated much interest. "Betting was immense" as the spectacle attracted upward of 20,000 spectators at its close. Once again, the Irish American was victorious, covering a record 520 miles in six days. Prompting Irish nationalist oratory at his victory functions, O'Leary returned to New York where he hoped to break his own record. Unable to do so in front of a sparse crowd, his strong Gaelic association was underscored by the following events of the final day: "While making his 458th mile a lady stepped on the track and presented O'Leary with a beautiful floral harp, which he carried around once with him amid thunders of applause . . . and to the strains of 'Garryowen,' 'The Wearing of the Green,' and 'Yankee Doodle.'"[9]

The London match might be considered to be the most important event in the history of pedestrianism as it prompted Sir John Astley, eager to promote the sport further, to establish the Astley Belt Championship. The year 1878 saw the first Astley Belt race held in London before 30,000 spectators. O'Leary beat his English challengers, winning the Astley Belt and $3,750 in prize and gate receipts. In October 1878, O'Leary returned to New York City to defeat John Hughes, a fellow Irish American, at Gilmore's Garden in the second running for the Astley Belt. Promised an opportunity to win the belt outright, the world champion took on all-comers in New York the following year. Among his challengers were John Ennis, who had arrived in Chicago from Ireland in 1869, and Patrick Fitzgerald, another Irish-American resident of New York. Despite O'Leary's anticipated victory, an Englishman by the name of Charles Rowell took the belt and $20,398 in prize money. Accused of having "thrown" the race, O'Leary went on to establish the O'Leary Belt Race for the Championship of America, the first running of which took place at Madison Square Garden in 1879.[10]

Rowing was the third sport that offered early Irish immigrants the opportunity to earn fame and fortune in a familiar sporting milieu. Although the professional rowing fraternity of northeast wherrymen was a world apart from the crew life of America's most prestigious universities, it appears that boat races among professionals were afforded some legitimacy by mainstream American society. Irish Americans took to rowing with great vigor forming the "Maid of Erin," "Young Men's Catholic Lyceum," "St. Mary's Temperance Society," and "St. James Young Men's Catholic Total Abstinence" boat clubs in Boston, Albany's "Celtic Board Club," New York's "Young Irish–American's" and "Emerald" crews, Buffalo's "Celtic," "Hibernian," and "Robert Emmet" clubs, the "Hibernian Rowing Club" of Newport, Rhode Island, and Portland, Maine's, "Emerald Boat Club." While the "Lincoln," "Starlight," "West End," "Charles River," "Shawmut," and "Ruddock" boat clubs of Boston, together with "Riverside Club" in New Orleans and the "Neptune Boat Club" of Lynn, Massachusetts, offer no nominal clue as to their ethnic patronization, close scrutiny of their crew lists indicates a strong preponderance of Caseys, Flynns, O'Neills, Ryans, and Sullivans. Challenges frequently appeared in the Irish-American press of the day with stakes set anywhere between $250 and $1,000 a side. Crowds of 30,000 spectators were not uncommon at these events. In 1874 the *Irish World* reported on "a very exciting boat race" in Norwich, Connecticut, concluding that "the victors were the popular Murphy brothers, Michael and John, both whole-souled and patriotic young Irish Americans."

The fact that Irish Americans dominated the professional rowing scene throughout the last three decades of the nineteenth century cannot be challenged. Among the leading scullers of the 1870s were Thomas C. Butler, George Faulkner, Patsy Reagan, J. J. O'Leary, and James O'Donnell. From 1885 through the turn of the century, the list of National Amateur Champions included Daniel J. Murphy (Crescent Boat Club of Boston), Martin F. Monahan (Albany Rowing Club), D. Donoghue (Nautilus Rowing Club), John J. Ryan (Sunnyside Rowing Club, Toronto), William Caffrey (Lawrence Boat Club), and Joseph Maguire (Bradford Boat Club). Following the Saratoga Regatta of 1874, the *Irish World* published a story entitled "Irish-American Muscle in the Ascendant," in which the author reviewed the results of the event: "And thus did Irish-American muscle bear off the palm in every contest of this the most important day of the regatta. This result should give an impetus to athletic organization among our young men. Of all healthful exercises, rowing is most to be encouraged, and there is not a more legitimate sport than boat-racing."

The following year brought an interesting thought from another contributor to the *Irish World*. After having discussed the successes of Ivy League universities at the intercollegiate regatta of 1875, the writer lamented:

Why cannot our Catholic colleges enter into competition of this kind every year. Most of them have crack ball clubs; would not rowing clubs be more creditable and beneficial? In St. Johns, Fordham, St. Francis Xavier's and Manhattan, New York, Seton Hall, New Jersey, Holy Cross, Worcester, and several other institutions here about there is splendid material for crews that would not discredit their alma mater even in the grand contest at Saratoga. In the task of developing the mind it is essential that the body be taken care of in Catholic Colleges as well as elsewhere.[11]

At the outset of the Civil War, cricket could well claim to be the most popular organized team sport in the United States. Largely due to its patronization by English immigrants, merchant and laborer alike, enthusiasm for the wicket slowly radiated westward from Boston, New York, and Philadelphia where it had flourished. Irish immigrants brought their knowledge of the game to the New World and made a moderate impact on the sport. America had been the destination of England's first touring cricket team in 1859. Twenty years later, an Irish cricket team was to visit the United States.[12]

Across the country, Irish teams sprang up with amazing regularity. The "Shamrock" (Holyoke, Woburn, and Boston, Massachusetts, Concord, New Hampshire, and Galt, Ontario), "Fenian" (Augusta, Georgia, and New Orleans), "Celtic" (Montreal), "Emerald" (Savannah, Georgia), "Hibernian Green" (San Francisco and Boston), and "Plaid Stocking" (Geddes, New York) baseball clubs suggest Gaelic affiliation. Further, teams were sometimes given the names of Irish national heroes such as the "Emmet" (Woburn, Massachusetts, and Savannah, Georgia), "Owen Garvey" (Pittsburgh), together with the "M. N. Nolan" and "Dillon" Baseball Clubs of Albany, New York. Other clubs, such as the "Carolina" (Charleston, South Carolina), "Mazeppa" (Newburyport, Massachusetts), "Strain" (Pittsburgh), "Old Vigilant" (Philadelphia), and "Our Boys" (Boston), together with the "Magnolia," "Empire," "Louisiana," and "Southern" teams of New Orleans, showed Irish players to be numerically prominent on their rosters. Baseball even found support among those Irish Americans who had entered higher education.

It was, however, the professional players who won the baseball laurels for Irish America. The Irish realized perhaps greater immediate success in baseball than any other immigrant group. By the turn of the century seemingly all the prominent clubs were captained by Irish Americans including Kelly (Brooklyn), Delehanty (Philadelphia), Collins (Boston), Donovan (St. Louis), Doyle (Chicago), Gleason (Detroit), McGraw (Baltimore), and Duffy (Milwaukee). A wander through the Baseball Hall of Fame in Cooperstown, New York, reminds one of the deep presence of professional Irish baseball players in the nineteenth century. Roger Patrick Bresnahan ("The Duke of

Tralee"), Tom Connolly, Joe Cronin, the Delehanty brothers, Hugh Duffy, Tim Keefe, "Wee Willie" Keeler, Joe Kelley, George Kelly, Cornelius McGillicuddy (better known as "Connie Mack"), "Iron Man" McGinnity, Tim Murnane, Jim O'Rourke, "Big Ed" Walsh, "Smiling Mickey" Welsh, and the incomparable Mike "King" Kelly could just as easily have constituted the passenger manifest of a steam packet arriving at Boston in the 1840s.

Michael Joseph Kelly was the son of an Irish immigrant papermaker, born at Troy, New York, in 1857. Making his debut with the Olympic Club of Paterson, New Jersey, in 1877, he went on to record a superlative professional career as a catcher, outfielder, and shortstop with the Buckeye Club of Columbus, Ohio, the Cincinnati Red Stockings, and the Chicago White Stockings. His subsequent "sale" to the Boston Red Stockings in 1887 was unprecedented in the sport and, while causing a furor in baseball circles, brought the "Ten Thousand Dollar Beauty" immediate renown. Best remembered for his baserunning and sliding abilities, his name was immortalized in the popular song entitled, "Slide, Kelly, Slide," celebrating the eighty-four bases that he "stole" during his first season in Boston. Later, in a stage adaptation of Ernest L. Thayer's "Casey at the Bat," Kelly was cast in the title role alongside the London Gaiety Girls. Thayer's ballad had first appeared in 1888. It is significant to note that even the mythical baseball players were Irish, as the lyrics included such characteristic Gaelic names as Blake, Cooney, and Flynn in addition to Casey. One wonders whether "mighty Casey," the hope of the Mudville Nine, might have hit a home run instead of striking out had his creator not been of the Brahmin stable and educated at Harvard University.[13]

Although Irish-American interest in track and field athletics might be viewed as a logical extension of their affinity for pedestrianism, the two sports possessed separate and unique characteristics. Foot races, hurdling, jumping, and throwing events, which had long been part of native celebrations in rural Ireland, were soon included in Gaelic festivals in America.

Yet the most significant contribution of Irish Americans to the sport was reserved for the highly respected, organized, and amateur track and field competition of the 1890s. Modeled on its London counterpart, the New York Athletic Club had opened its doors in 1868. Frequented by Astors, Belmonts, Roosevelts, Vanderbilts, and others of New York Knickerbocker society, it was to be the better part of three decades before the first Irish American athletes were found competing for the "Winged Footers." Due in large part to the exclusionary policies and practices of the New York Athletic Club, the Boston Athletic Association, and similar organizations, Irish Athletic Clubs were formed in New York City and Boston during 1879. Later changing their names to Irish-American Athletic Clubs, they became powerful forces in international track and field by the turn of the century. At its inaugural international track and field meet with the London Athletic Club in September 1895, the New York Athletic Club was represented by at least three Irish–American athletes including J. T. Conneff who was born in County Kildaire in 1866. Running for the New York club, he won both the one-mile and three-mile events, while Thomas E. Burke, "the Lowell Mercury," won the 440-yard race. The following year, while representing the Boston Athletic Association, Burke ran to victory in the 100-meter and 400-meter events at the first modern Olympiad in Athens. Increasing Irish-American representation in Greece was Tom Curtis who won the 100-meter hurdles race. At the Paris Olympics in 1900, Irish-born Mike F. Sweeney (high jump Champion of the World from 1892 to 1895), took home 750 francs in winning the 100-meter, high jump, and long jump events for professional athletes. Another Irish-American track man of this era was Charlie H. Kilpatrick who, born to Irish parents in Troy, New York, ran the half mile in 1:53.4 during 1895, a world record that would stand for fourteen years. While John F. Cregan's (Princeton University) second place finish in the 800-meter race and Myer Prinstein's (Syracuse University and later the Greater New York Irish American Athletic Association) victory in the triple jump at the Paris Olympics represented notable achievements, the Second Olympiad is important as it heralded the beginning of an Irish-American dynasty in throwing events.

In that year a New York City policeman by the name of John F. Flanagan (who was born in Limerick in 1868), won the Olympic hammer event for the New York Athletic Club. In third place was another Gaelic American, M. McCracken, who also recorded a second place finish in the shot putt. After winning the Metropolitan and Junior National Championships of the Amateur Athletic Union in 1904, the Greater New York Irish American Athletic Association was represented at the St. Louis Olympics by Flanagan, who retained his Olympic title in throwing the hammer, Martin Sheridan, who won the discus event, and Jim Mitchell (formerly of Tipperary), who had come to America with the Gaelic Athletic Association's "invasion" of 1888. The story continued in 1908, when Flanagan became the first modern Olympic athlete to win three successive titles in a standard event. Once again, Flanagan found ample companionship in Sheridan who won his second gold medal and another New York City policeman, Matt McGrath, who finished in second place in the hammer throw. Later joined by Pat McDonald and Pat Ryan, these men were collectively known as the "Irish Whales." Shrouded in legends beginning with their jovial, athletic demeanor, a contemporary recalled: "In their era, the Whales were giants . . . Some of them weighed in the area of three hundred pounds. They were all sons or grandsons of Erin and were mostly members of the New York City police force."[14]

Perhaps the most accomplished Irish–American athlete of these years was James Brendan Connolly. Born in South Boston in 1868, the son of Irish immigrants, Connolly is probably better remembered as the author of twenty-five maritime novels and 200 short stories than the first modern Olympic victor in 1896. After passing the entrance examination in October 1895, Connolly enrolled at the Lawrence Scientific School of Harvard University to study engineering. His hopes of playing football for the Crimson were dashed when he broke a collarbone in the first scrimmage. Joining the University track team, Connolly won the amateur hop, step, and jump championship of the United States in the same season. After his request for an eight-week leave of absence was turned down by the Harvard University administration, Connolly chose to forsake a college education in favor of paying his own way to the Olympic Games in Athens. Representing the South Boston Athletic Club, Connolly recorded a first place in the triple jump, second place in the high jump, and third place in the broad (long) jump. Traveling to Paris in 1900, to defend his Olympic triple jump title, Connolly placed second. Soon after, he left athletics to become a sportswriter for the *Boston Globe*, and went on to serve as correspondent to *Colliers Magazine* during World War I. Appointed Commissioner of American Relief for Ireland following the "Black and Tan" disturbances, Connolly eventually turned to writing maritime novels. Since that time James Brendan Connolly has been variously described as "the dean of American sea writers" and "the nearest thing to Homer the modern world has known." After receiving honorary degrees from Fordham University and Boston College, Connolly returned to Harvard University for the fiftieth reunion of his class whereupon he was awarded a letter in track. Perhaps the warmest testimonial came from President Theodore Roosevelt who once stated, "If I were to pick one man for my sons to pattern their lives after, I would choose Jim Connolly."[15] By the turn of the century, Irish-American athletes had begun to wrest the track and field laurels from the Scottish pioneers and members of the exclusive athletic clubs. Increasingly, the Greater New York Irish American Athletic Association's emblematic green fist set against a background of green shamrock inserts, transversed by a diagonal band of red, white, and blue stood victorious on the winner's podium in stadiums the world over.

Other North American sports attracted enthusiastic Gaelic patronization in the United States during the nineteenth century. After "The dauntless

Irish-American, Captain Boyton, [of Philadelphia] crossed the English Channel" enveloped in a buoyant suit in 1875, some two months ahead of Matthew Webb, the *Irish World* announced "A great swimming match between Coyle, the Irish-American champion, and J. B. Johnson, champion of England." Ignoring complaints of foul play, Johnson won the twenty-two-mile race from Chester to Philadelphia in the Delaware River.[16]

The turf presented immigrants with another viable pathway toward assimilation in America. As Dale Somers wrote, "The names of many jockeys suggest Irish youngsters frequently tried this avenue of escape from poverty." With the names of Burns, Murphy, and O'Conner foremost among jockeys and trainers in the South, Alexander Porter and Maunsel White found acceptance by the New Orleans Jockey Club. It was James Butler of New York who made the greatest social strides through horse racing. Born in Kilkenny, Ireland, in 1855, Butler arrived in Boston at the age of twenty. Working his way up from steward to hotelier and grocery store owner, by 1929 his wealth was calculated at $30 million. Readily welcomed into New York's fold of lace curtain Irish, "Squire" Butler became one of the nation's leading horse owners and owner of the Empire City racetrack in Yonkers. Although prominent among America's "First Irish Families," the Catholic Irishman was constantly at odds with the exclusive New York Jockey Club.[17] Such conflict between emerging Irish and mainstream America was not uncommon in the nineteenth century as competition and conditional acceptance became the precursors to assimilation.

SPORT, ETHNIC CONFLICT, AND ACCOMMODATION

It is important to note that the Irish immigrants' ready acceptance of, and participation in, the popular American sports of the nineteenth century did not constitute total assimilation. Greeley has shown that "an ethnic group can acquire many of the behavioral traits of the larger society without losing either its sense of identity or its desire to interact with other members of the group."[18] Sometimes described as "tentative assimilation," the intermediate stage of acculturation has been well demonstrated by the Irish-American athletes' insistence on using Gaelic names for their rowing, baseball, track and field, and lacrosse teams while taking every opportunity to "parade the green" in the sporting arena. It was inevitable that such demonstrations of ethnic pride would, at times, result in conflict best demonstrated by the burning of Catholic institutions and violent outbursts at labor and cultural rallies. Peculiar though it may seem, much of this conflict was waged between members of one ethnic group each vying for outright leadership.

Sport provides an abundance of evidence to support the existence of inter and intracultural conflict. While many sport and ethnic historians have long considered that the unparalleled success of nineteenth-century Irish prize-fighters did much to elevate the self-esteem of their fellow immigrants, others saw a counterargument. As early as 1871, the *Irish World* cautioned that:

The Irish, from their connection with the English, have unfortunately acquired some of the barbarous habits and customs of the Saxons, as they did their language. But Irishmen even in the prize ring are not wholly lost to honor. The genuine Celt fights, not for money, but for fame—such poor fame as it is—and he could never forget his manhood so far as to make himself, like the Saxon villain, a bull-terrier gladiator for the sport of a blackleg nobility.

To set the blame on English soil was not to be unexpected, but still questions surrounding the moral virtue and worthwhile qualities of prizefighting could not be denied, as J. C. Furnas has pointed out: "The rugged young men who survived [bareknuckle fights] did their share to give the Irish a bad name by being usually either Irish or of second generation Irish stock." While "The Boston Strong Boy" was honored as a civic hero, one local newspaper reported that "Blue-blooded Boston is disgusted with the notoriety the Hub has gained through the brutal victory of its hard hitting son, Sullivan." Middle class, literary Irishmen leapt onto this critical bandwagon, denouncing the Irish domination of the American prize rings as "human butchery" promoted by a "worthless, gambling class of lodgers" who frequented saloons, pool rooms, and other "gilded haunts." When, in 1888, John Boyle O'Reilly published a book extolling the virtues of pugilism, *Donahoe's Magazine* sharply criticized him for endorsing such a "barbarous" pursuit. The criticism of professional sports extended beyond prizefighting, as the *New York Times* observed in 1879: "It is very true that many of the men most interested in the walking match belong to the worst class of New York . . . And it cannot be denied that the crowd which surrounded the circus building was rough and unsavory in manners and atmosphere."[19]

While the Gaelic immigrant's physical proficiency often confirmed the Anglo–American Protestant stereotype that painted the Irish as having strong backs but weak minds, it also furnished an opportunity to advance the process of assimilation. As the nineteenth century wore on, the playing field increasingly became the pit in which cultural squabbles between immigrants and established America were settled. The annual encounter between the "Maid of Erin" and "Harvard" crews reflected a fundamental cleavage between Yankee Puritans and Irish Catholics in Boston. Yet perhaps such contests served as a cathartic outlet. The words of a ballad written by the Reverend William R. Huntingdon, of the Harvard class of 1859, reflect a disguised satisfaction at his boat's triumph over the Irish-crewed "Fort Hill Boy." Mocking all that is Irish, the accent, the dialect, and self-confidence, the author goes on to question the trustworthiness of the losing crew whose payment of bets is dependent upon victory, an indication of their poverty and professional status. Reversing Irish ridicule of the Harvard "lady pets," "fops," and "Beacon Street swells," the superiority of the University shell over the flat-bottomed ferry scow is put beyond all contention.[20]

If Irish-American athletes found increased pleasure in waging war with other ethnic groups in the sports arena, the English were their favorite adversary. John L. Sullivan always wore green breeches in the ring and readily exhibited the contempt for Englishmen so common among his oppressed fathers. On one occasion, in Canada, he declined to toast "Her Majesty," adding that "A true Irishman never drinks the health of a British ruler, King or Queen."[21] Recognizing that such oratorical displays might anger Anglophiles in the New World, he would often follow with a calm appeal to their sense of patriotism. Later, at the 1908 Olympic Games in London, the Irish-American disdain for the English resurfaced. The American team included at least ten members of the Greater New York Irish Athletic Association (among whom six were Irish-born). A *London Times* editorial went so far as to suggest that "owing to the number of Irish-Americans among their members, it might almost be said that the British athletes . . . competed with Irishmen, not Americans." The most notable feature of these Games was Ralph Rose's refusal, at the insistence of his "Irish Whale" teammates, to lower the stars and stripes before King Edward VII, explaining that the American flag "dips to no earthly king." Moreover, members of the Greater New York Irish Athletic Association showed that ethnic discord need not always result in conflict. Offering some evidence of cultural accommodation and eager to avoid replicating the exclusionary practices of the New York Athletic Club, Harry Cohn, Alvah Meyer, Myer Prinstein, and Abel Kiviat were granted membership. While the physical prowess of these Jewish athletes likely influenced the Irish-Americans' decision, Kiviat suggests that their action was quite genuine for "The Irish-American Athletic Club athletes wouldn't go where Jews had a hard time," while others chose not to venture beyond the secure confines of their Gaelic ghettoes wherein they consciously sought to retain their ethnic heritage.[22]

SPORT AND CULTURAL PLURALISM

Describing his native land, Walt Whitman wrote, "Here is not merely a nation but a teeming nation." Picturing a political state in which dwell a number of different nationalities, the cultural pluralists' thesis recognizes the natural tendency of immigrants to seek strength and security among ethnic enclaves in their new home. Arguing that national groups neither could not should be fused into one generic nationality, Horace Kallen suggested that

American democracy should provide the opportunity for a harmonious cultural mosaic to exist in the United States. Sport frequently strengthened this search for ethnic independence and persistence.

Following the 1873 "Irish National Games" in Philadelphia, the *Irish World* asked: "Few, if any, who either participated in, or were spectators of, those manly games, who were not forcibly reminded of home and fatherland.... The Germans, Scotch, English, and others have their national games, and why not we?" Eventually, an increasing number of Irish-American militia, religious, political, benevolent, and cultural organizations included "Irish Games" on the program at their picnics and annual excursions. From the Fenian Brotherhood to the Ancient Order of Hibernians, St. Patrick's Mutual Alliance Association, Catholic Total Abstinence and Benevolent Society, and the Young Men's Catholic Abstinence Society, members thronged to sites across the country to compete in foot races, hurdling, jumping events, throwing the light and heavy stone, boat races, and target shoots. By 1871 members of the Clan Na Gael Association of New York were joined at their second annual picnic by representatives from Troy, New York, Wilmington, Delaware, and Philadelphia. Including Gaelic football and hurling matches on the program, a reporter explained: "The object of these associations is not dissimilar to that of the German Turnverein. It aims at the physical, social, and intellectual elevation of the Irish in America. It promotes a love of literature and social life in its clubrooms and in its gymnastic exercises it helps develop the Irish muscle."

Advertisements appeared in the local press urging Irish-Americans to join native excursions to Spy Pond, outside of Boston and Jones' Wood in New York. By 1878 the Clan Na Gael picnic in New York attracted 13,000 participants. As bigger prizes were awarded, the festivals began to attract professional athletes. At the Emerald and Hamilton Rowan Clubs' picnic at Jones' Wood in 1878, "A leading feature of the occasion was the Irish national games and an athletic match between Duncan O. Ross, the Scottish champion, and James Lynch, the Irish athlete for $500 a side and the championship of the world." In their early years, many of these excursions were marred by "intemperate" behavior, but reports of such incidents all but disappeared as clergymen were invited to attend.[23]

Irish-American militia groups had appeared in New York City by mid-century and soon spread across the country. The "Irish Dragoons" (New York), "Hibernian Rifles" (San Francisco), "League of St. Patrick" (San Francisco), "Green Isle" (New York), "Shamrock" (New York), "Celtic" (New York), "Irish Jasper Greens" (Savannah, Georgia), "Irish Rifles" (Cincinnati, Greenwich, Charleston, New Orleans, and New York), "Meagher" (San Francisco),

"Montgomery" (San Francisco and New York), "Sarsfield" (New York and San Francisco), "Emmet" (New York, San Francisco, Savannah, Albany, and St. Louis), and "O'Connell Rifles" (New York) were named after Irish nationalist heroes. While some might argue that these organizations were a product of "native" companies, the Fenian agitation of 1866 and the deepest hope that one day they would return to liberate Ireland from the grip of "John Bull" implied an alternative motive. Moreover, an article in the *Irish World* suggested that the new-found democracy might play a part, as the author explained, "In Ireland the people are denied by law the right to bear arms; [whereas] in the United States it is deemed a patriotic duty in citizens to enroll themselves in military organizations." Nevertheless, Americans continued to condemn foreign-born militia for fostering divided loyalties and standing in the way of assimilation. By the turn of the century most groups had undergone a metamorphosis with the once active militia becoming competitive rifle clubs.[24]

In 1881 a reporter for the *Boston Pilot* noted that "a large number of the Irish people in Boston are becoming interested in the exhibition of the games and pastimes of their ancestors." Traditional Irish sports were not new to America. In New York, Irish Americans practiced handball throughout the city, while organized hurling teams first began to appear in the 1850s. Considered to be the most ancient of Irish sports, hurling ("Caman" in Celtic and "Iomain" in Gaelic) is a stick and ball game most closely resembling lacrosse. The earliest reference to organized hurling in the United States is the formation of a club in San Francisco in 1853. It was another four years before the Irish Hurling and Football Club was established in New York to revive that "truly Irish national sport." In the next thirty years the "New York," "Emmet," "Wolfe Tone," "Brooklyn," "Geraldine," and "Men of Ireland" teams promoted the game in New York, while, following its earliest introduction to "The Hub" by the Irish Athletic Club of Boston in 1879, the "Boston" and "Shamrock" hurling clubs led the way in New England. The Gaelic Athletic Association's "American Invasion" of 1888 had a positive impact upon hurling in the United States by the turn of the century. One correspondent optimistically reported:

Since the Gaelic Invasion of America . . . hurling has taken a firm root on American soil, and the present series of games at the magnificent grounds at Celtic Park for the James R. Keane Cup are certain to arouse an amount of interest and enthusiasm, and to make the Irish national pastime extremely popular with the exiled Gaels of Greater New York.

The Keane Gaelic Hurling Trophy was awarded, by the Greater New York Irish–American Athletic Association, to the city's champion team, while the

John Boyle O'Reilly Hurling Cup was competed for in New England under the auspices of the Irish-American Athletic Club of Boston.[25]

Gaelic football did not appear to share the widespread following that hurling claimed. The earliest account of an organized team is in New Orleans in 1859, where the game was first promoted by Irish fire companies and later by clubs bearing such nationalistic appellations as "Erin Go Bragh" and "Faugh a Ballagh." In Philadelphia the leading teams were the "Red Branch Knights" and the "Irish Nationalists," while San Francisco could boast the "Emmets," "Parnells," and "Geraldines." It seems that the names of national heroes were, once more, favored as the "Sarsfield" and "Geraldines" were foremost among the New York clubs. By 1899 the Dunn Trophy was donated to the Greater New York Irish-American Athletic Association "intended for the encouragement of the Gaelic football game and amateur sports for which Ireland was noted." That season it was competed for by the association's twenty affiliated clubs. The following year an advertisement appeared in *The Gael* for Spalding's "official" Gaelic Foot Ball costing five dollars.[26]

The ancient sports of Ireland received a boost in 1884 with the establishment of the Gaelic Athletic Association by Michael Cusack. Intended to return the control of sport to Irishmen, it might better be perceived as a manifestation of the ongoing struggle for independence by the impoverished Irish Catholic majority. In 1888 the "American Invasion" saw more than fifty Irish athletes travel to the United States competing at hurling and track and field in New York, Boston, Philadelphia, Newark, Paterson, Providence, and Lowell. Due in large part to the bad weather and popular preoccupation with the presidential campaign, attendance was low and the tour a financial disaster.[27] The first Gaelic Athletic Association in America was organized in Chicago in 1890. Three years later the Association had fifteen clubs (ten Gaelic football teams and five hurling teams) with a membership of 2,000. In Boston, a group of Irish-Americans actively sought to organize a Gaelic Athletic Union in 1985 for "those interested in the revival of Irish sports."[28] In New York City, at the turn of the century, the control of Gaelic football and hurling shifted from the Irish-American Athletic Association to the Irish Counties Athletic Union formed in 1904. Ten years later, the Gaelic Athletic Association of New York was established, taking over the role of athletic administration among the City's Irish-American sports teams.

The sheer magnitude of the wave of Irish immigration to the New World, throughout the nineteenth century, ensured its irreversible impact upon the infrastructure of American society. Sport was not to be forgotten as newly arrived denizens overlooked their frequent exploitation at the hands of professional managers in the quest for social amelioration. They were to represent a foundation in the process of ethnic succession which continues in some American professional sports today. While not all were provided the opportunity for complete assimilation through sport, Irish immigrants showed, by forming their own baseball teams replete with Gaelic appellations and brogue, that they could be as American as the next person engrossed in the national pastime. At the same time, evidence suggests that Irish-Americans (as well as other immigrant groups) fulfilled an important role in the early modernization of professional American sport. Yet their clannish attachments to the Land of Erin remained strong as national groups such as the Clan Na Gael promoted sport (particularly hurling and Gaelic football) to ensure that their fellow countrymen's Irish roots were never forgotten. Such ethnic consciousness is evident in the American athletic arena today, reminding us of the significant yet complex relationship between the Irish immigrant and sport.

NOTES

1. The plight of the nineteenth century Irish immigrant has been well-documented in William Forbes Adams, *Ireland and Irish Emigrants to the New World from 1815 to the Famine* (Baltimore: Genealogy Publishing Company, 1980); Stephen Byrne, *Irish Emigration to the United States: What It Has Been and What It Is* (New York: Catholic Publication Society, 1873); P. J. Drudy, ed., *The Irish in America: Emigration, Assimilation and Impact* (Cambridge: Cambridge University Press, 1985); Kerby A. Miller, *Emigrants and Exiles: Ireland and the Irish Exodus to North America* (New York: Oxford University Press, 1985); and Arnold Schrier, *Ireland and the American Emigration, 1850–1900* (Minneapolis: University of Minnesota Press, 1958).

2. Drudy, *Irish in America*, p. 14, Lawrence J. McCaffrey, *The Irish Diaspora in America* (Bloomington, Indiana: Indiana University Press, 1967).

3. Among the most useful sources dealing with Irish associationalism in the United States are Alfred Connable and Edward Silberfarb, *Tigers of Tammany* (New York: Holt, Rinehart and Winston, 1967); Michael Funchion, ed., *The Group Irish-American, Irish American Voluntary Organizations* (Westport, Connecticut: Greenwood Press, 1983); Edward M. Levine, *The Irish and Irish Politicians* (South Bend, Indiana: University of Notre Dame Press, 1966); and John T. Ridge, *Erin's Sons in America: The Ancient Order of Hibernians* (New York: 150th Anniversary Committee of the Ancient Order of Hibernians, 1986).

4. While there is not one comprehensive history of the Irish in America, the following volumes serve as important sources: Andrew M. Greeley, *That Most Distressful Nation: The Taming of the American Irish* (Chicago: Quadrangle Books, 1972); William V. Shannon, *The American Irish* (New York: Macmillan Company, 1974); Carl Wittke, *The Irish in America* (New York: Russell and Russell, 1970); William D. Griffin, *The Irish in America* (Dobbs Ferry, N. Y.: Oceana, 1973); William D. Griffin, *A Portrait of the Irish in America* (New York: Charles Scribner's Sons, 1981); Joseph P. O'Grady, *How the Irish Became Americans* (New York: Twayne, 1973); and Edward Wakin, *Enter the Irish-American* (New York: Thomas Y. Crowell, 1976).

5. Marcus de Burca, *The G.A.A.: A History of the Gaelic Athletic Association* (Dublin: Cumann Luthchleas Gael, 1980); Maurice Dineen, "The Game of Hurling," *The Gael* (September 1901): 290–92; Sean Egan, "The 'Aonach Tailteann' and the Tailteann Games: Origin, Function and Ancient Associations," *Canadian Association of Health, Physical Education and Recreation Journal* (May–June 1980): 3–5, 38; Alice B. Gomme, *Traditional Games of England, Scotland and Ireland* (London: Thames and Hudson, 1920); A. W. Long, *The Irish Sport of Yesterday* (Boston: Houghton Mifflin, 1923); W. F. Mandle, "The I.R.B. and the Beginnings of the Gaelic Athletic Association," *Irish Historical Studies* 20 (September 1977): 418–38; James S. Mitchel, "The Celt as an Athlete," *The Gael* (May 1901): 141–44; C. Short, *Ard Mhacha 1884–1984—A Century of Gaelic Athletic Association* (Drumang, Armagh: Gaelic Athletic Association, 1985); Herman Smulders, "Sports and Politics: The Irish Scene 1884–1921," *Review of Sport and Leisure* 2 (1977): 116–29; and P. P. Sutton, "The Ancient Games of Ireland at Tailten and Carmen," *The Gael* (July 1900): 209–12 and (August–September 1900): 255–58. See also Ralph C. Wilcox, "Rewriting Sport History. The Tailteann Games: An Ancient Irish Forerunner to the Greek Olympics?" (a paper delivered at the 1989 National Convention of the American Alliance for Health, Physical Education, Recreation and Dance, Boston, April 1989).

6. See *Irish World*, July 10, 1875, p. 8, *Wilkes' Spirit* 8 (May 2, 1863): 141. Cited in Melvin L. Adelman, *A Sporting Time: New York City and The Rise of Modern Athleteics, 1820–1870* (Urbana: University of Illinois Press, 1986), p. 228.

7. The relationship of Irish immigrants, the bachelor subculture, politics, and the prize ring is discussed in Alfred Henry Lewis, *Richard Croker* (New York: Life Publishing, 1901), pp. 42–68; Adelman, *Modern Athletics*, pp. 231–37; and Benjamin J. Rader, *American Sports from the Age of Folk Games to the Age of Spectators* (Englewood Cliffs, N. J.: Prentice-Hall, 1983), pp. 97–104.

8. Other prominent Irish-American fighters of the postbellum years included Mike McTigue, Terry McGovern, Tom Sharky, Packy McFarland, and "Philadelphia Jack" O'Brien. Finally, the original "Nonpareil" Jack Dempsey who was unbeaten as a middleweight from 1883 to 1891, was actually John Kelly from County Kildare. Also see Michael T. Isenberg, *John L. Sullivan and His America* (Urbana: University of Illinois Press, 1988).

9. John E. Tansey, *Life of Daniel O'Leary* (Chicago: n. p., 1878); J. Soler and Ed. Dodd, *Ultra Marathoning* (Mountain View, California: World Publications, 1979); *Irish World*, October 24, 1984, p. 8; May 12, 1877, pp. 3, 8; May 26, 1877, p. 3; June 30, 1877, p. 8; and July 14, 1877, p. 5.

10. *Irish World*, March 30, 1878, p. 8; March 22, 1879, p. 5.

11. *Irish World*, September 4, 1875, p. 8. See also Robert F. Kelley, *American Rowing: Its Background and Traditions* (New York: Putnam, 1932); Thomas Corwin Mendenhall, *A Short History of American Rowing* (Boston: Charles River Books, 1980), pp. 16–17, 60–70; *Irish World*, April 8, 1871, p. 7; March 2, 1872, p. 8; May 3, 1873, p. 8; September 6, 1873, p. 8; April 11, 1874, p. 8; June 27, 1874, p. 8; September 12, 1874, p. 6; September 19, 1874, p. 8; October 3, 1874, p. 8; June 12, 1875, p. 8, July 24, 1875, pp. 3, 8; January 13, 1877, p. 8; July 7, 1877, p. 8; July 28, 1877, p. 8; August 25, 1877, p. 8; June 8, 1878, p. 8; September 7, 1878, p. 8; Newport *Daily News*, May 19, 1902; July 5, 1902; September 20, 1902; and September 8, 1903.

12. The most comprehensive discussion of the rise and demise of cricket in America is found in George B. Kirsch, *The Creation of American Team Sports: Baseball and Cricket, 1838–72* (Urbana: University of Illinois Press, 1989); and Adelman, *Modern Athletics*, pp. 97–119. Also see William J. Baker, *Sports in the Western World* (Totowa, N. J.: Rowman and Littlefield, 1982), pp. 138–39; Rader, *American Sports*, pp. 90–91. George B. Kirsch, "American Cricket: Players and Clubs before the Civil War," *Journal of Sport History* 11 (1984): 33 has shown that 8 percent of cricketers in Newark, New Jersey, from 1855 to 1860 were Irish (while only 3 percent of baseball players were Irish), with their greater representation on the Mechanics Cricket Club (17 percent).

13. Steven A. Riess, "Race and Ethnicity in American Baseball, 1900–1919," *Journal of Ethnic Studies*, 4 (Winter 1977): 39–55. James S. Mitchel, "The Celt as a Baseball Player," *The Gael* (May 1902): 151–55. *Irish World*, October 31, 1874, p. 8; June 5, 1875, p. 8; June 26, 1875, p. 8; July 17, 1875, p. 8; July 24, 1875, p. 8; August 14, 1875, p. 8; June 3, 1876, p. 8; June 10, 1876, p. 8; June 17, 1876, p. 8; June 24, 1876, p. 8; November 11, 1876, p. 8; May 26, 1877, p. 8; July 28, 1877, p. 8; Harold Seymour, *Baseball: The Early Years*, vol. 1 (New York: n. p., 1960), pp. 327–28; Arthur Daley, "The American Irish in Sports," *The Recorder* 34 (1973): 100; and Jack Kavanaugh, "The Silver King Remembered," *Sports Heritage* (January–February 1987): 72–77. Ernest L. Thayer, "Casey at the Bat: (A Ballad of the Republic. Sung in the Year 1888)," San Francisco *Examiner*, June 3, 1888.

14. *Irish World*, June 7, 1879, p. 8; de Burca, "American Irish," p. 45; Daley, p. 95; Mitchel (May 1901), pp. 143–44; New York *Times*, July 18, 1900; August 2, 1904; William Simons, "Abel Kiviat Interview," *Journal of Sport History* 13 (Winter 1986): 249–50, Bob Considine and Fred G. Jarvis, *A Portrait of the N.Y.A.C.: The First Hundred Years* (London: Macmillian, 1969), pp. 98–105; David Chester, *The Olympic Games Handbook* (New York: Charles Scribner's Sons, 1971). James Brendan Connolly, "Oh, How They Ran!" *Colliers* 104 (September 16, 1939): 27, 75–76. For the most comprehensive source pertaining to the Scottish contribution to American track and field, see Gerald Redmond, *The Caledonian Games in Nineteenth Century America* (Rutherford, N. J.: Fairleigh Dickinson University Press, 1971).

15. Ernest Cummings Marriner, *Jim Connolly and the Fishermen of Gloucester* (Waterville, Maine: Colby College Press, 1949); John K. Hutchens, "Jim the Salty Penman," New York *Herald Tribune Weekly Book Review*, June 12, 1949, p. 2; in "Hats off to Connolly" *The Saturday Review of Literature*, September 16, 1933, follows the model of a classic novel about ancient athletics, focusing upon how a Greek peasant won the Marathon race. The autobiographical flavor is enhanced as he modestly alludes to the fact that an American won the triple jump. James Brendan Connolly, "The Spirit of the Olympian Games," *Outing Magazine* 48 (April 1906): 101–4 provides a colorful account of the events of 1896. James Brendan Connolly, "How Cronan Went to Athens," *Everybody's Magazine* (July 1910): 443–54; idem, "Record Breaking," *Colliers* 100 (November 13 1937), pp. 17, 68–69, and "Oh, How They Ran!" *Colliers* 104 (September 16, 1939), pp. 27, 75–76.

16. *Irish World*, April 10, 1875, p. 8; July 3, 1875, p. 3; January 29, 1876, p. 3; and July 27, 1878, p. 8.

17. ibid.

18. Greeley, *Distressful Nation*, pp. 7–8.

19. *Irish World*, June 3, 1871, p. 5; J. C. Furnas, *The Americans—A Social History of the United States 1587–1914* (New York: G. P. Putnam's Sons, 1969), p. 659, cited in John Rickards Betts, *America's Sporting Heritage: 1850–1950* (Reading, Mass.: Addison-Wesley, 1974), p. 222. *Donahoe's Magazine* 9 (May 1883: 466–77; 14 (November 1885): 444–46; and 20 (July–August 1888): 24–31, 148–57, cited in Ryan (1983), p. 115; *New York Times*, March 17, 1879. John Boyle O'Reilly, *The Ethics of Boxing and Manly Sport* (Boston: Ticknor and Company, 1888).

20. Reverend William R. Huntingdon, "Songs of the Harvard versus Fort Hill Boy Rowing Match of 1858," *Harvard Magazine* (July 1858).

21. Quoted in Nathaniel S. Fleischer, *The Boston Strong Boy: The Story of John L. Sullivan: The Champion of Champions* (New York: O'Brien, 1941), p. 35; also see Lewis, *Richard Croker*, pp. 60–61.

22. Bill Mallon, "To No Earthly King," *Sports Heritage. The Journal of Our Sporting Past* 1 (May–June 1987): 27–28; New York *Times*, August 7, 1904; September 2, 1904; and Simons, "Abel Kiviat," p. 256.

23. *Irish World*, September 6, 1873, p. 7. Roberta J. Park, "British Sports and Pastimes in San Francisco, 1848–1900," *British Journal of Sports History* 1 (December 1984): 311; *Irish World*, August 19, 1871, p. 7; August 25, 1871, p. 7; May 18, 1872, p. 8; August 10, 1872, p. 8; September 6, 1873, p. 5; August 8, 1874, p. 8; August 15, 1874, p. 8; August 29, 1874, p. 8; August 14, 1875, p. 8; May 27, 1876, p. 8; June 16, 1877, p. 8; June 30, 1877, p. 2; July 14, 1877, p. 8; July 28, 1877, p. 8; August 11, 1877, p. 8; August 25, 1877, p. 8; June 22, 1878, p. 8; July 20, 1878, p. 8; July 27, 1878, p. 8; August 10, 1878, p. 8; and June 7, 1879, p. 8.

24. Park, "British Sports," pp. 309–10; *Irish World*, February 21, 1874, p. 8; April 25, 1874, p. 8; September 19, 1874, p. 8; September 26, 1874, p. 4; May 8, 1875, p. 6; August 14, 1875, p. 8; August 25, 1875, p. 8; June 24, 1876, p. 8; September 8, 1877, p. 8; June 29, 1878, p. 8; August 17, 1878, p. 8; and September 7, 1878, p. 8.

25. Boston Pilot 4, June 25, 1881, cited in Stephen Hardy, *How Boston Played: Sport, Recreation, and Community 1865–1915* (Boston: Northeastern University Press, 1982), p. 138. *Irish World*, July 27, 1878, p. 8; and August 31, 1878, p. 8. Also see Robert P. Smith, "Heroes and Hurrahs: Sports in Brooklyn, 1890–1898," *Journal of Long Island History* 15 (Fall 1978): 11. *Daily Alta California*, May 4, 1853, cited in Park, "British Sports," p. 312; *Irish News*, December 12, 1857; *Irish World*, August 19, 1871, p. 7; August 14, 1875, p. 8; July 14, 1877, p. 8. Dinneen, "The Game of Hurling," pp. 291–92.

26. *Irish World*, August 19, 1871, p. 7; September 6, 1873, p. 7; June 17, 1876, p. 8; June 24, 1876, p. 8. *The Gael* (October 1899): 196; Park, "British Sports," p. 312, *The Gael* (March 1901): 102.

27. See de Burca, *The G. A. A.*, Mandle, "The I. R. E.," Short, *Ard Mhacha*, (1985), and Smulders, "Sports and Politics." The failures of the 1888 tour did not deter the Gaelic Athletic Association which returned to the United States in 1926, 1927, and finally in 1947 for the All-Ireland Football Final played before 35,000 spectators at the Polo Grounds in New York.

28. Funchion, *The Group*, pp. 128–29, Cull and Concannon, *Irish Directory*, p. 25; *Boston Journal*, May 6, 1895, cited in Hardy, p. 138.

5

Jews and Baseball: A Cultural Love Story

Eric Solomon

"I love baseball; you know it doesn't have to mean anything, it's just beautiful to watch"

—Woody Allen, *Zelig*.

Why Jews and baseball? Why connect a wave of immigrant tailors and Talmud scholars, and their descendants, to a game mostly played by American farm boys who were classified by their greatest bard, Ring Lardner, as barely literate? The answer does not necessarily lie in the fact that there have always been a number of Jewish-American major league ballplayers from Lipman Pike, who in 1866 earned credit for becoming the first professional player, to Hall of Fame members Hank Greenberg and Sandy Koufax. Interestingly, unlike most Jewish players, both of these greatest of all Jewish stars respected their ethnicity, not playing on Yom Kippur. And toward the end of his life, Greenberg changed his earlier desire to be known simply as a great ballplayer: "I find myself wanting to be remembered . . . even more as a great Jewish ball-player."[1] Although baseball historians may argue about numbers, Peter Levine's figure of 110 Jewish major league players from 1871 to 1980 (out of 10,000) seems accurate.[2]

More remarkably, the figure seemed low to many in the 1920s and 1930s. In 1926 *Baseball Magazine*'s F. C. Lane posed the question "Why Not More Jewish Ball Players?" in a game as "cosmopolitan as baseball." He quotes pitcher Ed Reulbach arguing that magnates should seek "some hook-nosed youngster who could bat and field" to supply a proper hero for Jewish fans.[3] John McGraw, who often carried as many as four Jewish ballplayers on his Giants roster, was always seeking a Jewish Babe Ruth, but the closest McGraw came was the brief career of the hopeless Moses Solomon, the ill-named

"Rabbi of Swat." Indeed, *The American Hebrew,* June 1, 1926, editorialized about McGraw's acquisition of second baseman Andy Cohen: "If Cohen comes through as his manager expects him to . . . he will rival Babe Ruth as a drawing attraction and stimulate the interest of the Jews of America in our great national pastime. . . . Baseball is the great American sport and as the Jew is thoroughly Americanized there is no reason why his name should not be prominently found upon the baseball roll of honor."[4] This, perhaps, appeared to refute Lane's conclusion that Jews were too much interested in the better odds for business success to apply their "keen and active minds" to baseball.

The percentage of Jewish-American novelists writing about baseball, however, seems to be quite the reverse: with the great exceptions of Ring Lardner, Robert Coover, W. P. Kinsella, and a few others, the number of Jewish novelists employing baseball as theme or trope has been massive. Baseball works its way into fiction about immigrants or family generational struggles by Gerald Green, Chaim Potok, Delmore Schwartz, J. G. Salinger, Paul Goodman, E. L. Doctorow, and Max Apple. The game provides the subject for early realists like Charles Einstein, Eliot Asinof, Irwin Shaw, Mark Harris; for authors of modernist baseball classics, combining in a very Jewish manner realism and fantasy, such as Bernard Malamud's *The Natural,* or postmodern popular culture parodies like Philip Roth's *The Great American Novel;* for feminists like Eve Babitz and Sylvia Tennenbaum; for a present generation of innovative baseball novelists such as Jerome Charyn, Jay Neugeboren, Eric Greenberg, Harry Stein, Robert Mayer, whose rhythms are Jewish and whose idioms baseball; for journalists-turned-novelists like Roger Kahn and Donald Honig; for science fiction and detective story writers; for authors of what has become a major American-Jewish genre, the lyrical memoir. According to Leslie Fiedler, "The writing of the American-Jewish novel is essentially . . . an act of assimilation: a demonstration that there is an American Jew (whose Jewishness and Americanism enrich each other) and that he feels at home."[5] The writer about baseball took on a traditional Jewish assimilationist role. The task, as set forth by Allen Guttman in "The Conversions of the Jews," "of the writer alienated from traditional Judaism is the secularization of Judaism's historic sense of mission."[6]

Baseball and Jews? American popular culture resonates with Jewish angles on the game—radio and television shows, plays, songs, ah, the songs. From Irving Berlin's "Jake, Jake, the Yiddishe Ball Player" to Paul Simon's "Where have you gone, Joe DiMaggio?" songwriters like Hy Gilbert, Sammy Cahn, or Ira Gershwin have attended to baseball. Baseball art includes work by Saul Steinberg, R. B. Kitaj, Roy Lichtenstein, Claes Oldenberg, Ben Shahn, and Harvey Dinnerstein.[7] In all this concentration of baseball, there is, of course, a "de-Semitization" process, a reflection as in Arthur Miller's plays or Hollywood films about the America of the assimilated Jews' hearts' desire, "a place where people have the same non-distinctive names, speak the same unaccented language, and share the same undivided national loyalties."[8]

Why? Among the many dimensions of the Jewish love affair with baseball, five concepts seem to predominate. The national game provided a superb avenue for acculturation—where a minority group emulates the dominant culture's values and customs—and assimilation—where a minority group is absorbed into the dominant culture. Baseball's original role for the immigrant, then, was not unlike that of the Yiddish theater, paradoxical as that might seem, which took as one of its missions the aim of teaching success and the transformation from *Yidn* to Yankee.[9] Next, baseball appealed, particularly in its remarkable historical and statistical documentation, to the argumentative, dialectical Jewish intellect, trained in Hebrew school in the methodology of *pilpul,* the close reading of religious texts. Torah study calls for simultaneous concentration on historical fundamentals and on logical interpretation—thus arguments as to who was the greater outfielder, Ruth or Cobb, or better pitcher, Johnson or Matthewson. Because this same Jewish sensibility was obsessed with the past—and remains haunted to our time by the Holocaust memory—the claims of history and folklore, the Old Testament and the family chronicle, baseball provided instant American nostalgia.

Third, since Jewish sons should not, according to their elders' beliefs, actually play baseball professionally, many wrote plays, novels, stories, songs, and poems about the national game; painted and sculpted the heroic moments; and wrote biography, history, reportage, using heads not hands. Then, baseball became a city game, and a preponderance of Jewish youth identified their urban roles by their ball clubs: if one grew up in Flatbush, one followed the Dodgers, in "the shadow of Coogan's Bluff," the Giants, in the Bronx (perhaps) the Yankees; other multiple-team cities like Boston or Chicago brought forth similar urban allegiances. Murray Baumgarten explains clearly the urban aspect of baseball in reference to Doctorow's *Ragtime:* "Baseball and city life are experiences in surprise, rewarding alertness to new situations where split-second judgments depend on knowing how to take advantage of the breaks. Like walking in the city, which is a matter of feeling your way through space, so baseball is a game of the individual's constant negotiation with his changing environment."[10]

Finally, it is baseball itself, the national game rich in folklore, deep in mythology, full of anecdote in the Scholem Aleichem mode, cabbalistic in numerology, quasi-religious in its gods, creative in language, reminiscent for some of an (invented?) rural past, denying time's rules while emphasizing the conflict between youth and age—mythic, historical, spiritual, simple and complex, harsh and beautiful, real and fictional . . . baseball, in simple, is America. And for the Jew who sought hyphenation—the 1930s Jewish-American, the 1950s American-Jewish, after 1990 what?—baseball provides a path into the cultural highway, the traditions, the rituals, the ceremonies, the society, the past, the secular religion of the United States.

As I have described elsewhere, baseball gave a focal point to the Jewish immigrant come to America to *stay,* more prepared to accept a full cultural transformation than, say, Italian Catholics who planned to return home or British Protestants who found little change, those who retained dreams of coming back wealthy to a beloved homeland or who kept emotional and familial ties.[11] For the Jewish arrival, baseball was a substitute for the *shtetl*—a center of perception and community with strong cultural traditions, psychological sanctions, and emotional commitments—and the *shul,* a center of belief and ritual. Thus, to know and love baseball was to know and love America. Certainly, the America the immigrant Jew found was depersonalized and dehumanized, in large part, not very different from the David Riesman-defined other-directed world their children and grandchildren would inherit. As Abraham Karp puts it, "The structured, ordered life of the *shtetl* was replaced by the socially fluid, economically frenetic, and religiously lax life of the American urban center."[12] In Peter Rose's terms, "Other immigrants also felt the sense of separateness. . . . But the Jews were bound and determined not to let any barrier divert their quest for a respected place in American society. For one thing, Jewish immigrants . . . had almost all taken one-way tickets to America."[13] Of course, for post–World War II European Jews who had escaped to America, there *was* no world to return to: "the Jew was cut off by birth, place, and circumstance."[14] My argument goes that the Jewish youth and adult alike could find America *in* baseball yet hold on to—just as the game itself lives on memories of nearly instant history, an invented past that in a Faulknerian sense ever looms over the present—a Jewish identity *through* baseball.[15]

In the game's fans, one found a community as well as rituals like Opening Day or the World Series or crosstown rivalries. Moses Rischin discovered this Jewish need for community, which I posit baseball's schedule and sports page reports helped to fulfill. "Unhinged from the old associations, the calendar guideposts to feasts and fasts appeared less reliable. Religious festivals, with their spontaneous, even pastoral charm, went limp, drained of communal relish, out of touch with the seasons."[16] That Jewish immigrants seemed to adjust more rapidly and successfully to American ways than did other immigrant groups[17] perhaps accounts for their interest in baseball and its changing seasons, reminding us of Jacques Barzun's apothegm that to understand America, one must first understand baseball. Steven Riess quotes a settlement house worker from a Jewish neighborhood in Chicago: "We consider baseball one of the best means of teaching our boys American ideas and ideals."[18] Baseball not only taught traditional values; it also helped newcomers join the mainstream through embracing the customs of the sport.

Baseball at its most sophisticated is memory; so too is the Jewish experience, especially as recreated in secular ways, in art and life. But it was never easy. "The immigrant father's view of life did not provide for sports, and he was distressed by his American son's concentration on sandlot ball in boyhood."[19] But when this youth became an adult, still "he has often bolstered his ego by identifying with brawn . . . Jewish sports heroes have an irresistible attraction for the American Jew. Against his better judgment he is prouder of a Sandy Koufax . . . than of a Marc Chagall."[20] The case of Moe Berg is instructive. Perhaps the most brilliant and best-educated man ever to play the game—in a journeyman fashion with fifteen years as a backup catcher and a .243 lifetime batting average—Berg's apparent dismissal of his degrees from Princeton, Columbia, and the Sorbonne, his seeming disdain for his advanced law and linguistic training coupled with his manifest love for baseball and the special male bonding involved in playing the game and even in hanging on in the most demeaning role on a major league club, that of bullpen catcher—all this confounded his family. "Moe could have been a brilliant barrister, but he gave it all up for baseball."[21] Baseball was fun; business or a profession was work. To Eddie Cantor's pious people of the ghetto, a baseball player was "the king of the loafers."[22] Still, Abraham Cahan, despite his firm beliefs in the Jewish work ethic, in education, in social responsibility, in the wonders of Yiddish culture, and in the honor of their being people of the book, reluctantly accepted the importance of baseball as an acculturating concept. He published in the *Jewish Daily Forward,* August 27, 1909, in Yiddish a diagram of the Polo Grounds with rules of the game, "Der iker fun di baseball game, erklert for mit keyn sports layt."[23] In those American cities that were beginning to house substantial non–Anglo-Saxon immigrant populations, baseball, according to Richard Crepeau, was expected to teach the Anglo-Saxon idea of play: "Baseball, the sportswriters averred, could play an important part in the Americanization of immigrants, since it was the purveyor of democracy."[24] This attitude was not limited to Eastern European immigrants in New York. The Sephardic

Jews of Los Angeles formed baseball teams in the 1930s, to instill pride and unity, and joined the B'nai B'rith League.[25]

Baseball supplied a source for generational conflict between parents who sought to retain religious and work traditions and sons who wanted to become as American as possible. On the other hand, the game would provide a source for community between these same sons, when they became adults, and their progeny. Conflict and love: sounds very Jewish and the stuff of innumerable baseball novels. And memoirs. The literary critic Leslie Fiedler speaks of the thirties, and the short story writer Max Apple describes the fifties, and the stories are different but the needs the same. Fiedler was looking for assimilated, really WASP parents, rather than his own "Yiddish-speaking grandparents and a father who never joined me at playing baseball."[26] Apple, from a later vantage point, grasped the generational distinctions. Even though his grandfather wanted Max to become a Talmud scholar, his grandmother a successful businessman, and his mother a lawyer, his working class father alone knew what the boy dreamed of: "to play second base for the Tigers and have a level swing like Al Kaline."[27] Irwin Shaw, Roger Kahn, Eric Greenberg, and Sylvia Tennenbaum have written movingly in novels about the moments of truth between generations engendered by a mutual love for the game of baseball. According to Marc Raphael, "Baseball served as one of the many 'American' cultural activities which attracted second-generation Jews, helped to define them as Americans, and thus differentiate them from the immigrant parents."[28]

Many of these immigrant parents denied their children the rights to become baseball players—a fact highlighted by there being seven major leaguers actually named Cohen, only one of whom, Andy, playing under his given name rather than Bohne, Kane, Cooney, aliases designed to protect the parental reputations in the neighborhood, not to avoid anti-Semitic slurs. (Not that anti-Semitism among ballplayers and fans didn't exist. Al Rosen, Sam Nahem, Saul Rogovin, and Cal Abrams have all joined Hank Greenberg's testimonies of verbal abuses.) Isaac Asimov is fascinating on the subject of why frustrated players like Shaw and Roth turn to baseball fiction. "To write great novels—yes, that was permitted Jewish boys, along with playing violins (not saxophones or guitars), playing chess (not poker or pool), and becoming a doctor or a lawyer (or, in an emergency, a dentist or an optometrist)—*but not a ballplayer*" (my italics). Asimov goes on to say, "The result is that a great many novels written in America deal with Jewish themes. After all, what else are all these great Jewish novelists going to write about? Methodists? to which I would reply, no, ballplayers."[29]

Baseball did not merely posit an intellectual or sentimental gathering place; the game was, as Cahan grudgingly came to understand, didactic, in the broadest sense of the term. Steven Riess has documented the ways baseball's anecdotes and records taught American values and beliefs.[30] Commitment to the progress of a professional ball club was an excellent assimilating tool. Gunther Barth has closely studied how the rules of the game taught immigrants to comprehend the possibilities of dissent within proscribed limits as they booed the umpire; how Yiddish speakers could still find urban pleasures and ways of belonging to the city; how newly-minted Americans could replicate Talmudic study by compulsively figuring club standings and batting averages; and how to attain—rather, have their children attain—new myths and folk legends, no longer Jewish, but American.[31] The "storehouse of myth" was no longer the Bible, but *Who's Who in Baseball.*[32] One writer, remembering his growing up in the 1920s, only partly ironically states that while he didn't actually believe Babe Ruth was Jewish, the boy nevertheless never thought of such heroes as anything else "in a period when most of New York's Jews were striving desperately to become Americanized."[33]

For the Jewish adult, either coming to America from Europe or studying American values for his generation, baseball was the objective correlative for comprehension of American rhythms, American dreams. Perhaps the most remarkable statement of what baseball could mean to an American was written by the distinguished Jewish philosopher Morris Raphael Cohen for the *Dial* right after the 1919 Chicago Black Sox scandal. Cohen adored baseball, thought of it as a secular religion and a moral equivalent of war. And his personal love affair with the game commenced in boyhood, naturally. He writes in his diary, "I begged Mama to let me go out and play baseball, but life was earnest on the Lower East Side"; he would go on to write about and teach ethics and metaphysics to generations of City College students, but he would also contribute complicated baseball questions to the radio quiz program *Information Please* in the 1940s. In his essay simply entitled "Baseball," Cohen compares the game to the fine arts of song, story, painting, sculpture, and music and asks what some later scholar might define as America's essence. "And when he comes to speak of America's contribution to religion, will he not mention baseball?" Cohen compares the game to Greek drama: "Is there any other experience in modern life in which multitudes of men so completely and intensely lose their individual lives in the larger life which they call their city?" Certainly, Morris Cohen writes with tongue in cheek when he tells of his dispute with the psychologist William James who had difficulty accepting Cohen's suggestion that baseball embodied all the moral force of war without the ultimate violence—"All great men have their limitations, and William James's were due to the fact that he lived in Cambridge, a city which, in spite of the fact that it has a population of 100,000 souls is not represented in any baseball league that can be detected without a microscope."[34]

The question as to why many new American intellectuals turned to a game such as baseball is perhaps best answered in a recent study of Leo Spitzer, the distinguished European philologist who ended up teaching at Johns Hopkins. Geoffrey Green writes that a literary person or an artist "who was trying to penetrate to the soul of the nation from an entry point within a literary work of art often, without fully realizing it, initiated his circle of understanding with an insight about the soul of the nation derived not from the literary text, but from his own experiences as a new American citizen; the scholarly materials would then be arranged to support this encompassing knowledge."[35]

Early and late, baseball has been a gateway to America's conceptualization, a game quintessentially faithful to youthful dreams and elderly memories. Delmore Schwartz, the poet who adored baseball, has a character in his short story "The Track Meet" who uses the game to explain America to an Englishman: "I suggested we go to a baseball game, since it was a purely American phenomenon."[36] Bernard Rosenberg and Ernest Goldstein posit that the Jews have always been great assimilators (their prime example is George Gershwin's ease in making Black music part of his own creative rhythm), a group that takes whatever useful materials a culture has to offer, en route, as it were. Thus baseball was of as great value for the educated refugee in the middle decades of the century as it was for the greenhorn earlier. They use Soma Morgenstern, a "Jewish Novelist in New York," as an informant. Confused by a sports joke in the *Daily News*—"I didn't even understand this type of reportage or what baseball could be. . . . At first I was biased against baseball; those uniforms reminded me of the chimney sweepers in Vienna"—unable to understand explanations offered by friends like the artist Al Hirschfield, Morgenstern is finally taken to a major league game by the critic Harvey Breit. "I will never forget this man for what he did because it was such a big part of my being Americanized. I don't think you can be Americanized if you don't understand baseball. All the other sports are not American."[37]

Of course, not all modern Jewish arrivals in the United States accepted baseball. The novelist Isaac Bashevis Singer felt only cultural shock at the strange sight of "boys holding sticks resembling rolling pins and wearing huge gloves on one hand [playing] ball in the middle of the street."[38] But for every Singer there were many more like the concert pianist Vladimir Horowitz who "when he left the Soviet Union . . . vowed never to return, and he became an avid baseball fan."[39] Perhaps the most interesting testimony of baseball's acculturating powers comes from the journalist Lesley Hazelton, often exiled, from Germany to England, where she had played a simple version of the game, then to Israel, finally coming to the United States as an adult. "I was fresh off the plane from Israel. It was only my second day in the United States, but my friends had made the shocked discovery that I had never seen a baseball diamond." Therefore, she comes to America's vital center, Yankee Stadium, home of America's true baseball God, Babe Ruth (flawed though he might be) and his acolyte Lou Gehrig (idealized though he was), the man who spoke some of baseball history's most moving words in his tragic farewell speech full of gratitude for his great good luck in once having been young and a Yankee. The game is specially ritualistic in part because it always repeats itself. So Hazelton arrives at Yankee Stadium on Catfish Hunter Day. "I gasped at the perfect greenness of it. What happened then was everything I expected of America." There was a band, a ceremony, speeches, gifts; the Catfish spoke, as had Gehrig, one of those traditional, elegiac, mystical baseball sentences that go to make up the folklore of the game: "'Thank you, God,' he said, 'for giving me strength and making me a ballplayer.'" For Hazelton, it was an epiphany: "And I too was up on my feet and cheering. It was the perfect American day, the perfect American place, the perfect American sentence." All the love for the game that veteran baseball journalists and historians from Dan Daniel and Arnold Hano to Richard Grossinger and Ira Berkow have written about rings again in Hazelton's immediate response. "That combination of faith and morality, sincerity and naivete was everything my Old-World preconceptions had led me to expect, and . . . I felt that I had my first glimpse of a mythical place called America."[40]

The idea of baseball can be relatively simple for the Jewish memoirist, like ACLU Executive Director Ira Glasser's paean to Dodger outfielder Carl Furillo: "We Dodger fans will miss him. . . . Your heart may have given out, but in our minds and memories your arm remains strong."[41] Or perhaps not simple: Roger Kahn's *The Boys of Summer* takes off from that same memory and combines nostalgia for the great Dodger teams he saw as a young reporter, memories of his father's ballplaying stories and shared love of the game, the anger of his Jewish mother's disdain for something as anti-intellectual as baseball, and, finally, Kahn's *memento mori* reportage of where those aging Dodgers came out in later life—that book, more a novel than a memoir, was very Jewish and complex. Then there is the case of Harry Ruby, the songwriter, who had a lifetime obsession with baseball, calling himself the world's greatest fan, writing baseball songs, meeting players, watching games, organizing softball contests. "Harry Ruby," recalled the sports columnist Red Smith, "felt deeply about music, yet given his choice of composing Beethoven's Third or ripping a line drive over second like Bill Dickey, he would have suited up on the spot. He loved the game but would infinitely rather have been Pete Rose than Arthur Rubenstein."[42] One hears the same sentiments from Philip Roth's Portnoy, who puts playing center field nearly over sex; and Gary Morgenstein entitles a novel *The Man Who Wanted To Play Center Field for the New York Yankees.* Somewhere between Ruby's obsession and Glasser's continuing interest is the position of Jules Tygiel, a labor historian who wrote a fine book on Jackie Robinson and the integration of baseball. Tygiel explains how while working in a library on his dissertation, he stumbled across an old *Life* magazine with Robinson's picture on the cover. Although only born in 1949, Tygiel was nurtured on the Robinson legend. "My favorite player was Jackie Robinson, largely because he integrated baseball. I was not sure what this meant, but I knew it was wonderful. I thus learned my first lesson in politics and race relations."[43]

Sometimes the knowledge of baseball must still be generational. For the writer who may well be the most intensely Jewish author of the twentieth century, as well as the most obsessed with the European past, Elie Wiesel, there was no place for baseball in his mind or heart. And when asked—one assumes because he was a Nobel Prize winner—to throw out the first ball in Game Two of the 1986 World Series, he at first refuses because it will take place on *Shabbat* (shades of Greenberg, Koufax, and, the baseball buff recalls, Art Shamsky), and the next game will be on Sukkoth. As a good Talmudist, with a fourteen-year-old son who loves baseball, Wiesel goes to his rabbi and gets permission to go since it's a night game—after sundown. "So when he came back for a third time, I took counsel with my son . . . a very great fan . . . I don't know for whom, for baseball anyway. And when he heard that, he was more impressed of that than of my getting the Nobel Prize. So, of course, I accepted doing it." A bit arch, but the Wiesels, father and son, go to the Series, "which apparently is an important event, I don't know."[44]

Certainly for this century in the United States baseball has held a remarkably strong grasp on youth's imagination. And for the Jewish boy baseball seemed special, a way of communicating with one's Christian peers as well as a method for employing memory and imagination. Whether playing the game or following the box scores, generations of Jewish young people distinguished their dreams by baseball metaphors. The national game supplies a theme, a litany, that stitches together decades of Jewish autobiographies.

Going back to the 1930s, the literary critic Irving Howe in his autobiography at once seeks to draw on collective Jewish memory yet continues to view himself as a semi-outsider, attached to and separate from Jewish life. Proud of having been a good ballplayer at age ten and ashamed when his parents broke through his American mask by calling him "Oiving," he resembled at that age the dramatist Clifford Odets who, said Harold Clurman, "wanted to be the world's greatest baseball player."[45] In the bad times of the Depression, Howe remembers, preparing to face the great world outside of the family, he escaped "the immigrant milieu" by attending a movie with his mother, and "another time I went with my father to Yankee Stadium and sat a few dozen yards from Babe Ruth, the greatest man in the Bronx."[46]

To become a ballplayer or to be part of fandom—the needs were similar. The sister of San Francisco newspaper columnist Herb Caen still feels the struggle between culture (Jewish) and sport (American) in her family. In 1930s Sacramento, "We both grew up with music. My mother was an opera singer, and I studied at Juilliard. Herb played a lot of piano until he was fourteen. Then baseball came along and he stopped entirely. I remember the neighbors used to say 'This is exactly what we need. A great Jewish baseball player'."[47] Rabbi Stephen Lerner, editor of *Conservative Judaism,* despite growing up in the Bronx, was not a Yankee fan because "I first fell in love with baseball, with the New York Giants, and with my hero, Johnny Mize." The boy responded to the big first baseman with the worshipful approach usually reserved for God: "I loved him with the irrational abandon that I suppose is true of all selfless love." When the slugger was traded to the Yankees, the future rabbi made the appropriate ethnic adjustment. "Many sleepless nights later, I decided that I would follow my hero into the world of *tumah* (Hebrew for impurity), and become a Yankee fan. Together with him I would endeavor to fan the spark of holiness that could be found in the most unholy places." Yet while watching Mize become a great pinch hitter for the Yankees, young Lerner returned his affections to the Giants, realizing that team loyalty was more important than Talmudic logic chopping, "bringing practical Kabbalah into baseball was ultimately unrewarding."[48]

The biographer of Vladimir Nabokov, Alfred Appel, argues for the distinction between the efficacy of baseball and that of other sports for the growth of one's mental agility. "As the war ended, and adolescence approached, we put down our guns in favor of bats and balls. Although we followed all major sports and went to every sports movie, baseball alone was an abiding, trans-seasonal pastime, offering mental giants an encyclopedic body of statistical lore that could be commanded more easily than a baseball field. History engaged us along with current events. . . . We impersonated the omnipotence of the great players, past and present."[49] Reading, perhaps especially for the Jewish boy, was crucial, and baseball certainly helped. The arts critic Gerald Nachman exaggerates, "I'm sure I'd read more classics if only they had little drawings and were more concerned with baseball, like most of the 538 books I read between the ages of nine and fifteen. Surely, 538 boys' baseball novels are worth one Paradise Lost or *The Communist Manifesto.*"[50] The Harvard sociologist David Riesman battled his intensely intellectual German-Jewish parents in the Philadelphia of the 1920s: "I was a disappointment to parents who learned Italian late in order to read Dante. It was not cultivated to know the batting averages of all major league players."[51] Not cultivated, perhaps, but very Jewish. The editor Theodore Solatoroff speaks for all of these Jewish boys looking backward on baseball memories (the present author included) in his analysis of the twin pulls of America and Jewishness being intensified by the game of baseball: "simply to say, 'Okay, you're a Jew!' after all and define myself accordingly would hardly account for all my sense of myself. I also grew up playing first base rather than in prayer. My boyhood idol was Lou Gehrig . . . I have a powerful immediacy about being American and a powerful hauntedness about being Jewish."[52]

While Jewish women's memoirs of their youthful involvement with baseball are rare, some exist—just as there are in the arena of popular culture some adult novels, particularly Sylvia Tennenbaum's *Rachel the Rabbi's Wife,* and a number of juvenile books—and one is especially pertinent. Ann Birstein the novelist has written a fascinating biography of her father, *The Rabbi on Forty Seventh Street;* he led the Slobodka Yeshiva whose congregation largely consisted of theatrical people such as Eddie Cantor, Sophie Tucker, Jack Benny, Ted Lewis, among others. Despite the daughter's assimilation, she was shocked when her father took her to the Polo Grounds on a Friday—but it was, after all, Ladies' Day. She was more surprised, she recalls, to discover her father knowledgeable about the game. "I went with Sam Rosh when you were in the *cockoleyn.* I've studied." (Such an aspect of Jewish-American rabbinical studies!) Introducing her to his friends—who come, literally, out of the pages of Damon Runyan—the Rabbi teaches her how to fill out a scorecard, "showing me how it was done. 1, Carl Hubbell, pitching, we're lucky. . . . 2, Hank Danning, catching, he's Jewish, you know." Yet her father remains clear as to the distinction between what is proper for a Jewish man and a Jewish girl to do in public: "Then Carl Hubbell was on the mound and it was 3 and 2 against Demaree, and my father leaped to his feet yelling, 'Come on, strike him out, you *goslin,* strike him out!' '*Momzer, Momzer!*' I cried, leaping up with him.

'Channela, sit down,' my father said, subsiding. The Jewish and baseball motifs come together, then separate. Although the Rabbi yells himself hoarse against the Cubs, he realizes that the sun is setting on the Sabbath eve, and he rises to leave, despite his daughter's pleas. "'What a shame you have to leave now, Rabbi,' Johnny Broderick said. 'It's only a game,' my father said, walking out backwards. In the lower grandstand, he popped his head in one more time, and shook it slowly." Unlike the youth, the adult still puts the Jewish religion above the American ball game, albeit reluctantly. But in his subsequent sermon delivered on the high holydays, he calls for a Jewish sense of community (the Giants?) and commitment (the religion): "It is sad that in Athens, the ones who were punished after a war were those who did not take part on one side or the other. To put it another way, and as Hank Danning will tell you, you can't get to first base without going to bat."[53]

If Jewish baseball art and fiction, at their best, wander from realism—as in Bernard Malamud's *The Natural* or in Ben Shahn's paintings—into a mystical importance much like the Talmud or American literature of the nineteenth century (which traditionally joins realism and romanticism), so baseball itself is most often logical and magical. In his account of a search for Jewish identity, *An Orphan in History,* Paul Cowan ponders baseball's strength, the love of professional sports that awakens "an immigrant's wonder" at the game "most second- and third-generation Americans take for granted." He realizes that *bar mitzvah* study resembles the "encyclopedia's worth of baseball statistics" one also memorizes and recalls a Chicago neighborhood thoroughly Americanized, "an environment where men and boys were still furious at the 1919 Black Sox scandal . . . and utterly indifferent to the Talmudic discussions."[54]

Further, many Jews, like one writer's grandfather who called himself the "Scorekeeper of Zion," collected famous Jews who as actors or athletes passed as Protestants. His greatest delight came when his grandson would bring him the name of another Jewish baseball player. "I can still remember the first great find that I brought to him: Jake Pitler, a Brooklyn Dodger coach. The entire world, of course, knew where Sandy Koufax went to pray, but Pitler was a Hebrew in the hole, a weapon my grandfather used for an inspired sneak attack in a crowded store one September day. 'If the World Series starts on Yom Kippur,' he loudly said, 'the Dodgers will be two men short.' Heads turned with puzzled looks as people counted Koufax and then wondered if Hank Greenberg had come out of retirement." This kind of collecting became more fun than gathering baseball cards, "unless, of course, the card was Al Rosen or Moe Berg." One can go too far in this Jewish search; I have a long-standing argument with Steven Riess over the Jewishness of the great Cub catcher Johnny Kling who identified himself as Lithuanian but who, according to materials in the Cooperstown Hall of Fame Library, saw both his daughters marry Jewish men and is himself buried in a Jewish cemetery. But we were all briefly fooled by the Orioles' John Lowenstein who was amused and went along with a misapprehension. This particular grandson was misled by the fact that New York mayor Robert Wagner once wore a *Yarmulke* into believing that the famous Pirates shortstop Honus Wagner was Jewish "because we need more than Greenberg in the Hall of Fame."[55]

While baseball indicates a subtext for many Jewish reminiscences about life in America, in six recent works the relationship to the national pastime is of great importance to the self-revelation of the author and his world. Joel Oppenheimer's *The Wrong Season* is a Jewish baseball book, the year-long chronicle of a complicated man: a poet, divorced, remarried, with children, literary friends, who is a recovering alcoholic and a totally driven New York Mets fan. He interweaves his personal responses to the Mets' 1972 season—when he is forty-two and feeling mortal—with memories of his own ball-playing days, his baseball poems, generalizations about the game, and his Jewishness. Oppenheimer concentrates on the theme that, for him, baseball encompasses both art and life.

The book is written completely in lower case, and its headnote avers that the author "is well aware that both e. e. cummings and don marquis were writing in lower case before he was born, which was 1930, a year that saw an astonishing number of batting averages over .300." *The Wrong Season* in many ways reads like a critical exposition of the Jewish-American baseball theme. Joe Flaherty's introduction strikes a familiar note: "When Macmillan published *The Baseball Encyclopedia,* he reacted like a lost soul who has found the original Torah in a train station locker."[56] The author quickly establishes the father-son conceptualization: "my father was born in 1893. he was a new york giants fan. my son nathaniel was born in 1966. he is a new york mets fan. i was born in 1930 and i was a dodger fan and am a mets fan."[57] Although his father never saw his grandson in a Mets uniform, the son played (badly) at summer camp before his father's eyes, and the three of them have observed much of the total history of baseball. Oppenheimer stresses that he finds the game "American" in its limits of time and space, love of trivia and statistics. He particularly remarks on the generational aspect—"so my father told me about pie traynor, and i tell nathaniel about eddie matthews, and he, perhaps, will remember brooks robinson"[58]—and a sense of historical metronomy in which players and plays from different time spans mix themselves in the mind's eye—"ernie lombardi lying stretched out by homeplate is inextricably messed up in my head with harrelson and milner crashing in left field,"[59] plays separated by four decades.

Oppenheimer insists that he is most Jewish in being a loser, starting out weeping when he is taken to a game at the Polo Grounds "by the jewish community center of yonkers"[60] to see his Dodgers lose 26–3. He follows countless Dodger heartbreaks and fights the usual Jewish familial resistance to baseball. "they're still hoping i'll become a dean or doctor or something," and takes the familiar Shaw-Roth way out by writing a baseball book: "writing a book about baseball seems infinitely preferable to them if it's a choice of that or poetry."[61]

In the dark war year of 1943, Oppenheimer, the Bar Mitzvah boy, employs baseball's nostalgia for a lyric past, a world that probably didn't exist, of rules that didn't change. "i'm trying to explain where i was then, a skinny Jewish kid who hadn't learned he could do anything but be, abstractly, smart . . . and in the whole city of yonkers i was one of the few who had cried when the ball went past owen in '41."[62]

The child's hidden pleasure of listening to a ballgame on the radio in bed, softly so his parents wouldn't hear, parallels the adult author's sneaking away to watch games on television in bars. Baseball, then, both connects with childhood and is also a way of grasping America and its history: "there were two great moments in my childhood where my father showed me the great world and one was hearing how my uncle served in the lost battalion in world war i and one was being told about an actual real ruth homerun he had seen."[63]

Baseball, to Oppenheimer, is like writing—in poetry and pitching one must get it right; athletes and artists share the right to rebel; and, inevitably, baseball is a prime Jewish-American metaphor. "the mustard at yankee stadium is yellow, which is a sign that they haven't lost their joyische tom even if they did manage to hire blomberg [Ron Blomberg, a hard-hitting first baseman] a large Jewish boy from atlanta . . . probably like yellow mustard. has anybody ever checked, officially, to see if he's indeed circumcised. i'll tell you one thing, art shamsky liked brown mustard."[64] The comic reference to Shamsky's more obvious ethnicity points up Oppenheimer's insistence on the personal linkage of his Jewish self with his American baseball fan persona. Even the calendar possesses this hyphenated aura. He notes that the Mets fell out of the 1972 pennant race on the eve of Yom Kippur, "and as passover is the promise of the spring, so is yom kippur the time for summing up, the time to look back on your sins of the last year. and so the mets lost to chicago 6–4."[65]

Ultimately, Joel Oppenheimer finishes his book with a pair of Jewish tropes realized by novelists like Neugeboren or Charyn. First, Oppenheimer conjoins Jews and Blacks as basically marginal Americans—in roles of ballplayers or fans—subject to historical change. He goes in 1947 to see Jackie Robinson play, "and i was surrounded by black faces . . . from somewhere near me is heard a voice from childhood, a Jewish tailor, yankel, yankel, yankel he yelled, as hard as all his neighbors shouting jack jack jack [Eric Greenberg employs a similar scene in *The Celebrant* for the Jewish fan]. that is very hard to believe this year when his children live in forest hills."[66] Then Oppenheimer moves on to all-star teams, decides to create his own, New York City team, which will include Hank Greenberg and "moe berg." And despite Oppenheimer's realization that the choice of an all-time Jewish major league baseball team is hackneyed, he carries it out anyway: Phil Weintraub on first; Andy Cohen, second; Buddy Myer, short; Al Rosen, third; Greenberg, Sid Gordon, and Lipman Pike in the outfield; Johnny Kling, catcher; Erskin Meyer and Sandy Koufax, pitchers. *The Wrong Season* is a quirky, indulgent, funny, unclassifiable book, hardly on the level of any of Roger Angell's grand seasonal studies or Arnold Hano's small classic, *A Day in the Bleachers*, but Oppenheimer's work documents powerfully the double emotional drives of American and Jewish identities that often coalesce around the idea of being a baseball fan.

The need for a Jewish boy to discover an American hero comes through equally strongly from the text of Ronald Sanders' *Reflections in a Teapot*. Sanders, who would become a historian of Jewish immigrants in New York's East Side, a biographer of Abraham Cahan, and a student of Jewish culture, had a gap, as a boy, that, he insists, a mystical communion with the glory of Joe DiMaggio filled.[67] The religious emphasis is clear. "To me, DiMaggio was for a long time the quintessential embodiment of the gigantic, solitary hero I dreamed of becoming . . . a truly great player of the game who seemed to maintain, even in moments of surpassing grandeur, a noble air of melancholy aloofness . . . my perennial quest for transcendence had found a new kind of religious affiliation . . . the New York Yankees were my sect, Yankee Stadium—the goal of a two-hour pilgrimage by subway—was my Jerusalem or Canterbury, and Joe DiMaggio was my sacrificial lamb and triumphant redeemer." Certainly, this emblem of Sanders' "church militant," this bringer of the "Millennium," is hardly Jewish, even though Sanders refers to the Stadium as his American *shul*, but the "mystery of sport," according to Sanders, educated him in American ways and assisted him in educating his father whom the boy took to semipro games near Prospect Park: "it was a great pleasure being his guide into something American like that."[68]

Despite his Christian rhetoric applied to the figure of DiMaggio, Sanders insists that his viewpoint is Jewish. He argues that from the perspective of "the Jewish world of Flatbush, this preference for the Yankees seemed vaguely goyish. For, strange as it may seem, the Brooklyn Dodger *mystique* . . . had taken a profoundly Jewish form among many of my Flatbush contemporaries."[69] The Jew, Sanders posits, found that the Dodgers reflected a certain typically Jewish urban typology, "the focus of a myth of some quirky New World *shtetl*," with loud accents, foolish chauvinism, and outlandish mannerisms. It helped that the Dodgers were, in Sanders' youthful years, losers—"the ultimate *schlemiels* in baseball." Here Sanders' anti-hero is Pete Reiser, the outfielder who seemed to specialize in running into fences and damaging what could have been a brilliant career. "Such doings represent the point at which the image of Don Quixote becomes a metaphor for Jewish history, at least if you are inclined to read things that way." My basic argument is that Jews are inclined to read baseball things that way, perhaps not as emotionally as Sanders who goes on to compare the Dodgers' final 1955 rise "from their *shtetl*" to defeat the Yankees in the Series with "a return to Zion," but to make a similar search for metaphors in baseball that will connect the American and the Jewish strain.

Joe DiMaggio becomes the basis for an entire book by another (partly) Jewish writer. Christopher Lehmann-Haupt echoes Sanders' main theme in the title *Me and DiMaggio: A Baseball Fan Goes in Search of His Gods.* While Lehmann-Haupt, the *New York Times* book reviewer, is only one-quarter Jewish, and while most of his book is a journalistic account of the player's career and of the writer's attempts to contact DiMaggio, the author reflects many themes we have identified as American-Jewish: "baseball as a transport to American culture"; "the museum of my own imagination";[70] fantasy and aging. What is interesting about Lehmann-Haupt's account is the consistent refusal of his German-Jewish intellectual father ever to bend from his disdain for the "silly game they play in little boys' knickers" or to depart from a rigid view of Babe Ruth as "a drunken bum in a monkey suit,"[71] even while reluctantly granting the game's acculturating force. The boy becomes hooked on baseball because of a boarder's radio and DiMaggio's three home runs, because of the (Jewish) announcer Mel Allen whose voice reassured the youngster that baseball was good despite his father's fear that this obsession with baseball would interfere with the real business of life.

Joe DiMaggio, we are reminded in David Halberstam's account of the 1949 Yankee-Red Sox pennant race, was extolled in song in Richard Rogers' *South Pacific* of that year, with the encomium to Bloody Mary whose "skin is tender as DiMaggio's glove." But Halberstam is initially fascinated by the youthful years of the *New York Times* reporter and editor Joseph Lelyveld who as a sixth grader was a serious Yankee fan "[who] owned some thirty books on baseball. . . . All his allowance went to the *Sporting News* and assorted baseball magazines . . . he knew all the baseball statistics, past and present."[72] Why? Again, Halberstam is bemused by the accommodation element. "He had become interested in baseball in 1946 when his family had moved to New York from the Midwest. Lonely and unsure of himself, in a new school where the kids seemed to be much tougher, he found order and symmetry in the universe of baseball as he did not in the world around him. . . . His father, later a prominent rabbi in the civil rights movement, was certainly not a fan."[73] Connecting with Rogers' use of DiMaggio's name in song, Halberstam shows Paul Simon, at age seven in 1949, becoming a Yankee fan "while sitting in his father's lap listening to Mel Allen's broadcast. DiMaggio was his father's hero." It follows that in 1966, when writing lyrics for the score of the film *The Graduate,* Simon "had sought for one song an image of purity in a simpler America. His mind flashed to the great Yankee player. He wrote down, completely by instinct, the words, 'Where have you gone, Joe DiMaggio? A nation turns its lonely eyes to you' . . . a lament for another time."[74]

Finally, Halberstam himself at the difficult age of fifteen, thin and wearing glasses, found the world of baseball more real and attractive than what he coped with daily. "I could understand what was happening in baseball. . . . I believed I knew the Yankees not only as players but as people—they were part of my extended family."[75] Unlike many memoirists who moved away from sports, Halberstam wrote not only this book but ones on basketball and rowing among his major works on war and studies of political and publishing powers. And it all goes back to his father taking him to Yankee Stadium, at age five, and explaining why DiMaggio was a great base runner.[76]

Baseball as a political litmus test is the controlling image of Carl Bernstein's *Loyalties* where he argues his father's case as a loyal American in spite of the FBI's and Congressional Committees' beliefs to the contrary as well as his involvement with the Communist Party as indicators that this Jewish Marxist labor organizer must have been suspect as an American patriot. In the son's eyes, what helps to prove his father's essential loyalty to the United States, for all Carl's own liberal suspicions, is the baseball connection. Born in 1910, his father adored major league baseball throughout his life. "His own grandmother died on the Sunday of the Cleveland-Boston Braves World Series. That's how he dates most things: baseball games. He remembers Larry Doby hitting a home run in the '48 Series, but he cannot remember his grandmother's first name."[77] An American childhood becomes persuasively plausible through baseball memories. "He and his friends would climb the rocks to

Coogan's Bluff and watch the Giants and the Yankees. . . . Sometimes they'd get inside on rain checks that the paying customers had thrown away."[78]

The son also adores baseball, plays it on long Washington summer evenings, and attempts to reconstruct the painful dates of his parents' political inquisition by a baseball fix: "I'm sure I would have looked at the paper—to get the afternoon baseball scores."[79] When times are worst, baseball provides some kind of healing as another family shows solidarity by taking the children "to see the Senators play the White Sox in Griffith Stadium."[80] The baseball references give the book its only external, concrete grounding beyond politics and the family, both to set time and to prove, consciously or subliminally, Americanism.

Toward the book's end, as the son struggles in the 1980s to understand his father's 1950s commitments and activities, the two leave the files they are discussing and go to Shea Stadium for a Mets game. The Mets beat the Reds, the suspicious son worries about his father's earlier politics, and one of baseball's fundamental characteristics—the enveloping of time, of seasons past, the yoking of a present game to one previously played—takes over and sustains the relationship, above suspicion, between father and son, both Jewish, both political, both baseball lovers. "Baseball was always our game. To go to Griffith Stadium which was down the hill from the laundromat, we rode the trolly. Once, sitting in the upper-deck grandstand, we saw DiMaggio hit three homers at a Sunday doubleheader; I was a Yankee fan, he always rooted for the Senators. On our way into the park old Clark Griffith would be standing on the ramp by the ticket windows, always dressed in a white linen suit against the heat, and he'd tip his hat to *those of us* he knew as regular customers."[81] The son who as a boy worried about his father's political notoriety as harmful to the youth's position as American among his peers, the son who as a man tries to understand how an American can be a communist, both boy and man can accept his father's basic American identity through the recalled epiphany, for the two Jews, of their acceptance from that most American of figures, the owner of a baseball club. And not just any owner, but Griffith appears as the essential Yankee, dressed in white linen like that most American of authors, Mark Twain, and tipping a hat to us, the term Twain employs to register loyalty as Huck Finn commits himself to Jim when slave catchers are after *us*, when in reality, they only seek one of them, the elder.

The most complex memoir employing a baseball thematic is *The Invention of Solitude* by Paul Auster, the author of the "New York Trilogy" of hermeneutic, self-reflexive, post modern detective novels. As a writer who works within closed systems, Auster makes baseball provide a bridge between his two autobiographical surges: to discover the dead father never really known and to establish an authorial philosophical/artistic persona that can find a place in the universe. In pursuing these aims, he combines baseball with an intense, yet secular, Judaism.

As a child, he desires to accomplish an act of heroism. "I was only ten years old and there was no child for me to save from a burning building, no sailors to rescue at sea. On the other hand, I was a good baseball player, the star of my Little League team, and although my father had no interest in baseball, I thought that if he saw me play, just once, he would begin to see me in a new light."[82] Naturally, when the father comes to the game, the boy fails—gets no hits, makes errors, and receives from his parent only a vague encouragement, "without feeling, an exercise in decorum," and the father forgets to buy the son a long-desired glove.

Auster makes clear that while the father comprehends *his* Jewish identity, taking his son to Jewish restaurants, eating borscht, pirogen, the boy is lost: "I, who was being brought up as an American boy, who knew less about my ancestors than I did about Hopalong Cassidy's hat."[83] Yet woven through this text of the boy's attempt to seize his father's past are references to a present where baseball exists. In order to avoid learning a particularly awful passage of family history, "All morning I have procrastinated. I have read the entire newspaper—right down to the line scores of the spring training baseball games."[84]

In important ways, baseball helps to supply the memoir's form. As Auster uses to develop a theory of coincidence the fact that in 1962 he meets someone in April at a Mets game, then meets the same person at another Mets game in May, so he sets the most powerful scene in his dying grandfather's apartment, watching a baseball game on television. "To immerse himself in these games was to feel his mind striving to enter a place of pure form. Despite the agitation on the field, baseball offered itself to him as an image of that which does not move, and therefore a place where his mind could be at rest, secure in its refuge against the mutabilities of the world." Then Auster describes, as do many of these Jewish memoirs, a childhood dedicated to playing the game. First, baseball requires devotion. "From the first muddy days in early March to the last frozen afternoons of late October. He had played well, with an almost obsessive devotion." Next, playing ball socializes him. "Not only had it given him a feeling for his own possibilities, convinced him that he was not entirely hopeless in the eyes of others, but it had been the thing that drew him out from the solitary enclosures of his early childhood. It had initiated him into the world of the other, but at the same time it was something he could also keep within himself." Third, baseball implies a dreamlike existence. "Baseball was a terrain rich in potential for revery," for fantasies of himself as a Giant, playing in the Polo Grounds before cheering crowds, while in actuality he is throwing a tennis ball against a stoop, replicating the actions of Neil Simon's Jewish lad Eugene in *Brighton Beach Memories.*

Most impressively, baseball binds present to past and vivifies his Proustian recall of the Jewish family. "As he sat through those long summer days in his grandfather's apartment, he began to see that the power of baseball was for him the power of memory. Memory in both senses of the word: as a catalyst for remembering his own life and as an artificial structure for ordering the historical past." He selects 1960 for an example, and much in the manner Philip Roth studies American geography through baseball teams' travels, Paul Auster recreates history, recounting 1960s key events: Kennedy becomes President, Paul has his Bar Mitzvah, but the special event, the controlling image, is the Pirate second baseman Bill Mazeroski's home run that beat the Yankees in the World Series: "by recalling the sensations of that moment, that abrupt and stunning instant of pleasure, he is able to re-enter his own past, to stand in a world that would otherwise be lost to him."

All of the above, necessarily, can be basically Jewish, mirroring the fundamentals of Days of Atonement, of Passovers, of memories of ethnic and religious past events and ideas and families. "To play the game as a child is simultaneously to imagine playing it as an adult," to be trained in a *shul* is to prepare for life in a *shtetl.* The writer can imitate Stan Musial or Willie Mays, or, in his own Jewish setting, "remember confusing the last words of the Passover Seder, 'Next year in Jerusalem,' with the ever-hopeful refrain of disappointed fandom, 'Wait till next year,' as if the one were a commentary on the other." To love baseball is to be Jewish, "to win the pennant was to enter the promised land. Baseball had somehow become entangled in his mind with the religious experience."

Baseball connects everything; this "baseball quicksand" joins Thurman Munson's, the Yankee catcher's, death with that of Lou Gehrig, with the grandmother who died of Lou Gehrig's disease, back with Munson who died in a plane crash on his way to visit his hyperactive son—and, intensely, with the memories of the dying Jewish grandfather. Similar to an urban version of a Faulkner hunting mentor, the grandfather "had taken him to his first game, had talked to him about the old players, had shown him that baseball was as much about talk as it was about watching." And at the end of this section, Auster reads to the dying man reports of the previous day's baseball games, deconstructing the messages implied in the box scores, working on the code just as one decodes the Talmud: "It was the one subject they could still come to as equals. . . . It was his last contact with the outside world, and it was painless, a series of coded messages he could understand with his eyes closed."[85]

Gunther Barth assumes the baseball-watching experience taught immigrants that rules regulated their new American world, and that these rules controlled whatever competition, beyond the ballpark, was necessary for success.[86] Further, baseball was special for the new arrival not only because it supplied a guidebook (*Spalding's Official Baseball Guide* first appeared in 1908), but also because observing the game became a major step "in their daily progress of becoming Americans"; and lacking sufficient English to read a book or to grasp the meaning of a stage performance, "they were natural sports spectators"[87] and discovered a "momentary unity as a religious bond."[88] Barth insists that baseball went beyond the teaching of rules and arguments, the code of competition, the "reports of records established one day and broken the next [that] diffused a historical consciousness in the modern city."[89] Beyond understanding came community since "rooting for a big-city team also gave rootless people a sense of belonging."[90] The ball park's message appeared in the form of statistics and standings, a clear numerical measure of victory and of history. "Such plain statistics appealed to the American passion for counting as a means of mastering reality."[91]

The Jewish needs for vague or mystical approaches to history yet at the same instance a Talmudic love for arguing for and against fixed details[92]—in essence a poetic/logical reconstruction of the past—are often met in baseball's similar combination of lyric, misty memory (Did Babe Ruth really call his home run against the Chicago Cubs in the World Series?), and minute arguments over set values (Are 100 runs scored more valuable than a old reinvent youthful achievements) meets the Jewish literal belief in "the magic potentiality of their dreams to transform even the physical world of action."[93] If much of baseball's pleasure is dream, much of at least the *chassid* approach is creative imagination. And how these assimilating Jews adored baseball! A perusal of Eliot Cohen's anthology of Jewish writing in *Commentary* discovers a litany of baseball memories. Baseball in the park and punchball in the gutter; a catcher's mitt acquired for two hundred United Cigar coupons awakes memory and dream: "I caught without a mask, chest protector, or shin guards. I just squatted behind the batter and caught, the United Cigar mitt between me and the lop-sided, black-taped ball. . . . Still, Hank Greenberg rose out of our neighborhood."[94] The intoxications of the past, of loyalty to sacred moments, accompanied by a love of fantasy, of a deeper truth, mark, according to Irving Malin, much Jewish writing.[95] Thus a Jewish fascination with baseball often helped counter senses of exile, suffering, and fear by acceptances of a present home (team) with its share of excitement and heroic possibility.

The sociologist Dennis Wrong posits two views of ethnicity, one showing a continuity between past and present—a traditional culture and contemporary flux—the other displaying a nostalgia for an exaggeratedly grim past and acceptance of the present culture as a creator of group identity.[96] This group has not been merely fellow Jews, but fellow Americans. The Dodgers, Pete Hamill insists, "provided common ground: Italians, Irish, blacks, Jews, Poles, all went to the games . . . they provided something to talk about that did not involve religion, politics, or race."[97]

American-Jewish writers, then, drew deeply from what baseball established as a common ground; if they needed an American language and structure, they took, often what was immediately available in youthful memories and present-day sports pages. Some Jewish writers wrote important baseball novels like Malamud's *The Natural* or Greenberg's *The Celebrant;* some wrote smaller works like Irwin Shaw's *Voices of a Summer's Day* or Mark Harris' *The Southpaw;* all may have sought, like Philip Roth, to write the great American baseball novel, but many settle for works of socio historical value. Even on this subject, the American-Jewish author can display a self-consciousness that draws on baseball rhetoric. In the words of Josh Greenfield, "No one ever sets out to be a minor writer any more than any would-be baseball player pictures himself winding up as a utility infielder. I remember as a boy growing up in Boston and Brooklyn I couldn't understand the Sibby Sistis and Whitey Wietelmans, the Oscar Melillos and the Johnny Hudsons, the fifth infielders who would rarely get to play. . . . How could anyone with the talent to reach the big leagues settle for a substitute—or minor—role? Yet that is the role I've settled for. I've never been anything but a minor writer."[98]

To return to the beginning—or perhaps to go into extra innings—why the strong connection between American baseball and Jewish creativity? Harold Bloom argues that post-Freudian, post-Holocaust Jews are now, paradoxically, fundamentally ahistorical, that they no longer can believe in the "lost coherence of Jewish memory at its strongest, which was messianic and so redemptive," so they choose myth over history, "a new, metahistorical myth for which the novel gives a temporary modern form."[99] My presumption is to argue that, in a great many cases, baseball provided many American Jews, who went on cultural record, with the substitute myth that unleashed creativity. Following T. S. Eliot's formulation in "Tradition and the Individual Talent," I discover baseball becomes art because it collects meaning from previous games and seasons; baseball is history because its actions only made full sense in the context of tradition, of past circumstances; baseball has a specially creative language because the vernacular, the demotic, becomes lyric and ironic in great baseball writing. William Carlos Williams comprehended the Jewish-baseball connection best as a kind of intellectual love affair. The crowd in his poem "At the Ball Game" includes "The Jew" who "gets it straight—it/Is deadly, terrifying—/It is the inquisition, the/Revolution/It is beauty itself."

NOTES

1. Donald Honig, *The Greatest First Baseman of All Time* (New York: Crown, 1988), p. 63.

2. Peter Levine, "If Only Don Drysdale Had Been Jewish: Professional Baseball and the American Jewish Experience" (paper delivered at Organization of American Historians Annual Meeting, New York, April 11, 1986).

3. F. C. Lane, "Why Not More Jewish Ballplayers?" *Baseball Magazine* 36 (January 1929): 341.

4. *The American Hebrew,* June 1, 1926.

5. Leslie Fiedler, *To the Gentiles* (New York: Stein and Day, 1972), p. 66.

6. Peter Rose, ed., *The Ghetto and Beyond* (New York: Random House, 1969), p. 444.

7. See James Mote, *Everything Baseball* (New York: Prentice-Hall, 1989) and Peter Gordon, ed., *Diamonds Are Forever* (San Francisco: Chronicle Books, 1987).

8. Sarah Belcher Cohen, ed., *From Hester Street to Hollywood* (Bloomington: Indiana University Press, 1983), p. 7.

9. Ibid., p. 2.

10. Murray Baumgarten, *City Scriptures* (Cambridge, Mass.: Harvard University Press, 1982), p. 148.

11. Allen Guttmann, "Out of the Ghetto and on to the Field: Jewish Writers and the Theme of Sport," *American Jewish History* 3 (March 1985): 274.

12. Abraham Karp, *Golden Door to America* (New York: Penguin, 1977), p. 10.

13. Rose, ed., *The Ghetto and Beyond*, p. 7.

14. Abraham Chapman, ed., *Jewish American Literature* (New York: New American Library, 1974), p. xxxvi.

15. Eric Solomon, "Jews, Baseball, and the American Novel," *Arete* 1 (Spring 1984): 43–46.

16. Moses Rischin, *The Promised City* (New York: Harper and Row, 1970), p. 146.

17. Charles Marden, *Minorities in American Society* (New York: American Book, 1952), p. 107.

18. Steven Riess, *Touching Base* (Westport, Conn.: Greenwood Press, 1980), p. 26.

19. Judd Teller, *Strangers and Natives* (New York: Delacorte, 1968), p. 26.

20. James Yaffe, *The American Jews* (New York: Random House, 1968), p. 91.

21. Moe Berg, *Scrapbook* (Cooperstown, N.Y.: Baseball Hall of Fame, n.d.).

22. Irving Howe, *World of Our Fathers* (New York: Harcourt Brace Jovanovich, 1976), p. 182.

23. Gunther Barth, *City People* (New York: Oxford University Press, 1980), p. 191.

24. Richard Crepeau, *Baseball: America's Diamond Mind, 1919–1941* (Gainesville: University of Florida Press, 1980), p. 59.

25. Stephen Stein, "Ceremonies of Civil Judaism among Sephardic Jews of Los Angeles," *Western Folklore* 47 (April 1988): 110.

26. Leslie Fiedler, *What Was Literature* (New York: Simon and Schuster, 1983), p. 8.

27. Max Apple, "My Love Affair with English," *New York Times Book Review*, November 22, 1981, p. 9.

28. Marc Raphael, *Jews and Judaism in a Midwestern Community* (Columbus: Ohio State University Press, 1979), p. 334.

29. Isaac Asimov, "Introduction," in *Wandering Stars: An Anthology of Jewish Fantasy and Science Fiction*, ed. Jack Dunn (New York: Pocket Books, 1975), pp. 15–16.

30. Riess, *Touching Base*, p. 14.

31. Barth, *City People*, 149 ff.

32. Walter Harrison, "Six-Pointed Diamond: Baseball and American Jews," *Journal of Popular Culture* 15 (March 1985): 217.

33. William Poster, "Twas a Dark Night in Brownsville," in *Commentary on the American Scene*, ed. Eliot Cohen (New York: Alfred Knopf, 1953), p. 55.

34. Morris R. Cohen, "Baseball," reprinted from the *Dial, Columbia University Magazine* (Spring 1981): 19.

35. Geoffrey Green, *Literary Criticism and the Structure of History* (Lincoln: Nebraska University Press, 1982), p. 140.

36. Delmore Schwartz, in *Dreams Begin Responsibilities* (New York: New Directions, 1978), p. 126.

37. Bernard Rosenberg and Ernest Goldstein, eds., *Creators and Disturbers* (New York: Columbia University Press, 1982), p. 93.

38. Isaac B. Singer, *Love and Exile: The Early Years, a Memoir* (Garden City, N. Y.: Doubleday, 1984), p. 12.

39. San Francisco *Chronicle*, November 6, 1989.

40. Lesley Hazelton, "Hers," New York *Times*, May 22, 1986.

41. New York *Times*, January 28, 1989.

42. New York *Times*, March 3, 1974.

43. Jules Tygiel, *Baseball's Great Experiment: Jackie Robinson and His Legacy* (New York: Oxford University Press, 1983), p. vii.

44. *Sports Illustrated*, November 10, 1986.

45. Rosenberg and Goldstein, eds., *Creators and Disturbers*, pp. 206, 186.

46. Irving Howe, *A Margin of Hope* (New York: Harcourt Brace Jovanovich, 1982), p. 5.

47. Estelle C. Barrett, San Francisco *Focus*, April 1986, p. 71.

48. Stephen Lerner, "Johnny Mize and the Birth of a Baseball Fan," New York *Times*, April 26, 1981, p. 25.

49. Alfred Appel, *Signs of Life* (New York: Alfred Knopf, 1983), p. 86.

50. Gerald Nachman, *Out on a Whim* (New York: Doubleday, 1983), p. 156.

51. David Riesman, "Quote," in *Harvard Magazine*, September, 1989, p. 32.

52. Rosenberg and Goldstein, eds., *Creators and Disturbers*, p. 419.

53. Ann Birstein, *The Rabbi on Forty Seventh Street* (New York: Dial Press, 1982), pp. 139–42, 173.

54. Paul Cowan, *An Orphan in History* (New York: Bantam, 1983), pp. 23, 36.

55. Ralph Shoenstein, "Let Us Now Claim Famous Men," *Village Voice*, November 24, 1974, p. 43.

56. Joel Oppenheimer, *The Wrong Season* (New York: Award Books, n.d.), p. 7.

57. Ibid., p. 13.

58. Ibid., p. 15.

59. Ibid., p. 17.

60. Ibid., p. 25.

61. Ibid., p. 30.

62. Ibid., p. 50.

63. Ibid., p. 86.

64. Ibid., p. 138.

65. Ibid., p. 152.

66. Ibid., p. 162.

67. Ronald Sanders, *Reflections in a Teapot* (New York: Harper and Row, 1972), p. 97.

68. Ibid., p. 99.

69. Ibid., pp. 97–98.

70. Christopher Lehmann-Haupt, *Me and DiMaggio: A Baseball Fan Goes in Search of His Gods* (New York: Simon and Schuster, 1986), pp. 13, 27.

71. Ibid., p. 13.

72. David Halberstam, *Summer of '49* (New York: William Morrow, 1989), p. 69.

73. Ibid., p. 70.

74. Ibid., p. 275.

75. Ibid., p. 287.

76. Ibid., p. 288.

77. Carl Bernstein, *Loyalties* (New York: Simon and Schuster, 1989), pp. 29–30.

78. Ibid., p. 49.

79. Ibid., p. 113

80. Ibid., pp. 123–24.

81. Ibid., p. 183.

82. Paul Auster, *The Invention of Solitude* (New York: Penguin, 1988), p. 23.

83. Ibid., p. 28.

84. Ibid., p. 35.

85. Ibid., pp. 115–18.

86. Barth, *City People*, p. 141.

87. Ibid., p. 185.

88. Ibid., p. 191.

89. Ibid., p. 152.

90. Ibid., p. 187.

91. Ibid., p. 188.

92. Louis Ginsberg, "Jewish Thought and the Halakah," in *The Menorah Treasury*, ed. Leo Schwarz (Philadelphia: Jewish Publication Society of America, 1964), p. 37.

93. Mordecai Grossman, "A Mystical Approach to Judaism," in *The Menorah Treasury*, p. 161.

94. Cohen, "Baseball," p. 245.

95. Irving Malin, *Jews and Americans* (Carbondale: Southern Illinois University Press, 1966), pp. 38, 138.

96. Dennis Wrong, "Making It," *New Republic*, August 28, 1989, p. 37.

97. Fredric Roberts, "A Myth Grows in Brooklyn: Urban Death, Resurrection, and the Brooklyn Dodgers," *Baseball History* (Summer 1987): 5.

98. Josh Greenfield, quote in "The Minor League of Literature," *New York Times Book Review*, March 1, 1987.

99. Harold Bloom, "Memory and Its Discontents" New York *Review of Books*, February 17, 1983, p. 24.

6

The Italian-American Sporting Experience

Carmelo Bazzano

Prejudice and discrimination are not easily eliminated. This is apparent from sport history books which do not mention the Italians' sport experience. It is as if five million people never passed on the American scene. Sport historians agree that English immigrants brought to America the love and knowledge of games, while German immigrants brought with them gymnastics. The Irish loved boxing, the Scotch-Irish showed propensities for track and field competition. The northern people, Scandinavians and Finns, loved snow sports. The Italians, who represented the third largest group among immigrants, apparently contributed nothing to the sporting life of America.

The intent of this essay is to examine the sporting experiences of Italian Americans. Although encountering various forms of discrimination, Italians were able to carve out an active sporting life that helped them maintain their cultural identity while at once assimilating them into the mainstream of American society. Like other immigrant groups, participation in sport proved invaluable to Italians as both a socializing agency and as a means to validate their self-worth in a society not always marked by its tolerance of newcomers.

AN IDENTIKIT OF THE ITALIAN IMMIGRANTS

Italian immigrants came from that area commonly called Italy which is a rather modern nation. It was united in 1861 by the armies of the king of Savoy and the volunteers of Garibaldi, a charismatic leader bent on freeing Italy from foreign domination. The north, south, and central parts of the peninsula had different traditions, and even the population of each area was quite different. In the north a lighter skinned, fair-haired type predominated. With the break down of the Roman Empire, Germanic tribes had pushed south and established themselves in the north of Italy. Their influence is visible among the inhabitants of the area.

The south and the islands had a different history. In these areas, the Mediterranean was the predominant type, characterized by a darker complexion, shorter stature, and dark eyes and hair. Even emotionally, the two types were different. The Southerners were more hot tempered, whereas the Northerners were more phlegmatic. The American government acknowledged these differences by keeping separate statistics for each group when they arrived in America. The central part of Italy was dominated by the Vatican, and it served as a buffer between the north and south. The Church's temporal state was interested in keeping the two portions of the peninsula separated physically and intellectually. A united Italy would have meant the loss of temporal power for the papacy. Its policies, therefore, aimed at maintaining the status quo.[1]

Thus for centuries the north and south went their separate ways. The north had sparkled during the Renaissance. Its city-states had tasted freedom and provided fertile ground for the cultivation of man. The physical and intellectual aspect of man had received equal attention. Sport had not disappeared, not even during the dark days of the Middle Ages. Dante, in his *Inferno,* noted that in the city of Verona an annual foot race was run. In the seventeenth and eighteenth centuries most of the north, after long and debilitating internecine wars, had fallen under the domination of the Hapsburg Empire. However, the Piedmont, a northwestern region, was controlled by the house of Savoy which eventually was to unite Italy. In the north of Italy, there was a tradition of emigration. For centuries builders and artisans had gone north and west to provide their specialized services. This was a seasonal migration; the workers usually returned in winter. In the nineteenth century many migrated to South America, a few to North America. According to the U.S. Census, prior to 1880 there were 44,230 persons of Italian foreign birth or parentage in this country. In general, these Italian immigrants were skilled laborers with few professionals among them. Since their number was small they blended more easily into American society and adapted earlier. Further, a sporting tradition existed in the north.[2]

THE NORTHERNERS' SPORTING TRADITION

During the Renaissance period, Italy had been the sporting center of Europe. "Calcio" was played on a regular basis by noblemen and students. Fencing schools were operating; Italian fencing masters could be found anywhere in Europe. Mass games were played by the commoners on holy days, and boxing had to be declared illegal by the duke of Urbino because its popularity interfered with the orderly running of the duchy, which was one of the many independent states.

With political decay also came a drastic slowdown in sport participation. By the late nineteenth century, however, sport was alive and well in northern Italy. Many sport clubs had already grouped themselves into federations. The Italian gymnastic federation was founded in 1869, the swimming federation in 1892, the boxing federation in 1916, the fencing federation in 1909, and the heavy athletic federation (which included weight lifting and wrestling—free-style and Greco-Roman) was founded in 1902. The most popular federation, in terms of number of participants, was the football (soccer) federation which was founded in 1885.

The years when the Italians were organizing their sport federations coincided with the period of heavy Italian emigration. Some four million Italians came to the United States between 1899 and 1924, with over two million returning to Italy during the same period. The persistent discrimination the Italians had to endure is demonstrated by the fact that, when the Nativists were able to carry the day by stopping the huge emigration from southern and eastern Europe, the yearly quota assigned to Italians was only 3,845.[3]

THE SOUTHERN ITALIANS

The southern Italians included people from the regions of Abruzzi, Campania, Apulia, Basilicata, Calabria, and the island of Sicily. Arriving in great numbers during a brief time period (1880–1920), these immigrants came to America because they were driven from Italy by poverty, maladministration, crop failure, and devastation caused by such plant diseases as the phylloxera, the olive fly, and many other insect pests. In any nation in periods of crisis those most affected are the poor. This was the case with southern Italy. When Italy unified, there was hope that things would change for the better. Instead, unification for the Southerners meant the substitution of one master for another. Under the Bourbons, the foreign tyrants, the south was called il Regno delle due Sicilie. After unification, it was called Italy; but the exploitation continued. The south was still a sort of colony which was to produce goods for the "real" Italy. The collected taxes and the wealth produced were not used to improve the land, which had been abused and impoverished by a long line of conquerors; instead they were used to fuel the industrial machine which was being developed in the north. The nobles owned huge tracts of land known as the *latifunda,* which they were hardly familiar with since most of them were absentee landlords and lived in their great palazzi in the cities. Their rapacious underlings tried to grab as much as they could for themselves. In reality, nobody was concerned with the improvement and/or maintenance of the land which, as a result, deteriorated.

Since there was plenty of manpower available, the landowners kept on squeezing the *contadini* (peasants) by lowering the pittance they payed for their services. Once the possibility of emigration was discovered, large numbers of *contadini* took advantage of the situation and came to America. The great majority were illiterate, unskilled laborers who did not possess the skills necessary to succeed and function in an emerging industrialized America. To further aggravate their situation was the fact, supported by the large number of returnees, that many wanted to stay in America only long enough to accumulate enough money to buy their own land back in the old country. Hence young men used their time to accumulate capital, unconcerned with acculturation or learning American ways.[4]

SPORTING EXPERIENCES OF SOUTHERN ITALIANS

The sporting experiences of the majority of southern *contadini* were virtually nonexistent because they had languished for centuries under the tyrants whose only aim was their exploitation. Pitre, an Italian sociologist of the last century, left a vivid picture of how the average Sicilian laborer spent his days. When he worked, he would get up very early to walk to the field. Sicilians preferred to live in towns and not on farms because it gave them a sense of security, easy social interaction with fellow townsmen, and a sense of identity. Sicilians were emotionally attached to their town much like the ancient Greek citizens of the city-states for whom a major punishment was to be exiled. This is one of the major reasons why first generation Italian immigrants tried to keep alive in the new land their old habits. As a matter of fact, the immigrants made every effort to recreate many of the sights, sounds, and smells of the Old World.

Farm hands would come home after sundown. After supper they would walk to the square for some discussion because someone would always be there willing to exchange views. After some time, they would either go home or journey to the nearby cantina for a glass of wine and a game of cards. Though holy days provided some relief to this routine, it remained constant year in and year out. The younger people followed a somewhat similar practice. By the age of twelve a youngster was considered capable of full-time employment and was asked to contribute his share to the family's welfare. According to Pitre, however, youngsters participated in a number of impromptu sports. For example, on Sunday afternoons they danced on one side of the square. These dances were for men only and were perfect opportunities to show off one's physical abilities. During the harvesting season, people remained in the fields to guard the collected grain. Young men would use the threshing area for wrestling contests or to compete in lifting sacks of grain. Although this was informal and occasional play, it helped establish a pecking order among the young men. Indeed, these activities literally helped to separate the men from the boys.

The conclusion of this modest survey is that there was little leisure, a short childhood, and no established sport participation among the southern Italians. Giovanni Schiavo, a pioneer Italian immigrant historian, had this to say about sport of the newly arrived in 1929: "It is well known that as a whole the Italian immigrant has not brought with him any traditions of national games . . . the only pastime for which the immigrant is noted is apparently bocce—an Italian game resembling lawn bowling."[5]

ARRIVAL, SETTLEMENT, AND SPORT PARTICIPATION

The great majority of Italian immigrants to America, then, were peasants from southern Italy and Sicily. Upon arriving in this country, about 80 percent of them remained on the eastern seaboard, mostly in the great cities of New York, Boston, and Philadelphia. They were forced to live in overcrowded and squalid conditions. For example, on the East Side of New York, 200,000 Italians lived in a territory less than one square mile in size. As many as five thousand persons were crowded onto one street, fifteen to a four-room flat, and four hundred in tenement buildings intended for fifty people. The creation of these slum conditions, combined with discrimination and continuous efforts by the immigrants to maintain their old ways of life, slowed down considerably the acculturation process. In spite of these conditions, Italians played sports.

There were a number of agencies which facilitated sport participation among the Italian immigrants. First of all, as noted earlier, the Northerners were more familiar with sport than the Southerners. This predisposed them to organize themselves differently. Very early on they established sport clubs which were copies of the sport clubs of Italy. The Royal Wheelmen Club of the Bronx was founded in 1900. The purpose of the club was to bring together people who loved bicycle racing. Its members participated regularly in racing and many times the club itself was the sponsoring agent of the races. This shows a high level of sophistication on the part of the club which could take upon itself to organize races.[6]

At the turn of the century, bicycle racing was a popular activity. It had supplanted pedestrian long distance running because its greater speed could create more excitement for the spectators. It was a well-organized sport. The Amateur League of American Wheelmen came to life in 1880. There were races for amateurs and professionals, and for a brief period—the late nineteenth and early twentieth centuries—it was the biggest sport craze. This sport had its share of followers among the Italian immigrants. The Unione Sportiva Italiana, at 254 West Fifty-Fourth Street, was one of the oldest Italian sport clubs and had a large number of bicycle racing devotees. Of its 250 members about 80 were expert cyclists who held races in the fall at the Harlem River Speedway in New York City. These races drew large crowds of enthusiastic fans. The membership of the Unione was formed mostly by Piedmontese immigrants or Northerners who carried out their sporting activities at night and on Sundays and holidays. They did well in this sport. By 1936 one of them, Franco Giorgetti, won the National Championship. Indeed, these immigrant sportsmen played a role in making Sunday a legitimate day for sporting activities.

The Italians also left their mark very early in Greco-Roman wrestling and bocce. The latter sport was certainly one of the favorite pastimes of the early Italian immigrants. This recreational game was played in New York, as far west as Seattle and San Francisco, in the southwest in Tontitown, Arkansas, and in Chicago in the north. Especially popular in Piedmont, Liguria, and Tuscany, the game was brought to America by northern Italian immigrants. It was very popular because it required mild exertion and was appropriate for people whose work was physically demanding. As late as 1967, there was an active bocce league in Tontitown and in Chicago where five clubs enjoyed active participation in the sport and maintained fine facilities.[7]

SPORT, SECOND GENERATION ITALIANS, AND
THE PROGRESSIVE MOVEMENT

It was with the second generation Italians that sport blossomed. Even as far back as 1905, historian Camillo Cianfarra understood that involvement with sport on a larger scale would be possible only with the American-born Italian children. He noted that in New York City: "In our public elementary school competitions, our children are not inferior to the children of other nationalities, in the lists of gymnastic [track and field] winners the Italian names appear quite frequently as they appear in the rosters of teams involved in inter-high school competition."

Cianfarra was certainly a keen observer of what was taking place. Indeed, sport during this period of intense immigration was to play an important role in the education of immigrant children. The Progressive movement, which intended to salvage a generation of children living and growing in an unhealthy environment, was organizing to meet the new challenge. The Progressive movement intended to socialize the children of immigrants who were seen as threats to the American way of life. The movement's leaders felt that their mission "was to train the urban young to think and feel in a regulated, efficient manner." The new man, as seen by the movement's leaders, should be a team player, able to work with others, willing to follow the rules, and able to put the good of the team ahead of individual accomplishments. The new thinking proposed to substitute the team for the gang. In addition, since many of these philanthropists tried to counterbalance the unhealthy conditions of the slums, securing a healthy body was one of their primary objectives. The Progressive movement's leaders believed in the unity of man, the healthy body being inter-connected with the healthy mind. It naturally followed, then, that sport would play a vital role in the movement.

It is hard to find fault with the objectives of the Progressives whose roots lay in the Muscular Christianity movement. It is particularly difficult for someone like myself who was trained at Springfield College, the school where Luther Gulick, one of the most important exponents of Muscular Christianity, had been president. But Italian fathers justly felt that there was a conspiracy by the Americans to imbue their children with a new set of values which ran counter to their own beliefs. On the one hand, Progressive leaders spoke about the importance of working with the group, while Italian immigrant fathers com-manded that their children trust nobody except very close family. Progressives argued that it was healthy and advantageous to play sports. Italian fathers, however, believed that play was a waste of time; children should get a job and contribute to the welfare of the family. This, the youngsters were told, was the highest obligation of every member of the family.[8]

Indeed, Italian parents were astonished that schools would provide recre-ation even at the high school level. Among other reasons, they felt that play could cause injury, hence loss of income and burden to the family. Perhaps the following utterance by an Italian mother is a fair representation of the belief held by other Italian mothers regarding sport: "I always thought of the school as a place where one has to study. But play? Questo gioco e la rovina della famiglia. [This play is the ruination of the family.]"[9]

Despite these differing philosophies, the fact remains that the Progressive movement, through the arms of the Public Schools Athletic League (PSAL) and the settlement houses which, as far as sport was concerned, complem-ented the work of the PSAL, exposed a considerable number of second gener-ation Italian children to sports. Initially, the PSAL offered Italian immigrant children and other youths competition in sports such as basketball, baseball, rifle marksmanship, and track and field events of running, soccer, cross coun-try, swimming, tennis, and lacrosse. This sports programs' model first developed in New York City and was promptly borrowed by many other cities throughout the country.

ITALIANS AND BASEBALL

One of the more popular sports among Italian immigrants was baseball. Together with boxing, it was a sport very much loved and quickly learned by young Italians. In Tontitown, Arkansas, an out-of-the-way Italian colony, youngsters learned to play baseball before they could speak more than a few words of English, and the game provided the only bridge between the Italians and the surrounding population.

Baseball was played by Italians not only where open spaces were available but also in the tenement houses and wherever Italian communities sprang up. In Barre, Vermont, baseball was played almost as early as the establishment of the community of stonecutters itself. Undoubtedly, the game was enjoyed from the very beginning by Italian immigrants who added a number of variations to it. Caroline F. Ware provided a colorful picture of the game played in Greenwich Village in New York City at the end of World War I:

The most general forms of sport were the street ball games. . . . The district abounded in block teams, ranging in age from eleven or twelve or more, who played the ubiquitous game of punchball—a sort of baseball played with a soft ball . . . or stickball—the same game substituting a broom handle. . . . These games revealed the height of adaptation to physical environment, for they took account in their rules of such physical conditions as stoops behind which balls could become lodged and traffic lanes which must be avoided. The players developed an almost unconscious reaction to passing vehicles, stepping out of the way to let vehicles pass and falling back into the game again, hardly sensing an interruption.[10]

The West Coast was also a hotbed of baseball with the first professional player of Italian descent coming from that area. His name was Francesco Stefano Pezzolo who, facing discrimination, was forced to change his name to the unlikely Ping Bodie. He was born October 8, 1887, in San Francisco, was five foot eight, weighed 195 pounds. A right-handed batter and outfielder, Bodie played from 1911 to 1917 with the Chicago White Sox and from 1918 to 1921 with the New York Yankees. His lifetime batting average was a respectable .275. It was the Depression years which proved to be a bonanza for Italian-American baseball players. Burger has argued that the decline of Nativism, which accompanied the economic hardship of the Depression, proved instrumental in the acceptance of the new immigrants in baseball. While it is difficult to substantiate Burger's argument, the fact remains that during the 1930s many Italian players began finding their way to the major leagues. By the close of the fourth decade, so many of them were active in the majors that the National Italian-American Civic League issued an "All-Italian Team" for 1939.

The march toward acceptance in baseball by Italian Americans was made most visible by Joe DiMaggio who became an all-American symbol and classical sport hero. DiMaggio, characterized by the *New York Times* as "the son of a humble San Francisco fisherman," was born the eighth of nine children to Giuseppe and Rosalie DiMaggio on November 25, 1914, in Martinez, California, near San Francisco. DiMaggio's parents had "emigrated . . . at the height of the European exodus at the turn of the century." DiMaggio did not want to follow in his father's footsteps. Whenever possible, he would sneak out of his duties as a hand on his father's boat and play baseball in the nearby sandlot. His father often became infuriated by his son's behavior, calling him *lagnusu* (lazy) and a *meschinu* (good-for-nothing). Yet DiMaggio's father was among the fishermen who carried him on their shoulders after he returned from his first season with the Yankees.[11]

From 1936 to 1951, DiMaggio led a Yankee onslaught that was only interrupted by his 1943–44 tour of duty with the Army. A career .325 hitter who blasted 361 home runs, he appeared in ten World Series; only once were "his" Yankees defeated. He appeared in a record high fifty-one World Series games. Finally, he was selected to play in the All-Star Game in each of his thirteen active seasons. The highlight of DiMaggio's career came in 1941 when he hit safely in fifty-six consecutive games, demolishing Wee Willy Keeler's major league mark of forty-four straight games with a hit. With these credentials, not only did the Yankee Clipper become the most popular baseball player but also the best paid. In 1949 he became the first player to receive $100,000 a year.

ITALIANS AND BOXING

Boxing also provided Italian Americans with great sport triumphs. Their involvement with boxing began early, the first wave of immigrants supplying new blood to the sport. The slums traditionally have been gold mines for boxing promoters and managers. Where else could a young man without marketable skills and ill-equipped to function in society hope for such a hefty payday? Boxing is the answer even today. Many observers have commented that in America, if one wants to know which ethnic group is at the bottom of the social ladder, one need only look at who is at the top of the boxing world.

The case of Giuseppe Carrora may be typical. An Italian boxer, this young man came to America in the early 1890s at the age of nine. His family found refuge in the overcrowded slums of the Lower East Side in New York. Carrora quickly learned to take care of himself because in the slums gang warfare was endemic. Scotty Monteith, a boxing manager, searched the slums for possible candidates for ring careers. He noticed that Carrora, although smaller and younger than many in the frequent street fights, always ended up on the winning side. Monteith proposed to the young man that he do his fighting in the ring and for money.

The proposition was very attractive to Carrora since fighting was a way of life for him. "If one could pick up some cash for something one did anyway for nothing, why not?" reasoned Carrora. Thus began his career, which was to take him to the championship of the world. The classical "rags to riches" story. What is not classical is that Carrora, in order to be a box-office attraction, had to Irishize his name. The boxing promoters knew that traditionally boxers and their followers were Irish; a boxer with a foreign-sounding name was simply not in their best interest. Promoters were also familiar with the xenophobia permeating society and were not about to jeopardize their business by promoting Italian boxers.[12]

Carrora was not the only Italian-American boxer to be transformed from Italian to Irish. Many world champions with Irish names were, in fact, Italian. Among the early title holders were the brothers Sam and Vince Lazzaro who fought under the assumed names of Joe and Vince Dundee. Both won championships of the world, the former in the welterweight and the latter in the middleweight division. The New York Italians Johnny Dundee, Joe Camorra "the Scotch Wop," and Lou Ambers were lightweight champions. Peter Gulotto, fighting as Pete Herman, was twice the bantamweight champion. Young Corbett was champion in the welterweight division, while Willie Pep, Bushy Graham, and Harry Jaffra were featherweight champions. This last boxer had also been bantamweight champion.

The only prizefighter to knock out Jack Dempsey was Andrea Chiariglione, an Italian, referred to by sports writers as Jim Flynn. Not to be forgotten was the classy boxer and champion of the world in the lightweight division, Sammy Angott. Discrimination toward Italians continued for some time and was a phenomenon not limited to the East Coast. For example, Joe Roche, a 1920s ranking San Francisco middleweight, was an Italian named Virgil Aschero. Even in the 1940s there were Italians fighting under assumed Irish names. For example, the real name of Joe Maxim, the light-heavyweight champion of the world, was Giuseppe Antonio Bernardinelli. Willie Pep's real name was Papaleo. Based on the aforementioned examples, one has to be careful about utilizing the table compiled by S. Kirson Weinberg and Henry Arond in their often-quoted article, "The Occupational Culture of the Boxer." Weinberg and Arond contend that in 1909 the Irish had the largest number of active boxers, the Germans were second, and the English were third. In 1916 the order was as follows: Irish, Germans, Italians. In 1928 it was the Jewish Italians, and then Irish fighters who predominated. In 1936 the

Italians finally achieved predominance. It appears that many of those earliest Irish boxers were Italians with Irish surnames.[13]

ITALIANS AND SOCCER

In addition to baseball and boxing, soccer was a game the Italians of the old and new world played with passion and skill. It is doubtful that the first wave of immigrants played the game with much regularity. But later immigrants brought with them the knowledge and love for the sport which was very popular in Italy at the turn of the century. During the 1920s, many Italian soccer clubs had been established in the Italian neighborhoods of many eastern cities.

In 1929 the Italian Soccer Club was organized in Chicago. This team, according to the organizers, was the first step in uniting the Italian soccer players into a club of their own. Previously, many Italian players had been playing for teams of other ethnic groups.[14] St. Louis was also a hotbed of soccer in the 1920s, and Italians of the second generation were conspicuous by their participation. According to historian James Robinson: "The Hill, a southwestern district in St. Louis, populated by Italian immigrants and derisively called by the natives Dago Hill, was important breeding ground for soccer players. Since 1929 the Hill has been an outstanding center for soccer activity in the St. Louis area."[15] During the 1928–29 season, the first in which players from the Hill played together defending Calcaterra Undertakers colors, they won the city title. This was no small accomplishment. The Germans and the Irish had played soccer in St. Louis for many years and were proud of their records. Yet the Italians established superiority in the sport. According to historian Gary R. Mormino, by 1955 the Hill had spawned a half dozen professional baseball players—Joe Garagiola and Yogi Berra being the most famous—twice that number of professional soccer players, and several national soccer club championships.[16]

In New York City, because of the large Italian immigrant population, soccer clubs had been active for a long time. Yet the most amazing event in early Italian soccer participation took place in 1909 when the Coal City Maroons Soccer Club, which had been active since the turn of the century in that downstate Michigan Italian mining community, challenged and tied the Olympic Soccer Champs from England who had won their title in 1908.

SUMMARY AND CONCLUSION

It is apparent from this essay that Italian immigrants of the first and second generations had to operate under difficult conditions. Some of the obstacles were self-imposed. Many of them had come to America without any sporting traditions and were primarily intent on making as much money as possible and eventually returning to Italy. Further, because of their cultural background, immigrants' parents exercised tight control over their children. The immigrants started work very early in life and expected their children to do the same without governmental interference.

The first two generations of Italians had to fight various forms of discrimination. Indeed, they were crowded into ghettoes, utterly misunderstood, and did not accommodate themselves to American society as easily as other early immigrants. This discrimination was also reflected in sport. But Italians learned to play and contributed to the growth of sport in this country. They did not bring with them their own national game, hence their contribution was in playing the games, thus improving and popularizing them. Improvement was the result of competition, and Italians had to compete for their spot. This they did and did it well.

In the process, they helped change the vision that the dominant culture had of Italians. Indeed, things have changed. The third and fourth generations have experienced new living conditions and are better adapted to America. For these generations, thanks to the sacrifices of the two previous ones, participation in baseball, football, basketball, tennis, golf, and other sports has been much easier. As far as sport is concerned, the opportunities are now available, and the Italian-American outlook is positive. Perhaps this optimism is best expressed by the comment of Raymond J. Barbuti (400-meter Olympic champion at Amsterdam in 1928) in a recent interview: "I'm so pro-American. I believe in this great Country. It has given me my opportunity. This is the greatest Country in the world." Not bad for the son of immigrants who were considered incapable of becoming Americans.

NOTES

1. Alfonso Manaresi, *Storia contemporanea* (Milan: Casa Editrice Luigi Trevison, n.d.); Andrew Rolle, *The Italian Americans: Troubled Roots* (New York: Free Press 1980), pp. 64–66; Luciano J. Iorizzo and Salvatore Mondello, *The Italian Americans* (Boston: Twayne, 1980), p. 54; Jerre Mangione and Ben Morreale, *La Storia* (New York: Harper Collins, 1992), pp. 31–40.

2. Francesco Quintavalle, *Storia dell'unita italiana: 1814–1924* (Milan: Hoepli, 1926), pp. 199–251; Humbert S. Nelli, *From Immigrants to Ethnics: The Italian Americans* (New York: Oxford University Press, 1983), p. 42; Bruno Zauli, *Contributo materiale e spirituale dell'educazione fisica al Risorgimento italiano* (Massa Carrara: Casa Editrice Le Pleiadi), pp. 15–18.

3. Carmelo Bazzano, "Dal calcio fiorentino all'Association Football," *Didattica del Movimento* (Rome: Società Stampa Sportiva, luglio–ottobre 1987), pp. 25–28; Carlo Bascetta, ed., *Sport e giochi* (Milan: Edizioni Il Polifilo, 1978), p. 355; *Spectacle (Sport)*, Italian Olympic Committee Publication, no. 15 (March–April 1960) (IX-2), pp. 3049–52;

Humbert S. Nelli, "Italians," in the *Harvard Encyclopedia of American Ethnic Groups,* ed. Stephan Thernstrom (Cambridge, Mass: Harvard University Press, 1980), p. 556.

4. Zeffiro Ciuffoletti and Maurizio Degl'Innocenti, *L'Emigrazione nella storia d'Italia* (Florence: Vallecchi, Editore, 1978), p. 422; Salvatore Saladino, *Italy from Unification to 1919* (New York: Thomas Crowell, 1970), pp. 52–93; Benedetto Croce, *A History of Italy: 1871–1915,* trans. Cecilia M. Ady (New York: Russell & Russell, 1929), pp. 163–96; Nelli, *From Immigrants,* p. 20; Mangione, and Morreale, *La Storia,* pp. 159–60.

5. Caroline F. Ware, *Greenwich Village: 1920–1930* (New York: Harper & Row, 1935), p. 38. Giuseppe Pitre, *Usi e costumi, credenze e pregiudizi del popolo siciliano,* ed. Arnaldo Forni ed. (n.d.), pp. 71, 89; Giovanni Schiavo, *The Italians in Missouri* (Chicago: Italian Publishing, 1929), p. 81.

6. Rolle, *Italian Americans,* p. 6; Camillo Cianfarra, "Lo Sport nelle colonie italiane," in *Gli Italiani negli Stati Uniti* (New York: Andrew H. Kellogg Co., 1906), p. 6.

7. John A. Lucas and Ronald A. Smith, *Saga of American Sport* (Philadelphia: Lea & Febiger, 1978), p. 145; Cianfarra, "Lo Sport," pp. 1–6; Maurice R. Marchello, *Crossing the Tracks* (New York: Vantage Press, 1969), p. 174; Carmelo Bazzano, "The Sporting Life of Tontitown's Italian Immigrants" (paper delivered at the sixteenth annual NASSH Conference, Arizona State University, 1988.)

8. Cianfarra, "Lo Sport," p. 5; Dominick Cavallo, *Muscles and Morals* (Philadelphia: University of Pennsylvania Press, 1981), pp. 10, 6; Thomas J. Jable, "The Public Schools Athletic League of New York City: Organized Athletics for City School Children, 1903–1914," in *The American Sporting Experience,* ed. Steven A. Riess (Champaign, Illinois: Leisure Press, 1984), pp. 221, 222. Leonard Covello, *The Social Background of the Italo-American School Child* (Totowa, N. J.: Rowan & Littlefield, 1972), pp. 325–26, 274.

9. Cecil L. Griel, M.D., "I problemi della madre in un paese nuovo," in *Italians in the U. S.: A Repository of Rare Tracts and Miscelleana* (New York: Arno Press, 1975), pp. 50–51; Jable, "Public Schools," p. 228.

10. Bazzano, "The Sporting Life," p. 6; Center for Migration Studies of New York, *Images: A Pictorial History of Italian Americans* (New York, 1981), p. 232; Ware, *Greenwich Villager,* p. 144.

11. Marchello, *Crossing the Tracks,* p. 173; Joseph A. Burger, "Baseball and Social Mobility for Italian-Americans in the 1930s" (unpublished paper at the Center for Migration Studies), p. 6; "All-Italian Team," *New York Times,* August 13, 1939, sec. V, p. 8, col. 5; George De Gregorio, *Joe Di Maggio: An Informal Biography* (New York: Stein and Day, 1981), p. 13; Gay Talese, "The Silent Season of a Hero," in *Thirty Years of Best Sports Stories,* ed. Irving T. March and Edward Ehre (New York: W. P. Dutton, 1975), p. 213.

12. S. Kirson Weinberg and Henry Arond, "The Occupational Culture of the Boxer," in *Sport, Culture and Society,* ed. John W. Loy, Jr. and Gerald S. Kenyon (London: Macmillan, 1969), p. 440; Giacomo Rodorigo, "Quel picciotto di Dundee," *America Oggi,* Anno 2 no. 53, February 20, 1989, pp. 22, 23; Maurice R. Marchello, "Italian American Sport Heroes," in *A Documentary History of the Italian Americans,* ed. Wayne Moquin (New York: Praeger, 1974), pp. 425–29.

13. Michael A. Musmanno, *The Story of the Italians in America* (New York: Doubleday, 1965), p. 229; *Images,* p. 65; Interview with Willie Pep, October 4, 1992; Carmelo Bazzano, "The Irish-ization of Italian Boxers at the Turn of the Century" (paper delivered at the twentieth annual NASSH Conference, Dalhousie University, 1992).

14. Marino Mazzei and Bobby Finder, "Sports," *La Parola del popolo,* Anno 68, vol. 26 (settembre/ottobre 1976): 344–45.

15. Quoted by Gary R. Mormino, "The Playing Fields of St. Louis: Italian Immigrants and Sports, 1925–1941, *Journal of Sport History*, 9. (Summer 1982): 12, 6.

16. Ibid., p. 14.

7

The Recreation and Leisure Pursuits of Japanese Americans in World War II Internment Camps

Alison M. Wrynn

Yoshiko Uchido's *Desert Exile* recounts the story of family life in the assembly centers and internment camps established during World War II. These camps, opened in March 1942, displaced more than 100,000 Japanese Americans from their West Coast homes.[1] Sitting in the converted horse stall in the Tanforan Assembly Center which had become her family's home, Uchido reflected upon the bleak and dreary surroundings, commenting that the "north wind tore through the camp each day, sweeping with it the loose dirt of the track and its surrounding grounds." Although only across the San Francisco Bay from her former Berkeley home, she observed that the sun "seemed harsher and less benevolent.[2] This description surely does not conjure up images of leisure, diversion, and recreation.

On the contrary, Tanforan Assembly Center, like the other camps, brings to mind the conditions that so many Japanese Americans experienced from 1942 to 1945: dust, wind, desert, mountains. These are impressions that those who did not experience the cruel restriction of civil rights that Japanese Americans did during World War II can only imagine. Those who survived life in the camps, however, recall the endless boredom, limited opportunities, and lack of freedom. Since the publication of Dorothy S. Thomas' *The Spoilage* (1946) and *The Salvage* (1952), a growing number of scholars have examined the political purposes for the evacuation as well as the effect of the internment on the structures of Japanese-American society and family life. Others, such as John Tateshi, have published works based upon personal testimony of life in the camps.[3]

In recent years some scholars have begun to use games and sport to study the experiences of individuals who have been interned or whose ability to come and go freely has been in some way restricted. Though vastly different in many ways, there are certain similarities between recreation at the Japanese-American internment camps discussed in this paper and those of Theresienstadt, the showcase ghetto of the Nazis during the Second World War. As George Eisen has indicated, the German authorities permitted play in Theresienstadt because they felt that "such an outlet might have a calming effect upon the agitated population." Not only were these games seen as a diversion for the children; but they provided, for the adults who attended the children's games, an "opportunity to escape from a reality over which they had no control."[4] These are motives which echo some of the statements made by the United States government with regard to the internment of Japanese Americans during World War II. David Wiggins' research has shown that plantation owners in the Antebellum South provided recreation for their slaves in part to take their minds off their labor, a purpose the United States government also ascribed to internment camp recreation for the Japanese Americans. Victoria Paraschak has studied the sporting experience of Native women who lived on the Six Nations Reserve in Ontario, Canada. Whereas at Theresienstadt, and in the Japanese-American internment camps, individuals had no choice, the women whom Paraschak studied had opportunities to compete in the "All-Indian" leagues as well as in the larger society.[5]

Recently, historians have also begun to examine life in the Japanese-American internment camps by looking at the recreations and diversions of the internees. Sam Regalado's "Sport and Community in California's Japanese American "Yamato Colony' 1930–1945" presents a focused view of the maintenance of pride and community among Japanese Americans, prior to and during their internment, through baseball. This essay provides a different perspective on the functions that recreation and sport played for the Japanese Americans in the camps. As will be discussed in subsequent portions of this paper, although participation did provide the Japanese Americans with pride and solidarity, at another level, athletics and recreation reflected generational differences between individuals interned in the same location. Upon initial inspection the programs that were run during the internment seem inclusive, entertaining, and well-organized. Closer examination, however, shows that this was not always the case. In certain instances the programs were initiated by the internees; in other instances the United States government took the initial steps. However they emerged, the role of the Japanese Americans was of paramount importance to the programs. For the most part, programs were separate for *issei* (first generation, immigrant Japanese) and nisei (children of the *issei*, born in America), and not all the activities were enjoyed and supported by the internee community. In a few instances leisure time activities even became a disruptive element in the camps.

As sociologist Sylvia Yanagiasako and others have shown, the evacuation and internment disrupted the normal patterns of family life. Additionally, community structures which Japanese-Americans had established over a period of decades were uprooted. *Issei's* parental and economic control over the community was diminished. The basic necessities of life were provided for by the United States government, not the head of the family, and opportunities for gainful employment for Japanese American fathers were eliminated. Prior to the war, *issei* women had a great deal of control over their children's lives, especially in the social and educational realms.[6]

Diaries of internees frequently indicate that in the camps this relationship was markedly changed. For one thing, they had no real choice in the school they attended. In many instances they had rich and varied recreational and social outlets, most organized and run by the *nisei* themselves. In the assembly centers and internment camps, leisure time activities for the *issei* provided an especially important way to keep alive some aspects of Japanese cultural life. They participated primarily in games including *goh* and *sho-gi* for the men and *mah jong* for the women.[7] Japanese shows and entertainments became an important part of the recreational life of the *issei* in the internment camps. The *nisei*, for the most part, continued to participate in the types of activities which they had prior to the war, mostly athletics, dances, talent shows, and social events.

EVACUATION AND THE ASSEMBLY CENTERS

In mid-February 1942 President Franklin Delano Roosevelt signed Executive Order 9066 which directed the removal of suspected enemy aliens from the West Coast of the United States. Although the wording of the order was broad enough to include immigrant aliens from Germany and Italy, very few individuals residing in the United States who had been born in those countries were effected. Additionally, no American-born citizens of German or Italian descent were detained. Executive Order 9066 was directed at the Japanese Americans living in California, Oregon, and Washington State.

Public demand for the internment of Japanese Americans was immediate. Swept up in the forced relocation that ensued were both *issei* and *nisei*. Japanese Americans had begun to immigrate in small numbers to the United States in the late nineteenth century. As early as 1850 Americans, especially on the West Coast, had already begun to express concern about the influx of the Chinese. Formalized in the Chinese Exclusion Acts (1882), these sentiments were well established when the Japanese began to arrive at Angel Island in San Francisco Bay. By the turn of the century, the number of immigrants from Japan was only 10,000. The "Gentlemen's Agreement" of 1907 affirmed the ongoing antipathy of Californians to immigration from Japan. Among its other clauses, this diplomatic agreement between the United States and Japanese governments restricted the further immigration of Japanese males. The Alien Land Act (1913) further limited the rights of the *issei*. The National Origin Act (1924) imposed another impediment by restricting the immigration of Japanese women to the United States.[8] Following the bombing of Pearl Harbor on December 7, 1941, the already established anti-Japanese sentiments made the evacuation an almost forgone conclusion.

In March 1942 the first "Civilian Exclusion Order" was issued by the United States Army. This signaled the beginning of the relocation of Japanese Americans. Most were given only seven days to prepare to leave for the assembly centers. Told that they could bring only what they could carry, they were forced to dispose of nearly all their possessions. Assembly centers were located relatively close to centers of Japanese-American populations. Hastily arranged at converted fairgrounds and racetracks, these were dismal and depressing places. Among them were Tanforan, located near San Francisco, Santa Anita and Pomona, both located near Los Angeles, the Portland (Oregon) center, and a score of others.

Upon arrival men, women, and children were appalled to find that their accommodations were horse stalls swept clean of hay and given a coat of paint. The furnishings were sparse, and internees were obliged to struggle to obtain scrap wood to build furniture. There was a general lack of privacy in living quarters and lavatory facilities. There were few if any opportunities for employment. The abrupt departure had occurred near the end of the school term; thus recreation was the only substantial way to fill hours of forced inactivity.

Executive Order 9066 had placed the assembly centers under the direction of the Army and the Wartime Civil Control Administration (WCCA). In May 1942, an Operation Manual was issued. The evacuation (assembly) center's purpose was explained within the manual. The primary mission, as stated in the manual, was "to care for Japanese who were moved from certain military areas and placed in the camps under guard as a matter of military necessity." The manual specified that great care was to be taken not to refer to these as "concentration camps" to avoid comparison with events in Nazi Germany. There were, however, some similarities. The Japanese Americans, too, had been forcibly removed from their homes and communities. The camps were guarded, and internees could not leave in most instances. Moreover, considerable regimentation was imposed in the operation of the camps. The rules, regulations, and organizational structures are reflected in the large amount of paperwork that was generated by the internment. This useful body of plans, reports, and correspondence includes information on such things as construction, supply, special services, operations, and planning. Of these, the last two had as part of their assigned task the organization and development of recreation programs at the newly opened assembly centers.[9]

A preliminary report addressed to the WCCA by E. Rodney Overton, a Field Recreation Representative from the Office of Defense Health and Welfare Service and the Federal Security Agency, specified that programs of recreation should be as encompassing as possible since the internees had so much enforced leisure. The government hoped that recreation would fill the void that work and school had previously filled. This recommendation was aimed at eliminating discontent and the social friction that the government feared might result from boredom and inactivity. The report also maintained that a well-organized recreation program would contribute directly to the overall efficiency of the center. Throughout the approximately six month duration of the assembly centers, government administrators believed that the programs were a positive addition. One government official expressed it in this manner: the recreation program helped the center to "assume its own tempo and [attain] a good natured general feeling about the center which was reassuring."[10] Recreation programs, the report concluded, should be started immediately. They should include a pre-school play center, games and athletics, dances, musical entertainment, movies, and a library.

Although optimistic about the ways in which recreation might be used to fill the leisure hours, administrators were concerned that organized programs would be difficult to establish for the *issei*. There was some concern that they would be resentful of government attempts to organize a program for them. However, there is nothing in the report on recommended activities to indicate that the government authorities understood the types of recreation that would be preferred by *issei*. The report's bibliography consisted solely of pamphlets on community recreation available from the National Recreation Association. The report also stated that the government was afraid that it would be difficult to find personnel to run these programs as "it was not a characteristic of the Japanese to volunteer."[11]

Notwithstanding this general report for all centers, in some instances there seems to have been a recognition of the need for nonwestern activities. There was an Adult Activities Division which made attempts to provide recreation for the *issei* at the Tanforan Assembly Center. An area was set aside for the men to play *goh* and *sho-gi*. The women were given room to play *mah jong*. Spectating was apparently quite popular among the *issei* as it is mentioned in several sources, especially in connection with athletic events. There were, in fact, many of these to observe. In addition to playing *goh* and other games, and spectating, once a month a program consisting of Japanese songs and dances was performed.[12] Among the participants as well as spectators *issei* were especially prominent. Through these programs they were able to continue to express what they deemed to be their own culture, even though the content had to be approved by the center administrators. Although officially prohibited in the assembly center regulations, many administrators believed that, within certain constraints, there should be some opportunities for internees, especially the *issei*, to participate in activities traditional to their culture.

Among the *nisei*, "American" activities were the more popular. A talent show at Tanforan featured popular songs, skits, and college cheers. It drew an audience of nearly 2,000, the vast majority of whom were *nisei*. Dances to contemporary music were also very well liked among the *nisei*. Movies were a favorite of all the internees. Up to three showings an evening were necessary to accommodate all who were interested. Reports of playing basketball and softball, and comments about the games, occur often in the diaries of internees and appear to have been popular. Internees also played tennis and badminton and constructed their own facilities for outdoor sports. Although anyone might spectate, almost all participants were *nisei*. Softball games might attract 200–300 fans. Not everyone shared in the same enthusiasm for sports. One *nisei* college student stated that he was unable to understand why people got all "worked up" over recreational activities. He believed that they should be spending their time in more constructive pursuits. A diarist recorded that another individual characterized as a "prominent fellow" had expressed concern that recreation was overemphasized and could lead to problems of juvenile delinquency.

There were those among the *issei* who wanted children to participate in traditional Japanese cultural activities, such as sumo wrestling, rather than American activities. One *nisei* man expressed concern that non-American activities were overemphasized and this could have negative results for the children. As indicated earlier, camp directors permitted a certain amount of latitude. This is not to suggest that traditional Japanese activities and programs conducted in Japanese were not concerns of the administration. For the most part the administration did not understand the Japanese language, and in some instances their concern was warranted. These differences notwithstanding, both the internees and camp officials believed for the most part that recreation was a positive force in both the assembly center and the internment camps.

In accordance with traditional culture, prior to the evacuation, many of the older men and women had some "work" to do. They would be needed to help out in the home, on the farm, in the shop or other family business. Within the centers these opportunities were not available. Nonetheless, many of the older *issei* managed to attain a certain level of complacency with their existence within the center. They could visit with friends, or play *goh* or *sho-gi* whenever they pleased. This is how they spent a considerable amount of their time. Among the younger *issei* men (approximately 40–60 years of age) there was less contentment. They had lost their businesses and money as a consequence of the evacuation. Although these individuals were not very interested in participating in the various forms of organized recreation, they might frequently be spectators at *nisei* activities. As former heads of households and the focus of the family's presence in the community, the loss of status as well as material goods was especially painful. *Issei* women, however, still had family responsibilities. These occupied appreciable amounts of their time. Sewing or flower arrangement classes rather than more vigorous forms of recreation were their choice of leisure activities.[13]

Not even the most elaborate of recreation programs, however, could have filled the long hours of enforced idleness. Men, women, and children became restive. One indication of their discontent was the discovery of chalked signs in the Santa Anita Assembly Center which supported the Axis. The closing of the assembly centers in the fall of 1942 probably prevented further, more serious outbreaks. But the relocation of the Japanese Americans to internment camps created other types of issues that both the government and the internees had to deal with for another two and a half years.[14]

INTERNMENT CAMP RECREATION

The government had decided to set up ten internment camps to be the more permanent homes of the Japanese Americans during the war. These were located in California, Arizona, Arkansas, Utah, Colorado, Wyoming, and Idaho. With the transfer from assembly centers to internment camps in the fall of 1942, administration of the camps passed from the WCCA to the War Relocation Authority (WRA), a newly created civilian agency. By its official policy, the government continued recreation as an important aspect of the camp's program. A separate recreation section for each camp was established. According to the WRA, the aim of this program was to organize varied leisure activities and to see that no age or interest group was omitted from the process. Although there were variations from camp to camp, typical programs included sports and athletics, arts and crafts, movies, girl scouts and boy scouts, dances, and an *issei* program.

The WRA lifted many of the official restrictions imposed by the WCCA, so that the *issei* could more fully participate in the recreation program at the internment camp. Some *issei* appear to have been enthusiastic about these programs and were given considerable latitude in the organization of activities. They welcomed the opportunity to maintain some aspects of traditional Japanese culture. Greater attention was given to such things as Japanese food, *goh* and *sho-gi* clubs, and sumo wrestling teams. These types of activities were the recreational focal point of older Japanese Americans. Additionally, there were "study clubs" (some authorized by camp administrators, others not) which gave the *issei* a forum in which to discuss their internment.[15] Since very few of the camp administrators understood the Japanese language, all of these activities provided opportunities to discuss and complain about a variety of personal and community issues.

Although it was official WRA policy that organized recreation was to be an important part of the internment camps, difficulties were encountered when implementing the program. Initially, the government failed to provide sufficient funding, materials, or space. The development of teams and leagues was also hampered by interruptions caused by the departure of residents from some camps for agricultural work furloughs or relocation, either to another camp or to one of the designated inland cities (such as Chicago, Denver, or Cleveland). The recreation program at most of the camps, by and large, followed guidelines established by the WRA. At Arizona's Gila River Internment Camp, the first program to be organized was for the *nisei*. Spontaneous activities such as block talent shows and picnics were encouraged. Since ministers of churches they had attended in their home communities were among the internees, some aspects of the services that churches had previously provided were retained. The minister served as the locus for the reestablishment of churches. Among the many things the churches did was start talent shows. The participants were almost exclusively *nisei,* and the shows were conducted in English. The types of activities frequently included were comedy acts and community songfests. Most *nisei* found their social outlet within their own age group, keeping busy with games, dances, and social events.[16]

These activities, for the most part, did not involve young children. During the early days at Gila River, there were no organized educational opportunities. Concerned that school-age children did not have constructive outlets, *issei* organized Japanese games and activities for them. They also busied themselves by attending sporting contests, especially softball and sumo wrestling. The Closing Activities report for Central Utah's Topaz Internment Camp recorded that *issei* had participated in a wide range of activities during their stay. These included games and contests such as *goh* and *sho-gi*. In addition, the report records that *issei* enjoyed a variety of traditional songs, ballads, old tales, and the like, referring to these as *utai, naniwabushi, naga-uta, gida-yu, biwa.*[17]

To provide a more complete picture of recreation and leisure in the internment camps, two will be examined in more detail. The following sections will examine Arizona's Colorado River Relocation Center, also known as Poston, and the Tule Lake Internment Camp in northern California. Tule Lake is unique as it eventually became a segregation center for those *issei, nisei,* and *kibei* (*nisei* who had attended school in Japan for some period of time) who were deemed to be "disloyal" by the United States government.

Recreation at Poston

In its basic structures, the recreation program at Poston was similar to those at Topaz, Gila River, Manzanar, Heart Mountain, and the other internment camps. Administered as one unit, the Poston camp was so large it was divided into three separate communities. Each had its own recreation programs administered by the War Relocation Authority. Within the government-sponsored Community Activities Department, there were four major divisions: girls and women's activities, boys and men's activities, skills and crafts, and fine arts. The unit referred to as Poston 1, the largest of the communities, will be the focus of this study.

Poston opened in July 1942. The evacuees themselves initiated the recreation program shortly after their arrival. They developed a plan which they presented to the WRA-appointed "Recreation Officer" who approved of it and set about hiring a staff of recreation leaders from among the internee population. (Indeed, the federal government had intended to use internees as a majority of the workforce in the camps and most of the departments in the camp were so staffed.) Shortly after its inception, the Recreation Department was merged into a larger unit called the Community Activities Section. Athletics such as softball and basketball were the first activities offered by the new recreation department. Shortly thereafter the boy scouts, girl scouts, YMCA, and YWCA were organized as well. Whereas efforts to establish the YMCA were hindered by the lack of qualified male leaders, initial steps were taken in the summer of 1942 by trained Japanese-American "Y" secretaries to establish the YWCA.[18]

Young children played catch and running games; there were all sorts of sports for boys, including judo and sumo. In addition to sewing, girls might participate in baseball, volleyball, or other sports. There was an entertainment committee, staffed mostly by *nisei*, which was responsible for supervising the weekend dances, selecting movies, developing talent shows, and planning major campwide activities. The main problems encountered by the recreation department were finding enough space to run all of the programs and obtaining funding from the WRA to support them. The *issei* were primarily interested in traditional Japanese forms of literature, music, and drama. One of the popular activities was *shibai*, a dramatic program that included the traditional *kabuki* drama. One of the features quickly incorporated into the *shibai* were contemporary skits about life in Poston. The skits, at times, would be critical of the camp's administration. Although there is no evidence that this provoked the same level of response that it did at the Tule Lake Internment Camp, the camp administrators kept a watchful eye that this criticism did not get out of control.[19]

As has been noted, the recreation program at Poston included a substantial number of contemporary social activities and recreational forms that had the support and encouragement of the WRA. There were also covert activities. Gambling drew the greatest number of objections from both the WRA and some internees. When the *nisei* gambled, the preferred game was poker. The *issei* played a Japanese card game, *hana*. Although initially widespread among the Poston community, the gambling was not highly organized. High stakes were rarely bet; and as long as the players remained circumspect, the administration did not bother them. Neither did the "internee police force," which the administration had established to assist it in overseeing the camp. Gambling was usually confined to small groups of friends; *nisei* and *issei* typically referred to it as a source of "recreation." As gambling became more organized on a campwide basis, however, there was a concerted effort on the part of the administration to put a stop to it. An investigation was begun. When it was discovered that there were payoffs to members of the "internee police force," threats, and even violence, a trial was held. Those found to be implicated in the organized gambling were split up and sent to other internment camps or sentenced to terms in the local jail.[20]

Although there were disruptions of various kinds at Poston, of which the gambling incident described above is one, the majority of the internment camps were like the one located near Arizona's Colorado River. The Tule Lake Internment Camp, however, had a special status among the internment camps as it was designated as a segregation center in late 1943. This influenced many facets of life at Tule Lake, one of which was recreation.

Recreation at Tule Lake

Tule Lake, located in extreme northern California near the Oregon border, was unique among the internment camps; in late 1943 it was designated as a segregation center. It was here that those *issei, nisei,* and *kibei* whom the federal government had determined were disloyal to the United States were relocated. Begun as a regular camp, the change to a segregation center was precipitated by the registration crisis of 1943. This crisis resulted from a "leave clearance questionnaire" that the government required all internees to fill out. Two questions, numbers 27 and 28, were used by the government for making decisions about the probable loyalty of internees. Question 27 asked if an individual would be willing to serve in the United States armed forces, and question 28 asked if an individual would foreswear allegiance to the imperial government of Japan.

The respondent was in a difficult position. If one replied "no" to either or both questions, he would be sent to Tule Lake. Question 28 was especially problematic for the *issei* who, by law, were unable to become naturalized citizens of the United States. If they rejected allegiance to the emperor of Japan, they were relinquishing their Japanese citizenship and therefore were without citizenship in any country. In addition, internees who had requested repatriation to Japan were also likely to be sent to Tule Lake. Not everyone who was placed in Tule Lake, however, was labeled "disloyal." Some were family members of those who had been segregated; some had been residents of Tule Lake prior to the segregation and did not wish to move again.

W. E. Dimon, who was the recreation director at Tule Lake, recorded that the program there was similar to that of other camps. After its conversion to a segregation center in late 1943, the WRA made a point of telling the general public that no funds were to be spent on Japanese forms of recreation. Although this continued to be the official position of the WRA, judo and sumo programs, as well as Japanese language films and dramatic shows, were permitted. While concerned about public perceptions of the use of general funds to support such activities, Tule Lake's administrators seemed to believe that allowing some of these Japanese-oriented activities might reduce unrest and protest against camp conditions. Support for this assertion is that *issei* were permitted to have their own recreation staff which helped to provide Japanese types of entertainment.[21]

These entertainments at times contained pro-Japanese nationalistic songs and jokes. This led to conflicts with the administration. During an *ahodarakyo,* a satirical or comic monologue, some anti-American comments apparently were made. When the camp administrators learned of this they told community leaders "every trouble that occurs [here] ... is just laying another plank that makes the bridge right over to Japan for you." In an effort to convey their resolve in the matter, the camp administrators stated that if such activities persisted there was the chance that the camp might be changed over into a "concentration camp."[22]

Whereas Tule Lake shared with other internment camps such things as stage shows, music, arts and crafts, and athletics, there were areas in which it seems to have been markedly different. Contemporary dances were very popular at Poston, Topaz, and other camps, but not so at Tule Lake. Dimon, who had taken over the recreation division in late 1944, reported that the primary reason was an influential group of *issei* and *kibei* who felt that dances were too American in character. Younger *nisei* who wanted these, Dimon continued, were afraid of physical violence; hence few such dances were attempted.

In the summer of 1942, Dimon had been in charge of recreation at the Pomona Assembly Center. Of his tenure there he stated that he had been "thoroughly impressed" with the Japanese Americans with whom he had worked. Dimon's experiences at Tule Lake resulted in rather different reactions. During his year and a half of association with the internees at the northern California camp, he claimed that he had not been able to find "a single intelligence level comparable in any way with the mass intelligence of the Japanese American people." whom he had met when the relocation first began in 1942. The Japanese Americans at Tule Lake, he believed, were not a representative gathering of their people. Although Dimon refers to a lack of intelligent leadership at Tule Lake, the context of his report strongly suggests that what he means is a lack of cooperation. Despite the resistance of many individuals, at Tule Lake Dimon was still able to organize a recreation program that saw 10,000 spectators attend the opening day of the camp baseball league. Apparently baseball attained considerable popularity because an all-star team was selected and actually played two games against a semi-professional team from nearby Klamath Falls. In commenting upon these, Dimon indicated that the Tule Lake internees had been the winners by substantial margins.[23] Although there is nothing in his report which speaks directly to this, it is interesting that the internees accepted baseball, a sport identified almost exclusively with America, while at the same time rejecting dances labeled as "too American" in character.

THE CLOSING OF THE CAMPS

As Allied victories in the Pacific mounted and the end of the war was in sight, the relocation of internees from the camps to inland areas of the United

States proceeded. Recreation programs were slowly dismantled as fewer and fewer internees remained in the camps. Most of the Japanese Americans returned to their former communities on the West Coast, to be greeted by bigotry and even violence.[24] By late 1945 most camps had been closed.

During the three years of internment, the camps had become the homes of nearly the entire population of West Coast Japanese Americans. Uprooted from the structures of both their own communities and the larger American society of which they were a part, they had reestablished as much normality of family and community life as was possible. In the camps they had few opportunities for gainful employment, but a great deal of enforced leisure. Recreation, both organized and unorganized, helped to fill the void. Through camp-wide dances, talent shows, and athletic events, recreation was a unifying force among the Japanese Americans. For the *issei*, it provided them with the opportunity to sustain their traditional culture. Upon deeper inspection it is also apparent that the recreation programs in the internment camps created some tensions between the *nisei* and the more traditional *issei*.

Both federal officials and the Japanese-American leadership within the camps saw recreation as important. The United States government hoped that the ten internment camps would become "little cities" and that the Japanese Americans would become involved to the maximum extent in the organization and operation of the camps. The recreation program was designed to keep varied groups interested during their leisure time and to provide for all segments of the internee population. Noted most frequently by the Japanese Americans was that recreation filled time, gave them a sense of pride, and kept alive some aspects of their traditional Japanese culture.

This paper has focused on only a small number of the many centers to which Japanese Americans were directed during World War II. As increased attention is focused on the recreation and leisure programs at these assembly centers and internment camps, our understanding of the function these programs performed will expand. Continued research is needed. Fortunately, a massive collection of primary sources exists, for example, the Japanese Evacuation and Relocation Collection of the Bancroft Library at the University of California, Berkeley, and the Japanese American Research Project Archives at the University of California, Los Angeles. These and other collections should provide useful information. A better understanding of the evacuation and internment may help us never again to engage in such a shameful event.

NOTES

This chapter is a revised version of a presentation given at the annual meeting of the National Association of Ethnic Studies in March 1991. I would like to thank the editors of this book, George Eisen and David K. Wiggins, for encouraging me to submit this work; and my dissertation advisor, Roberta J. Park, for suggestions on its revision.

1. Both first generation, *issei*, and second generation, *nisei*, were evacuated during the internment. Although the *issei*, who had emigrated from Japan, were denied the right to become naturalized citizens of the United States, their children who were born in the United States (*nisei*) were citizens of this country by virtue of *jus soli*.

2. Yoshiko Uchido, *Desert Exile: The Uprooting of a Japanese American Family* (Seattle: University of Washington Press, 1982), p. 91.

3. A few of the many works on the evacuation and internment include: Roger Daniels, *Concentration Camps in North America: Japanese in the United States and Canada during World War II* (Malabar, Florida.: Krieger, 1986); Peter Irons, *Justice at War: The Story of the Japanese American Internment Cases* (New York: Oxford University Press, 1983); John Tateshi, *And Justice for All: An Oral History of the Japanese American Detention Camps* (New York: Random House, 1984).

4. George Eisen, *Children and Play in the Holocaust: Games among the Shadows* (Amherst: University of Massachusetts Press, 1988), pp. 44 and 46.

5. David K. Wiggins, "Good Old Times on the Old Plantation: Popular Recreations of the Black Slave in the Ante-Bellum South, 1810–1860," *Journal of Sport History* 4 (Fall 1977): 260–84; Victoria Paraschak, "Organized Sport for Native Females on the Six Nations Reserve, Ontario from 1968 to 1980: A Comparison of Dominant and Emergent Sport Systems," *Canadian Journal of Sport History* 21 (September 1990): 70–80. H. L. Stafford and John Bigelow, "Minidoka Report No. 71," Japanese Evacuation and Relocation Collection, the Bancroft Library, University of California, Berkeley (hereafter cited as JERS).

6. Sam Regalado, "Sport and Community in California's Japanese American 'Yamato Colony' 1930–1945," *Journal of Sport History* 19 (Summer 1992): 130–43; Sylvia J. Yanagiasako, *Transforming the Past: Tradition and Kinship among Japanese Americans* (Stanford: Stanford University Press, 1985), pp. 4, 54.

7. *Goh* (also known as *Go*) is a popular Japanese board game, derived from the ancient Chinese game *Wei-ch'i*. *Sho-gi* (also known as *Hasami shogi*) is a board game which is the Japanese form of chess. *Mah jong* is a table game for two to four players, and is played with tiles. J. A. Cuddon, *The International Dictionary of Sports and Games* (New York: Schocken, 1979), pp. 362, 714, 522.

8. "Total Japanese by Sex," 15.17, JERS; Roger Daniels, *Asian America: Chinese and Japanese in the United States since 1850* (Seattle: University of Washington Press, 1988), p. 126; John Modell, *The Economics and Politics of Racial Accommodation: The Japanese of Los Angeles, 1900–1942* (Urbana: University of Illinois Press, 1977), p. 161.

9. Daniels, *Concentration Camps*, pp. 244–45; "Operation Manual," B1.11, JERS; "Organization for the WCCA and CAD," B1.08, JERS.

10. E. Rodney Overton, "A Recommended Program of Recreation Activities for the Induction and Reception Centers Operated by the WCCA," B1.15, JERS, 1; anonymous author, "Inspection of Centers," **B9.50, JERS.

11. "Recommended Program of Recreation," B1.15, JERS, 1.

12. "Tanforan Recreation Program," B4.01, JERS, 35.

13. "Anonymous Diary," Tanforan, B12.10, JERS, 33–34; Western Defense Command and Fourth Army, WCCA "Assembly Center Regulations," B3.02, JERS, 8–9; "Recreational Activities in the Gila Community," K8.56, JERS, o–q.

14. Anonymous author,**B9.50, JERS, 7; anonymous author, **B12.10; **B12.43, JERS.

15. Robert F. Spencer, "Gila in Retrospect," in *Views from Within: The Japanese American Evacuation and Resettlement Study*, ed. Yuji Ichioka (Los Angeles: Resource Development and Publications, Asian American Studies Center, UCLA, 1989), pp. 166, 170.

16. "Minidoka Report No. 71," Carton 3, JERS; "Recreational Activities in the Gila Community," K8.56, JERS, a; "Recreational Activities in the Gila Community," K8.56, JERS, q–r.

17. "Recreational Activities in the Gila Community," K8.56, JERS, c–d; "Closing Report, Community Activities Division," H3.40, JERS, 3.

18. "Youth Organizations [Poston]," J2.81, JERS, 1 and J2.81, JERS, 23.

19. "Report on Various Activities," J2.85, JERS.

20. Anonymous author, "Gambling at Poston," **J6.09, JERS, 56–57.

21. "Description of the [Tule] Center," R1.00, JERS, 1; "Tule Lake Segregation Center," *Life*, March 20, 1944, 25–35.

22. Frank Miyamoto, "Tule City Council Meeting," R20.20, JERS, 17.

23. W. E. Dimon, "General History and Outline of the Community Activities Program at Tule Lake," R1.10, JERS, 5; W. E. Dimon, "Personal Narrative," R1.10, JERS, 1–2; W. E. Dimon, "General History and Outline of the Community Activities Program at Tule Lake," R1.10, JERS, 1.

24. "Returning *Nisei* Find Home Ruined by Fire," Fresno *Bee*, September 21, 1945, p. 3.

8

The Notion of Double-Consciousness and the Involvement of Black Athletes in American Sport

David K. Wiggins

W.E.B. Du Bois wrote in his classic book, *The Souls of Black Folk*, that blacks in this country have always felt a sense of being "an American, a Negro; two souls, two thoughts, two unreconciled strivings, two warring ideals in one dark body whose dogged strength alone keeps it from being torn asunder. . . . The history of the American Negro is the history of this strife."[1] This double-consciousness of being both black and American, which Du Bois pointed out in 1903, was evident in the careers of the most successful black athletes involved in American sport since the latter half of the nineteenth century.

Outstanding black athletes in this country were similar to other members of their race in that American discriminatory practices compelled them to live split existences. On the one hand, black athletes were proud of their race for its forbearance and ability to survive, and fought against the negative images of black inferiority. At the same time, black athletes aspired to success in American sport which necessitated that they adhere to values upheld in the dominant society. This duality was intertwined with a number of other important considerations, including economic issues, questions of gender, and the fact that black athletes strove for success in an institution not only controlled by whites but whose basic structure was defined by white standards.

The likelihood of maintaining a black identity, let alone gaining admission into sport, was made difficult for black athletes because the white American's stereotype of blacks inverted their own Protestant ethic. Blacks were variously categorized as docile or savage, faithful or tricky, pathetic or comical, childish or oversexed. This broad range of black character deserved no rewards and did not accommodate the ideal white image of the athlete. In addition, black athletes were involved in an institution which fashioned itself as the great

leveler in society but in actuality was one of the most conservative, tradi-
tion-laden institutions in America. The success of black athletes required
them, even more so than their white counterparts, to submit to the dictates of
coaches and other support personnel, display evidence of moral rectitude, and
exhibit high levels of conformity and respectability as well as physical skills. In
contrast to a black cultural form such as jazz, there was less room in American
sport to deviate from accepted white standards of performance and forge any
notion of racial consciousness.

Black athletes devised an assortment of responses to their uncertain position in American sport, responses that served as both a palliative and source of
liberation. They were similar to other minority group athletes in that they
dealt with their institutional constraints with a high degree of fluidity, periodi-
cally speaking out against racial injustice and other forms of discrimination
while knowing full well that reticence and conformity were the usual set of
behaviors necessary to survive in sport. Although not politically conscious as a
group and sometimes even choosing to disassociate from lower class blacks
who they believed were largely responsible for the stigmatized condition of all
blacks, many outstanding black athletes felt an obligation to reach out to less
fortunate members of their race while at once striving for individual success in
sport. This balancing of individual ambition and more collective action, which
obviously varied by degree from one athlete to another, was tied to the black
athletes' quest to realize a sense of identity amid the constraints of organized
sport. In a very real sense, then, black athletes moved in and out of their
respective roles as blacks, athletes, and Americans with a high degree of regularity in an attempt to foster a positive self-image and realize success in one of
this country's most prominent institutions.

In the years immediately following Reconstruction a number of black
athletes would make their mark in predominantly white organized sport and
become household names for sports fans of both races. Though involved in
almost every sport in America during the last half of the nineteenth century, it
was in horse racing and boxing that black athletes became most prominent and
had the largest representation.[2] Black athletes gained greater access to these
two sports partly because the sport establishment believed they were suitable
to the black man's abilities and partly because of the stigma attached to the
sports themselves. The prominent role played by black jockeys during this
period, for example, was primarily due to the horse racing establishment's
approach to blacks and the jockey profession in general. The profession was
closely identified with life on southern plantations where slaves had been
exploited as jockeys by their masters. Owners of thoroughbreds believed

success on the track depended on the bloodlines of their horses rather than who rode them and that the jockey profession was ideally suited for intellectually inferior but physically gifted blacks. In other words, riding horses for a living was, for a time, nothing more than "nigger work" with white riders generally not challenging the black jockeys' preeminence because of the stigma attached to working at the same job as a black.[3]

Regardless of these circumstances, successful black athletes in the latter half of the nineteenth century sometimes realized the numerous benefits typically reserved for whites. Each one of them received their share of plaudits and adulation from America's sporting public, earned large sums of money from their athletic exploits, and attained a standard of living unknown to most blacks. Success in sport allowed them not only an opportunity to support themselves and their families but a chance to bolster their self-esteem. They enjoyed a degree of self-respect and sense of accomplishment generally denied blacks during the late nineteenth century. As a group, successful black athletes of the period worked extremely hard at their particular sports and parlayed physical skills and connections with white employers into better lives.[4]

One of the most visible signs of their better lives was property ownership. Several well-known black athletes in the latter half of nineteenth-century America held some type of real estate. Besides furnishing income and adding a degree of comfort, property ownership had enormous symbolic importance to black athletes as it did to other black Americans. Whites might downplay their athletic skills, but land, houses, and other material evidence were impossible to disregard. These possessions furnished challenging evidence of the black athletes' capabilities while at once countering the white stereotype of the lazy and incompetent black. Isaac Murphy, the celebrated black jockey who captured the Kentucky Derby three times, used his wealth to purchase real estate in his home town of Lexington and as far away as Chicago. Moses "Fleetwood" Walker, the first black to play major league baseball, owned a hotel and several motion picture theatres in Steubenville, Ohio, and an opera house in nearby Cadiz.[5]

Although successful black athletes in the latter half of the nineteenth century worked hard to achieve their privileged positions, they never fully escaped the dictates of the American sport establishment. Regardless of the success they enjoyed on the playing field and the possessions they accumulated, black athletes of the period were unable to realize the degree of independence granted white athletes of comparable abilities. In efforts to climb the ladder of success, black athletes curried favor with the sport establishment which frequently increased their dependence on whites. Even though physical skills were a necessary prerequisite for athletic achievements, black athletes of the period often depended on alliances with white employers and customers for their ultimate success. The upshot of all this was that close ties frequently developed with white benefactors that sometimes strengthened the black athlete's concern for white opinion and the distance they felt between themselves and the majority of blacks in American society. This certainly seemed to be the case for Isaac Murphy who was compelled to establish a close relationship with Mrs. Hunt Reynolds, Ed Corrigan, and other members of horse racing's upper crust in order to realize success in the sport.[6]

Establishing ties with white employers did not necessarily mean that black athletes lost a sense of their separateness. The success of these athletes can be explained partly by their deftness at concealing their drive for success so thoroughly and by their ability to express their individuality at the appropriate times. Fluidity, in other words, was one of the greatest gifts of black athletes involved in American sport. Depending on the situation, they could either be cleverly docile, verbally persuasive, or very forceful. They were prepared to be passive if they knew they were in a vulnerable position or if it assisted them in maintaining status. They could also become combative when encountering discrimination, even though it might temporarily negate the reticence on which they most commonly relied. They realized early on that their physical skills placed them in an enviable position because white society often stood to benefit handsomely from their performances and that their status allowed them an opportunity to air grievances and express their opinions without the constant fear of reprisals. Early in his career, Peter Jackson, the celebrated black heavyweight from Australia, chided Jack Burke, a popular boxer known as the Irish Lad, for repeatedly refusing to cross the color-line and fight him. He attacked Burke in a manner that belied his generally quiet nature. For instance, immediately following one of Burke's exhibition matches, Jackson stepped to the side of the ring and angrily challenged Burke: "He [Burke] says he draws the color-line. Well John L. Sullivan, who also draws the color-line, says he has no objection to meeting a colored fighter in private. If Mr. Burke is of the same way of thinking, I will gladly meet him tonight, tomorrow or any day he might select in a cellar, barn or any private room he chooses to name and will wager him 1,000 pounds on the result."[7]

The success of black athletes in nineteenth-century American sport never freed them from their sense of being exemplary. Although they consciously strove to gain acceptance as great American athletes, they never completely escaped from being defined by race. Each triumph showcased their individual talents and was a symbolic nail in the coffin of racial inferiority, while each loss was considered an individual tragedy and evidence of racial limitations. Marshall "Major" Taylor certainly became a representative figure in his races against white riders. His biographer, Andrew Ritchie, noted that "crowds wanted action and drama and a strong whiff of danger and the struggle between Taylor and his white rivals was basic and easily understandable, like a young David taking on several Goliaths at once—full of an unstated but obvious racial symbolism."[8]

Late nineteenth-century black athletes were often disturbed by their inability to be classified by anything other than race. They recognized the symbolic importance of their triumphs to the black community, but wanted to be acknowledged as outstanding athletes rather than simply outstanding black athletes. To do otherwise only served to demean their accomplishments and denied them full recognition as Americans who had achieved success in one of this country's most visible and cherished institutions. Their views were similar to those expressed by other well-known blacks of accomplishment. For instance, E. Franklin Frazier, the prominent sociologist known for his work on the black family, remarked shortly after a trip to Brazil in 1941 that in the United States an "Afro-American scholar was regarded first as black, secondarily as a scholar." "When his work is recognized," stated Frazier, "it is usually pointed to as the work of a negro. He is a competent negro sociologist, an able negro economist, an outstanding negro historian. Such recognition is as much the product of the racist mentality as the negro rest rooms in the Montgomery airport are."[9]

Although they desired full recognition as people who had achieved success by means of the American virtues of individualism and self-reliance, their shared color and experiences of discrimination ultimately led some black athletes to be group conscious and collective.[10] In the most extreme cases it meant loyalty to only race and family. Moses Fleetwood Walker, for example, struggled for some seven years to establish himself in organized baseball. Lured by the chance to gain prestige and status, he wanted to participate in America's national pastime with color being irrelevant to his success. Walker would also become, however, a leader in the back to Africa movement that was popular among some blacks around the turn of the century. In his 1908 book, *Our Home Colony*, Walker advocated separation of the races, arguing that blacks would never become equal participants in American life. "There can be given no sound reason against race separation," wrote Walker. "All experience, and every deduction from the known laws and principles of human nature and human conduct are against the attempt to harmonize two alien races under the same government. When the races are so differentiated in mental and physical characteristics, as the Negro and Anglo-Saxon, the government that undertakes the experiment rests at all times on a volcano."[11]

The American dream of unlimited possibilities was ultimately shattered for black athletes. By 1900 most of them had successfully been excluded from American sport and were forced to establish their own separate sporting organizations. The most famous of these were the black baseball leagues, a loose aggregate of teams that did not achieve much organizational structure until Rube Foster founded the National Negro Baseball League (NNL) in 1920. Similar to other black cultural institutions of the period, black baseball offered a viable alternative for black athletes excluded from the major leagues. Hidden from the view of most white Americans, black baseball was considered by many in the black community to be a temporary institution that would cease to exist once integration in organized baseball was realized. Although black Americans were concerned about the survival of their own leagues, they were not preferable to having black players in the major leagues. Not unexpectedly, those with a vested interest in black baseball took a different view of baseball integration than the majority of black Americans, realizing the entry of blacks into the major leagues would jeopardize their business or, worse yet, put them out of business. They did not actively oppose, however, the campaign for baseball integration waged throughout the first half of the twentieth century because to do so would have been considered, in the words of historian Janet Bruce, "racial treachery in the black community."[12]

It was also unrealistic to expect talented black athletes to forego their chance of success in organized baseball in order to sustain the black leagues. Black players were no different than their white counterparts in that they had always dreamed of one day participating in major league baseball. Organized baseball would not only give them a chance to gain money and prestige, but would furnish them an opportunity to compete against the best players in the world and showcase their abilities to a larger audience. Even though black players enjoyed their own leagues and occasionally competed against white major leaguers in exhibition games, they yearned to be a part of organized baseball because it would help define themselves and verify their talents. Participation in the national game would give black players a chance to measure their achievements against white players who had always been used as the standard for success.[13]

The leaders in black baseball realized that regardless of what happened in organized baseball, black Americans should make an effort to maintain their leagues for a time so as to promote their own interest in the sport and to supply employment for the largest number of black players. More specifically, the leaders in black baseball were determined to make their leagues successful institutions because they served as an example of black enterprise, and concomitantly, helped prove that black players belonged in America's national game. The enormous gap between ideal and practice in organized baseball forced most blacks, in other words, to desire access into that institution while at the same time feeling obliged to support their separate leagues operating with very little white interference.[14]

Perhaps no one expressed these sentiments more clearly than the architect of black baseball himself, Rube Foster. For example, in 1922 Ed Bolden, the black owner of the Hillsdale, Pennsylvania, baseball club, withdrew from the NNL because of travel difficulties and the following year organized the rival Eastern Colored League (ECL). Foster opposed formation of the new league for obvious business reasons, but he was also troubled by the fact that the majority of owners in the ECL were white. Although he realized the races could work together for mutual benefit—as indicated by the amicable working relationship he established with the owner of the Kansas City Monarchs, J. Leslie Wilkinson—Foster was fearful of the intentions and possible deleterious effect white owners in the new league would have on black baseball. "There can be no such thing," said Foster, "as [a black baseball league] with four or five of the directors white any more than you can call a street car a steamship. There would be a league all right, but the name would have to be changed."[15]

The consequence of all this was that black baseball was at once remarkably similar in organizational structure to the major leagues and a distinctive entity that reflected, in many ways, black culture. Like the major leagues, black baseball was divided into two leagues, played an all-star game composed of the best players from the two leagues, and at season's end held a championship series between the winners of the two leagues. Many of the black teams used major league ballparks and copied everything from uniform styles to special-order baseball bats. For example, when Bill Robinson, the famous dancer known affectionately as Mr. Bojangles, purchased the New York Black Yankees, one of his first acts was to buy year-old Yankee uniforms.[16]

In actual play, black players were generally more daring, unpredictable, and prone to improvise than their white counterparts. They emphasized speed and played "tricky baseball" or "unwritten baseball." Black players viewed their sport more as a form of entertainment in which each player could express his individuality and at the same time contribute to his team's overall effort. Perhaps the primary reason why the annual East-West All Star game was the premier event in black baseball and overshadowed the leagues' World Series, was the fact that it was a perfect opportunity for black players to display their unique performance styles. The most noteworthy example of an individual performance style was expressed by Leroy "Satchel" Paige, one of the black leagues' most legendary players. Always the master showman, Paige captured newspaper headlines and the imagination of baseball fans with his hesitation, Model T, and windmill windups. He threw, in his own words, "bloopers, loopers, and droopers . . . [a] jump ball, bee ball, screw ball, woobly ball, whipsy-dipsy do, a hurry-up ball, a nothin' ball and a bat dodger."[17]

Notwithstanding these apparent differences, black leaguers were still subject to the same rules, regulations, and code of ethics as those players in major league baseball. They also had undisputed home run hitters in the league and could play the power game that dominated organized baseball by the 1920s. In addition, the men in black baseball sometimes emulated and frequently identified with players from both leagues. Having played against Dizzy Dean, Bob Feller, and other barnstorming major leaguers in exhibition games, black leaguers came to admire their more famous white counterparts and sometimes patterned their play after them. Perhaps most important, many leaders in black baseball exhorted their players to "be like major leaguers." Individual performance styles were recognized and appreciated in the black leagues, but many people in black baseball disapproved of the more flagrant clowning and funny stunts used to heighten the entertainment value of games because they believed this approach to the sport merely perpetuated the negative stereotypes whites had of blacks. One sportswriter who covered the black leagues on a regular basis castigated the Indianapolis Clowns for capitalizing on "slap-stick comedy and the kind of nonsense which many white people like to believe is typical and characteristic of all Negroes."[18]

While blacks were fashioning their own separate world of black baseball, several individual black athletes successfully participated in predominantly white organized sport. The most notable of these were Jack Johnson, America's first black heavyweight boxing champion, Joe Louis, the second black boxer to capture the heavyweight crown, and Jesse Owens, the famous track star from Ohio State who won four gold medals in the 1936 Olympic Games in Berlin. Of the three, Johnson was certainly the most controversial. Perhaps no black athlete has incurred the wrath of such a broad segment of the white population and part of the black population as Johnson. To whites, he possessed many of those personal qualities found so reprehensible in blacks. He was ill-mannered, defiant, and absolutely incorrigible. He had also ignited their worst fears by marrying three white women and capturing the heavyweight championship which had come to symbolize the Ango-Saxon belief in racial superiority. By the same token, many blacks, including the likes of Booker T. Washington and to a lesser extent Dubois, were appalled by Johnson's actions and believed he hindered the progress of the race. Though a hero to many in the black community, others considered him an embarrassment and the worst possible representative of black Americans because he refused to assume the subservient role assigned to him by whites.[19]

Much of what Johnson did, however, was merely an expression of the American way of life. His entire career was a quest for freedom to choose his own definitive style while gaining access to the material things of this world.[20] In the ring there was seldom any doubt about how Johnson felt about himself. Like other black boxers, he adopted a defensive style of fighting, relying to a great extent on feints, cross-counters, and deceptive maneuvers. As Randy Roberts has noted, this reflected black culture which has always found it necessary to place a high value on the ability to retort and defend.[21] Perhaps even more significant was that Johnson resembled other black performers in consciously adopting a style that was undisputably his own. It was extremely important to him that he fashion an individual performance style that was personally developed and publicly acknowledged. He wanted clear and unquestioned claim to the image he had cultivated.

Johnson's life outside the ring was much more complex. He adopted no apparent political stance and would not hesitate to shift his allegiance when he found himself in a vulnerable and dangerous situation. In spite of all this, Johnson never stopped identifying with other blacks and receiving his basic sustenance from America's black community. His resentment of outstanding black boxers such as Sam Langford, Harry Wills, and Joe Louis indicated more his longing to be recognized as black America's only true champion rather than any need to divorce himself from other blacks. His numerous relationships with white women were one way he could exert a sense of power and control, and not necessarily an indication of a lack of interest in his race or that he yearned to be a part of the white world. Johnson's apparent lack of political consciousness should not be construed as a disregard for other members of his race. He protested discrimination by proving himself as a black man and American. His ring triumphs and refusal to accept any limitations was Johnson's statement for racial justice and civil rights. Lawrence Levine, in his well-known book *Black Culture and Black Consciousness*, wrote that Johnson "was not prone to see himself as a representative of any larger cause" but "was inevitably affected by the clamor" made over him by the black community. By the time he fought Jim Jeffries, says Levine, Johnson realized that not just the championship was at stake but also his "own honor, and in a degree the honor" of his own race.[22]

Johnson's career was more controversial and tumultuous than those of Joe Louis and Jesse Owens. While these two famous athletes had things in common with Johnson, they generally lived their lives much differently and with more restraint than America's first black heavyweight champion. White Americans continually expressed the belief that other blacks would do well to emulate Louis and Owens who always acted like gentlemen and were cognizant of their proper place in society. In public, they usually adopted an ingratiating and compliant manner with members of the dominant culture. Their manner and gestures were deliberate and almost always understated. Perhaps most important was the fact that Louis and Owens regularly spoke about how much they loved their country and owed America. Louis, for instance, donated his share of two title defenses to the Army and Navy relief funds during World War II. When criticized by some blacks for giving away his prize money while being fully aware of the racially discriminatory policies maintained by the Navy, Louis responded by saying: "I'm not fighting for nothing, I'm fighting for my country."[23]

The irony in all of this was that Louis and Owens were not necessarily submissive. It took ambitious and determined men to make it as far in American sport as they had. They were merely experts at concealing their drive for recognition. Owens and Louis adhered to traditional athletic expectations by being highly disciplined, obedient, and respectful of authority. As black athletes, they were also aware that they were allowed far less room to deviate from expected modes of behavior than their white counterparts. Both of them genuinely believed, moreover, in the American dream of individual success and the moral formula needed to realize that success. Owens and Louis were no different than most American-bred youths in that they had been taught that the path to success was contingent upon them displaying proper decorum, courteously yielding to the opinions or wishes of others, showing deference to the good tastes and sensibility of others, and being industrious in one's calling. Bad manners, uncontrolled emotions, and similar types of behavior were inappropriate, particularly in black culture where the ability to control oneself and exercise constraint was highly valued. Louis' mother told him that "a good name" was "better than money" and encouraged him to work hard and become somebody. His managers, John Roxborough and Julien Black, urged him to be clean living, sportsmanlike, and to practice restraint.[24]

No degree of decorum could stop Louis and Owens from identifying with the black race. It was not always evident, but neither one of them abandoned the larger black population. While family, friends, and individual success were of paramount importance to Louis and Owens, the two athletes eventually recognized their significance to black society and strove to set positive examples for the whole race by maintaining a public image that was at once attractive and non-threatening to all segments of society. Exhibiting an occasional sense of noblesse oblige, Owens and Louis also reached out to other blacks, even though it was often done very cautiously and only after being persuaded to do so by other blacks. Louis and Owens were aware that openly negative reactions to racial discrimination were often seen by whites as unreasonable, over-reactive, hypersensitive, and even "un-American." They often couched their complaints of racial discrimination in words acceptable to whites. Both men went to great lengths to avoid any interpretation by whites that their complaints of racial inequities were an expression of their merely being black or, perhaps stated more explicitly, "acting like a Nigger."[25]

At the same time, the help Louis and Owens gave other blacks seemed to border on the type of paternalism practiced by many whites. For this reason, as well as generational differences, Owens, and to a much lesser extent Louis, were sometimes viewed with suspicion if not overt hostility by younger blacks in this country. Taking a more conservative approach to racial issues and having isolated themselves somewhat from the black masses, the two athletes never completely won the confidence of more forceful and politically conscious blacks during the latter stages of their lives. Vince Matthews, who was involved in the proposed boycott of the 1968 Olympic Games in Mexico City, recalled the cold reception he and his fellow black athletes gave Owens when the former track star met with them the day after Tommie Smith and John Carlos gave their much publicized black power salutes. "When Jesse walked into the room," noted Matthews, "most of us tried to show him respect because of his age and his athletic accomplishments. But when he got up at the meeting and said he wanted the white athletes in the room to leave because 'these are my brothers,' and I want to talk to them, you could see the snickers on some of the faces."[26]

All things considered, Louis and Owens were like other black Americans in that they responded in various ways to racial discrimination in order to rid themselves from an imposed sense of inferiority and transcend their stigmatized condition in American society. Significantly, these efforts often proved futile for Louis and Owens because American society typically relegated blacks to a single, racially inferior category. The stereotypical notion of black inferiority seemed so strong in America that regardless of how great their individual prestige, Louis and Owens could never be fully disassociated from the lesser privileged members of their race or completely extricated from the "black image in the white mind." Although white Americans would refrain from identifying them by the color of their skin and trumpet their victories as symbolic triumphs of "America over Nazi Germany" or "America over Fascist Italy," the two athletes would always be linked with character traits supposedly innate to their racial group. It is precisely for these reasons that Owens tried to rise above his color and insist that he be seen as a "human being first and last, if not always," and questioned if there was not "something deeper, richer, better in this world than the color of one's skin."[27]

America's black community never forgot that Louis and Owens were black and that they were, to some extent, being exploited by this country's sports establishment. The success of two black athletes in international competition could not erase the fact that Jim Crow America continued to prohibit black athletes from participating in all sports. The sport that best illustrated the precarious status of black athletes and the injustices of American society was professional baseball. The "Gentlemen's Agreement" by major league owners prohibited any black players, regardless of ability, from entering white organized baseball. This form of discrimination was terribly frustrating to black Americans who believed that until blacks could participate fully in the national game, they could not lay claim to the rights of full-fledged citizenship.[28]

Fortunately, America's entrance into World War II gave blacks more reason and opportunity to protest discrimination in the national game than at any other time in history. The hypocrisy involved in fighting a war for the four freedoms against aggression by a country proclaiming a master race ideology while concurrently upholding racial discrimination in organized baseball and society at large, provided blacks with a perfect opportunity to expose the gap between America's creed and its practice. The democratic ideology with which the war was fought kindled hope in black Americans because they could fasten their racial demands to the same ideology in their attempts to integrate the national game. Blacks used the war to illustrate that the game of baseball was not the great leveler in society and a sport within the reach of all Americans.[29]

It was in this kind of atmosphere that Branch Rickey took the bold step and signed Jackie Robinson to a contract with the Brooklyn Dodgers. The signing of Robinson was received with unabated enthusiasm by America's black community. Robinson immediately became a hero in black America, surpassed in popularity perhaps only by Joe Louis. Some black Americans questioned, however, whether Robinson's sometimes volatile personality would prevent him from achieving success in organized baseball. He was an intensely proud black man who was quick to defend his rights and seldom, if ever, backed down from racial confrontations. He had spoken out against discriminatory practices while at UCLA and during his brief stint in the military. If Robinson was to survive in organized baseball, he would have to do his best to avoid racial conflicts with prejudiced white players.[30]

Serious altercations between Robinson and white opponents never materialized. As things turned out, Rickey chose the ideal player to integrate the game. Although Robinson had a tendency to be high-spirited, he also knew his responsibilities as organized baseball's first black player and was careful to avoid any skirmishes that might jeopardize his chances for success. Robinson wanted a long-lasting career in organized baseball. Like other young men in America, he had dreamed of one day participating in major league baseball and frequently spoke of ultimate integration in the sport. For him the segregated black leagues signified second-class citizenship. He supported it in principle, but never grew accustomed to the loose scheduling and erratic play that was so much a part of black baseball.[31]

On a more collective level, Robinson grudgingly ignored racial slurs thrown at him by white players and fans partly because Rickey wanted him to, partly out of fear of retribution at the hands of the dominant culture, and partly out of a genuine concern for his race. He realized that the hopes of many black Americans rested on his shoulders and, rather than take the more forceful approach he had adopted in previous interracial contacts, he acquiesced and let his athletic performance do the talking. As modern day baseball's first black player, Robinson was suddenly catapulted into the public eye and, as a result, almost immediately realized a sense of being exemplary. If he handled himself properly, he could point the way to other black ballplayers and perhaps make it possible for them to participate someday in the national game. As a role model, he could become a symbol of possibility and a much needed example of black achievement. In many ways, Robinson was similar to great black athletes who preceded him in that he was inevitably defined by the color of his skin. In his autobiography, Robinson commented on his role as a representative of black Americans: "Many [blacks] who came to the ball park had not been baseball fans before I began to play in the big leagues. Suppressed and repressed for so many years, they needed a victorious black man as a symbol. It would help them believe in themselves."[32]

Following Robinson's breakthrough with the Dodgers, a number of blacks gained entry into organized sport at both the professional and college levels. These athletes shared many of the same attitudes toward racial issues and the American sport establishment. Although occasionally speaking out against discriminatory practices, they tended to deemphasize black consciousness and redefined themselves in accordance with the integration-orientation policies established by the leaders in organized sport. They were similar to other black Americans in that the gradual desegregation of sport, combined with the post–World War II propaganda about the brotherhood of man, caused them to think less about blackness as a cultural identity and more about their loyalty to this country and its ideals. Black athletes were concerned about their rights as human beings, but were reluctant to protest for fear that their actions would be construed as un-American and possibly jeopardize their careers in sport. Althea Gibson, the first black player to participate in the United States Tennis Championships at Forest Hills, wrote in her autobiography that she did not consider herself a racially conscious person or a crusader. "Someone once wrote," noted Gibson, "that the difference between me and Jackie Robinson is that he thrived on his role as a Negro battling for equality whereas I shy away from it. That man read me correctly."[33]

The patriotism exhibited by black athletes during the 1950s was not wasted on the youthful Cassius Clay. From the time he captured a gold medal in the 1960 Olympics to his defeat of Sonny Liston for the heavyweight championship some four years later, Clay was universally hailed as a great athlete whom all Americans could admire. During this period, Clay was variously described as loyal, patriotic, witty, charming, articulate, and clean living. He seemingly had no interest in civil rights issues and mounting tensions between the two races. Many of his public statements were reminiscent of those made by Joe Louis nearly twenty years earlier. When asked by a Soviet reporter in 1960 about racial discrimination in America, Clay responded by saying, "Tell your leaders we got qualified people working on that, and I'm not worried about the outcome. To me, the U.S.A. is still the best country in the world, counting yours."[34]

Shortly after his title fight with Liston in 1964, Clay stunned the sports world by announcing he had changed his name to Muhammad Ali and joined the Black Muslims. Ali's conversion to a black separatist group like the Muslims, his sudden willingness to speak out against racial inequities, and his eventual refusal to join the military resulted in a myriad of reactions from the American public. He became a hero in the black community and was admired by many liberal-minded Americans, but was looked upon with utter disdain and branded a traitor by those who supported the war and followed traditional societal values. Gene Tunney and Jack Dempsey both castigated Ali, telling him that he was undeserving of the heavyweight title and that his actions were un-American. Similar comments were made by sports writers, governors, U.S.

senators and representatives, and such organizations as the American Legion and Veterans of Foreign Wars.[35]

Ali's refusal to be inducted into the military was just one reason members of the establishment found him disruptive. He was also not the type of athlete the conservative white sporting world appreciated. While the sports establishment expected their heroes, particularly black ones, to be humble and accommodating, Ali was always flamboyant, immodest, and defiantly confident. Perhaps most troubling to whites was that Ali never sacrificed a degree of his racial identity, but chose instead to emphasize his cultural distinctiveness, the merits of a black lifestyle, and the value of his negritude. To the white majority, Ali's celebration of black culture challenged the existing social order because it helped eliminate the negative self-image prevalent among some blacks and encouraged black consciousness which was a necessary foundation for the promotion of black political and economic power. Members of the establishment were, moreover, infuriated by Ali because he exposed, for all the world to see, an America that was unwilling to honor its own precepts. With no need to nourish this country's dreams and myths, Ali continually made clear that freedom, equality, and fair representation were not available to all Americans.[36]

The willingness to express pride in his blackness was not an indication that Ali wished to sever himself from American society. In fact, one of the truths of Ali's career was that, even while preaching a separatist position, his very actions indicated he was a man who believed that the American dream of unlimited possibilities, while imperfect and perhaps even fanciful, was worth striving for. Ali wanted to participate in American life and realize the numerous benefits that derived from being successful in sport, but not if it implied the supremacy of everything white and the inferiority of everything black. America would have to compromise and accept him on his own terms or not at all.[37] A composite of several types of heroes in black folk culture, Ali was always his own man, someone who clung tenaciously to his racial past while at once seeking immortality in the boxing ring and resisting the standards of behavior imposed by white society. "In the context of boxing," wrote Eldridge Cleaver in his well-known autobiography *Soul on Ice*, "Ali was a genuine revolutionary, the black Fidel Castro of boxing." Every black heavyweight champion of the past had been a puppet, said Cleaver, "manipulated by whites in his private life to control his public image." In regards to Ali, however, "the puppet-master was left with a handful of strings to which his dancing doll was no longer attached."[38]

Ali's refusal to succumb to the dictates of the dominant culture was particularly significant because it helped spawn a black athletic revolution. Inspired by the champion's racial consciousness, a number of black athletes followed Ali's lead and began to speak out against racial discrimination and other inequities in American society. Perhaps the most noteworthy phase of this revolution was the proposed boycott of the 1968 Olympic Games in Mexico City. The planned boycott, which was spearheaded by Harry Edwards, an instructor of sociology at San Jose State, was aimed at exposing the racism prevalent in the United States and around the world. While civil rights legislation was sometimes responsible for the increased participation of blacks in American society, the implications of this type of participation were greater than Edwards and a growing number of black athletes were prepared to accept. It was apparent to them that participation in American society was possible, but only at the expense of being denied their own identity and their African heritage. In brief, black athletes involved in the proposed boycott were similar to other black Americans in that they were interested in disclosing this country's racial inequities while at the same time expressing the distinctiveness of black culture, the quality of black life, and the value of race pride. Tommie Smith, the great sprinter from San Jose State, explained shortly after the announcement of the boycott in December 1967 that he would not only give up participation in the Mexico City Games but his life if it meant the elimination of injustice and oppression in American society.[39]

Smith did not give up his life or participate in any boycott. Other than the black power salute given by himself and John Carlos, the games went on without interruptions. The overriding reason for the failure of the boycott was that Edwards never succeeded in unifying the black athletes. While black Olympians supported the boycott in principle, the vast majority ultimately concluded that the price to pay for non-participation was simply too high. First of all, South Africa was eventually kicked out of the games by the International Olympic Committee because of their discriminatory practices against blacks. This fact softened the militant stance of many black athletes who originally agreed upon a boycott because of their desire to expose the racial inequities existing in South Africa and ultimately to see that the country was barred from Olympic competition. Edwards was also wrong to think black athletes would follow through on something as radical as a boycott. Almost everything Edwards asked of the black Olympians was in direct opposition to what they had always been taught was the proper behavior of a competitive athlete. While black athletes—and white athletes for that matter—were expected to be humble, tolerant, and respectful of power, Edwards encouraged them to be outspoken, defiant, and disrespectful of authority. In essence, Edwards urged black athletes to be something they were not. Participation in Olympic competition was also the highlight in the careers of most black athletes and perhaps their ticket to a brighter future and more rewarding way of life. Public adulation awaited those black athletes who came home from Mexico City victorious. It was nearly impossible for any athlete, regardless of color, willingly to squander that type of attention and forego a chance to compete against the best athletes in the world. Black athletes eventually concluded, with varying degrees of conviction, that achievement in sport was an ideal starting point for wiping out inequities due to race.[40]

The boycott was hurt, moreover, by Edwards' reluctance to take advantage of all the resources available to him. Conspicuous by their absence from the movement were black female athletes. Such outstanding performers as Wyomia Tyus and Jarvis Scott were not consulted by the men, privy to the inner workings of the Olympic Project for Human Rights (OPHR) or invited to the various strategy sessions and meetings organized by Edwards and his cohorts. This was particularly disconcerting to the black female athletes because they realized, as did black women of the past, that they needed to work alongside men for the ultimate liberation of black Americans. It was absolutely essential to black female athletes that the struggle for civil rights be done in concert with black males, since the root cause of their problems was not sexism but the racial oppression in American society.[41]

The unwillingness to involve black female athletes in the boycott stemmed largely from what historian Paula Giddings called the "male-conscious motif" that dominated American society in the 1960s.[42] The boycott masterminded by Edwards was as much a "male revolt" as it was a "black athletic revolt." Confronted by racial discrimination, challenged by a caste system that left little room to display one's masculinity, and having their honor attacked by more radical members of the black community who were emphasizing the need for the celebration of black lifestyles caused Edwards and his followers consciously to exert both their sense of racial pride and manhood to the exclusion of black female athletes. There simply was no room for women in a movement where black men were trying to rid themselves of their imposed status as "Negroes" through the raising of black gloved fists, threats of nonparticipation in the world's greatest athletic festival, and other exhibitions of "black power." Like the men in many black civil rights organizations, the boycotting black athletes' desperate need for male affirmation necessitated that their female counterparts be pushed into the background and not permitted to take an active role in the rebellion. The unstated fear on the part of the boycotting black athletes was that they would be robbed of their manhood if women such as Wyomia Tyus and Jarvis Scott were allowed to share in decision making and strategic planning. "We were most disappointed that our feelings were not brought out," noted Scott about the boycott movement. "While the men issued statements and held conferences, finding out what we felt was only a last minute thing."[43]

All things considered, then, the most telling aspect of the boycott was the interplay not only between Edwards and the black athletes, but among the black athletes themselves. The situation required a sophisticated assessment of both individual and group costs on the part of black athletes and whether either line of action—that is, resisting or yielding to group pressure—would yield the most benefits. There certainly was no question in Edwards' mind as to what the black athletes should do. Notwithstanding the exclusion of women from the movement, Edwards tried to convince black athletes that the problems of blacks were common to them as a group rather than as individuals. He continually emphasized that the fight for equality was by necessity a collective struggle and could not be based solely on individual achievements. Personal accomplishments were praiseworthy, but they could never completely eliminate the discrimination experienced by blacks because the rights and freedoms of individuals in American society depended to a great extent upon the status of the group to which they belonged. In essence, Edwards urged the kind of race consciousness that marked the larger black protest movement of the 1960s. In the end, however, black Olympians took an approach that seemed to be, at least on the surface, less race conscious and collective. They ultimately answered in the negative to questions posed by well-known long-jumper Ralph Boston prior to the games: "Will a boycott advance the cause of freedom? If it doesn't is it fair to ask the athletes to make the sacrifice needlessly?"[44]

The revolts staged by black athletes would decrease dramatically after the early 1970s. The women's movement, lessening racial tensions in American society, and problems associated with inflation and unemployment would converge with a host of other factors to take some steam out of the black athletic revolt just as it had the larger black power movement. The decline in number of protests did not mean, however, that black athletes no longer occupied the attention of the American public. If anything, they began receiving unprecedented attention. Evidence of this fascination with black athletes can be gleaned from the outpouring of popular articles and research studies published over the last two decades dealing with such topics as inadequate reward structures in sport and racial differences in sport performance.[45]

Of the aforementioned topics, perhaps none has been more reflective of the black athletes' continued stigmatization and sense of being both black and American than the discussion concerning racial differences in sport performance. Although such a debate had been waged in American society since at least the beginning of this century, the last two decades have witnessed a heated discussion revolving around the outstanding performances of a disproportionate number of black athletes in sport. Notwithstanding the fact, as historians Randy Roberts and James Olson have contended, that whites have increasingly come to see black athletes as a more diverse group of individuals, people of all races and backgrounds have continued to explain away the overrepresentation of blacks in sport by arguing that they are endowed with innate physical skills that lead to superior athletic performances.[46] The implication is that blacks have come by their great athletic performances naturally and not through hard work, dedication, and other character traits so admired in American society.

Black athletes, while not always verbalizing their anger, have been disturbed about being characterized differently than other athletes merely because of skin color and stereotyped as athletes who realized success through no effort of their own. They are similar to other athletes in American sport in that they want to be acknowledged for the hard work and dedication that go into their performances. To do otherwise demeans their accomplishments and only serves to perpetuate long-standing beliefs about the black race's lack of intelligence and faulty character.[47] One black athlete who publicly expressed his resentment over the divergent characterizations of black and white athletes was Isiah Thomas, the outstanding guard of the Detroit Pistons. Shortly after the Pistons lost the seventh and final game to the Boston Celtics in the 1987 Eastern Conference Championship, Thomas told reporters he agreed with the earlier comments of his Piston teammate, Dennis Rodman, that Larry Bird was a very good basketball player, but if he were black, "he'd be just another good guy." In an attempt to explain what he meant by this comment, Thomas later told reporters that he was not referring to Bird so much as he was "the perpetuation of stereotypes about blacks." "When Bird makes a great play, it's due to his thinking and his work habits," noted Thomas. "It's all planned out by him. It's not the case for blacks. All we do is run and jump. We never practice or give a thought to how we play. It's like I came dribbling out of my mother's womb."[48]

The frustrations expressed by Thomas have been heard less frequently from black athletes in the recent past. Although they continue to be sensitive to discriminatory practices, cognizant of the stigmatized condition of blacks in American society, and burdened by the pressures of the white world, black athletes in contemporary sport have generally refrained from speaking out on racial matters and larger issues of the day. This is partly a result of black sportsmen adhering to the traditionally conservative athletic role and the fact that more blatant forms of racial discrimination have largely disappeared from highly organized sport. It is also a result, however, of the marginalized position of black athletes in the African-American community and the larger American society. Having garnered millions of dollars and realized a heightened sense of accomplishment and prestige as a result of their performances in sport, black athletes feel a distance between themselves and the masses of black people that has created barriers to the notion of group consciousness and led to a more cautious approach to racial protests.

The burden for black athletes of today, regardless of the distance they feel between themselves and other blacks, is that they continue to be defined by race and expected to serve as symbols of possibility and "role models" for members of the black community. While more thoughtful and sensitive blacks have constantly lamented the fact that the entry of a disproportionate number of blacks into sport is delimiting the conditions of black identity within American society, they also believe black athletes are obligated to lead exemplary lives that are above reproach.[49] Michael Jordan and Charles Barkley are just two of the great performers who are not only expected to fulfill their role as athletes, but counted upon to serve as positive examples for members of their race. Insisting that black athletes such as Jordan and Barkley serve as role models is a reflection, perhaps more than anything else, of the lack of leadership in a black community sensitive to white America's continued questioning of their character and competence. The late Arthur Ashe was troubled by the obsession with role models in the black community, particularly when they were drawn from the sport and entertainment industries. "The very fact that we [black community] speak of 'Leaders' and 'Role models,'" wrote Ashe in his last book, *Days of Grace: A Memoir*, "as much as we do tells of our lack of power and organization. . . . We even think of athletes and entertainers in this way; we see basketball players and pop singers as possible role models, when nothing could be further, in most cases, from their capabilities."[50]

In sum, the struggle to maintain an ethnic identity while actively participating in organized sport and the larger American society was not an easy task for black athletes. Burdened by the desire to sustain group loyalties, and at the same time striving to uphold the American virtue of individualism, caused black athletes to exert their racial pride in different ways depending on particular circumstances. Although some black athletes were more adept at this approach than others, the vast majority proved to be remarkably flexible and honored the basic tenets of their own culture while simultaneously accommodating themselves to adverse situations. Outstanding black athletes were able to compete with other Americans for status and social equality because they realized early on that success in this country was ultimately linked with the process of adaptation and differentiation and the need to assume multiple roles. It was a complex situation that clearly indicated that the careers of black and white athletes, though quite different in many respects, were always intertwined and mutually dependent. From the moment they were first allowed into organized sport, then, black athletes were involved in a continually changing and sometimes ambivalent relationship with white athletes and American society that contributed to their sense of identity as black people and Americans. The achievements of black athletes perhaps have done little to change racial attitudes among the dominant culture, but their successes did serve, ironically enough, as symbols of possibility for members of the black community who strove for recognition with the same earnestness as their white counterparts and who attempted to forge their own identities in an America that held fast to racial stereotypes and refused always to honor its own precepts.

NOTES

1. W.E.B. Du Bois, *The Souls of Black Folk* (New York: Fawcett, 1961), p. 17.

2. See, for example, Edwin B. Henderson, *The Negro in Sports* (Washington, D.C.: Associated Publishers, 1939); A. S. "Doc" Young, *Negro Firsts in Sports* (Chicago: Johnson, 1963); Peter Chew, *The Kentucky Derby: The First 100 Years* (Boston: Mifflin, 1974).

3. Dale A. Somers, *The Rise of Sports in New Orleans* (Baton Rouge: Louisiana State University Press, 1972); Charles Stewart, "My Life as a Slave," *Harpers New Monthly Magazine* 69 (1884): 730–38; David K. Wiggins, "Isaac Murphy: Black Hero in Nineteenth Century American Sport, 1861–1896," *Canadian Journal of History of Sport and Physical Education* 10 (May 1978): 15–32.

4. Marshall "Major" Taylor, *The Fastest Bicycle Rider in the World* (Brattleboro, Vermont: Stephen Green Press, 1972); Moses Fleetwood Walker, *Our Home Colony: A Treatise on the Past, Present, and Future of the Negro Race in America* (Steubenville, Ohio: Herald Printing, 1908); Wiggins, "Isaac Murphy"; idem, "Peter Jackson and the Elusive Heavyweight Championship: A Black Athlete's Struggle Against the Late Nineteenth Century Color-Line," *Journal of Sport History* 12 (Summer 1985): 143–68.

5. Wiggins, "Isaac Murphy"; Walker, *Our Home Colony.*

6. Wiggins, "Isaac Murphy."

7. Wiggins, "Peter Jackson," p. 148.

8. Andrew Ritchie, *Major Taylor: The Extraordinary Career of a Champion Bicycle Racer* (San Francisco: Bicycle Books, 1988), p. 73.

9. Anthony M. Platt, *E. Franklin Frazier Reconsidered* (New Brunswick: Rutgers University Press, 1990), p. 67.

10. Wiggins, "Isaac Murphy"; idem. "Peter Jackson."

11. Walker, *Our Home Colony,* p. 46.

12. Janet Bruce, *The Kansas City Monarchs: Champions of Black Baseball* (Lawrence: University of Kansas Press, 1985), p. 112.

13. John Holway, *Voices from the Great Black Baseball League* (New York: Dodd, Mead, and Co., 1975); Don Rogosin, *Invisible Men: Life in Baseball's Negro League* (New York: Atheneum, 1983).

14. Ibid.

15. Bruce, *The Kansas City Monarchs*, p. 32.

16. Rogosin, *Invisible Men*, p. 71.

17. Leroy Page, *Pitchin' Man*, ed. Hal Lebovitz (N.p.: by the editor, 1948), p. 67.

18. Rogosin, *Invisible Men*, p. 148.

19. See Al-Tony Gilmore, *Bad Nigger! The National Impact of Jack Johnson* (Port Washington: Kennikat Press, 1975); Randy Roberts, *Papa Jack: Jack Johnson and the Era of White Hopes* (New York: Free Press, 1983); William H. Wiggins, "Jack Johnson as Bad Nigger: The Folklore of His Life," *The Black Scholar* 2 (1971): 4–19.

20. Ibid.

21. Roberts, *Papa Jack*, p. 26.

22. Lawrence W. Levine, *Black Culture and Black Consciousness: Afro-American Folk Thought from Slavery to Freedom* (New York: Oxford University Press, 1977), p. 431.

23. Roi Ottley, *Inside Black America* (London: Eyre and Spottiswoode, 1948), p. 157.

24. Dominic J. Capeci, Jr., and Martha Wilkerson, "Multifarious Hero: Joe Louis, American Society and Race Relations during World Crisis, 1935–1945," *Journal of Sport History* 10 (Winter 1983): 6.

25. Joe Louis, "My Life Story," *Life* 25 (1948), p. 142; Jesse Owens with Paul G. Neimark, *Blackthink: My Life as Black Man and White Man* (New York: William Morrow, 1972).

26. Vince Matthews with Neil Amdur, *My Race Be Won* (New York: Charterhouse, 1974), p. 194.

27. Owens, *Blackthink*, p. 182.

28. David K. Wiggins, "Wendell Smith, the *Pittsburgh Courier-Journal* and the Campaign To Include Blacks in Organized Baseball, 1933–1945," *Journal of Sport History* 10 (Summer 1983): 5–29.

29. Horace R. Clayton, "Negro Morale," *Opportunity* 19 (December 1941): 371–75; Cornelius C. Golightly, "Negro Higher Education and Democratic Negro Morale," *Journal of Negro Education* 11 (July 1942): 322–28.

30. See, for example, Harvey Frommer, *Rickey and Robinson: The Men Who Broke Baseball's Color Barrier* (New York: MacMillan Publishing, 1982); Carl T. Rowan, *Wait Till Next Year* (New York: Random House, 1960); Jules Tygiel, *Baseball's Great Experiment: Jackie Robinson and His Legacy* (New York: Oxford University Press, 1983).

31. Jackie Robinson as told to Alfred Duckett, *I Never Had It Made* (New York: G. P. Putman's Sons, 1972), p. 36.

32. Ibid., p. 11.

33. Althea Gibson, *I Always Wanted To Be Somebody* (New York: Harper and Brothers, 1958), p. 124.

34. Quoted in Benjamin Rader, *American Sports: From the Age of Folk Games to the Age of Spectators* (Englewood Cliffs, N.J.: Prentice Hall, 1983), p. 330.

35. Frederic Cople Jaher, "White America Views Jack Johnson, Joe Louis and Muhammad Ali," in *Sport in America: New Historical Perspectives*, ed. Donald Spivey (Westport, Conn.: Greenwood Press, 1985), pp. 145–92.

36. Muhammad Ali with Richard Durham, *The Greatest: My Own Story* (New York: Random House, 1978).

37. Ibid.

38. See Eldridge Cleaver, *Soul on Ice* (New York: McGraw-Hill, 1968), pp. 90–96.

39. "The Angry Black Athlete," *Newsweek* (July 15, 1968): 59.

40. See Harry Edwards, *The Revolt of the Black Athlete* (New York: Free Press, 1969); idem, "The Olympic Project for Human Rights: An Assessment Ten Years Later," *The Black Scholar* 10 (March–April 1979): 2–8; idem, *The Struggle That Must Be: An Autobiography* (New York: Macmillan, 1980).

41. Donald Spivey, "Black Consciousness and Olympic Protest Movement, 1964–1980," in Spivey, ed., *Sport in America*, pp. 248–49.

42. Paula Giddings, *When and Where I Enter: The Impact of Black Women on Race and Sex in America* (New York: Bantam Books, 1988), pp. 314–24.

43. Spivey, "Black Consciousness," pp. 248–49.

44. Chicago *Tribune*, July 4, 1968.

45. See, for example, John W. Loy, Jr. and Joseph F. McElvogue, "Racial Segregation in American Sport," *International Review of Sport Sociology* 5 (1970): 5–23; Sandra C. Castine and Glyn C. Roberts, "Modeling in the Socialization Process of the Black Athlete," *International Review of Sport Sociology*, 9 (1974): 63–69.

46. Randy Roberts and James Olson, *Winning Is the Only Thing: Sports in America since 1945* (Baltimore: The Johns Hopkins University Press, 1989), p. 178.

47. See David K. Wiggins, "Great Speed but Little Stamina: The Historical Debate over Black Athletic Superiority," *Journal of Sport History* 16 (Summer 1989): 158–85.

48. *New York Times*, June 2, 1987; see also ibid., June 5 and 9, 1987.

49. See Earl Graves, "The Right Kind of Excellence," *Black Enterprise* 10 (November 1979): 9; Anthony Leroy Fisher, "The Best Way out of the Ghetto," *Phi Delta Kappan* 60 (November 1978): 240.

50. Arthur Ashe and Arnold Rampersand, *Days of Grace: A Memoir* (New York: Alfred A. Knopf, 1993), p. 153.

9

Sport in Philadelphia's African-American Community, 1865–1900

J. Thomas Jable

The Civil War, although divisive, destructive, and debilitating to our nation and people, brought an end to slavery. For African Americans that meant freedom, citizenship, and franchise, amenities guaranteed by the Thirteenth, Fourteenth, and Fifteenth Amendments to the U.S. Constitution. But in postbellum America, such constitutional protections meant little for America's blacks. Whatever gains they made as a result of the war and its aftermath quickly dissipated during the ensuing decades when the emergence of Jim Crow initiated discriminatory practices that institutionalized segregation. What followed was a period of racial repression that relegated African Americans to second-class citizens.

To cope with the torment of racial discrimination, some African Americans turned to sport. Entertaining and diversionary, it temporarily took their minds off the harsh realities of surviving in a segregated society. Sport sometimes served as a rallying point which brought blacks together. Baseball, for instance, was a unifying force for segments of Philadelphia's African-American community. Games between local clubs and intercity rivals attracted hundreds of supporters who came chiefly from the city's black middle and upper classes. Boxing attracted the lower classes and at best was a mixed blessing. On the one hand it provided an avenue for black heroes to emerge and generated revenue for prizefighters, but on the other it was more a source of entertainment and gambling for whites who looked upon these Black Samsons as mere gladiators. Horse racing, like boxing, was a means of livelihood for a few poor blacks who became successful jockeys. Bicycling and athletics (track and field) were healthful diversions that offered both competition and relaxation. Day excursions to nearby watering holes and recreation sites gave black city dwellers temporary relief, while the more affluent could seek longer refuge from the summer heat at Cape May, New Jersey, or Saratoga Springs, New York, two resorts with black populations large enough to accommodate African-American visitors.

Sport, however, did not always benefit African Americans. In fact, it worked against them, serving as a conduit for separating the races and reinforcing segregation. The color line, once drawn in baseball, bicycling, and horse racing, was a constant reminder to African Americans that they were not equal to whites. By extending Jim Crow to sport, white America closed what little opportunity there was for blacks in the nineteenth century to gain recognition and ultimately equality. This essay examines the experiences of Philadelphia's African Americans in sport during the latter third of the nineteenth century. It explores the course they followed in sport, and it depicts the plight and obstacles that confronted them. Some experiences brought them joy and excitement, others grief and pain. In presenting the involvement of African Americans in the sporting arena, this essay focuses on some of Philadelphia's premier black athletes not only because they were visible and their performances recorded, but because their actions give us a glimpse of sport in African-American culture. It also depicts, though to a much lesser extent, some of the sporting and recreational practices of the African-American community at large. This information, in conjunction with the activities of premier athletes and their followers, provides a more definitive picture of African Americans' involvement in sport and helps us to determine its role and meaning in Philadelphia's African-American community during the years following the Civil War.

Philadelphia in postbellum America was a diverse, industrializing city. Its population doubled from 408,000 in 1850 to 840,000 in 1880 and then increased by nearly another 60 percent to 1.3 million at the century's close. A sizeable portion of the increase was due to the influx of immigrants—Irish, Germans, British—before the Civil War and Italians, Poles, and Russian Jews afterward. The total foreign-born residents in Philadelphia was consistently higher than 20 percent throughout the 1850 to 1880 period, while African Americans never exceeded 5 percent of the city's population during that time. With the odds stacked against them, African Americans had fewer opportunities for economic success and social acceptance than European immigrants. As a consequence, they were victims of racial and economic discrimination. The city's residential patterns forced large numbers of African Americans into the seventh ward where they were within easy access of 23,000 manufacturing jobs, yet they could secure only a few. Most went to Irish and German immigrants and their offspring. In the few instances where African Americans held manufacturing jobs, they did not live close to white workers employed in the same industry. African Americans thus lived close to one another "regardless of industrial affiliation," while other groups—Irish, Germans, and native whites—lived in neighborhoods on the basis of occupational affiliations.[1]

Within the African-American community itself, there was stratification based on color or, more appropriately, shades of color. Theodore Hershberg and Henry Williams have hypothesized that color functioned "as an important stratifier of social consequence." They based their supposition on the disproportional representation of African Americans with lighter skin among the wealthy and powerful of the community. Mulattoes had greater mobility and usually lived on blocks with decent reputations and a lower incidence of crime than did blacks. Mulattoes were "occupationally differentiated" in that they held a disproportionate number of professional, proprietary, and skilled artisanal positions among African Americans. In the artisanal ranks, mulattoes were twice as likely as blacks to have skilled rather than laboring jobs. Similarly, mulattoes held twice as much real property as did blacks with the property value being three to five times as great as that held by blacks.[2]

Stratification based on skin color within Philadelphia's African-American community was typical of African-American urban communities throughout America. In a comprehensive study of America's colored aristocracy, Willard Gatewood found patterns of discrimination and stratification within the Negro community based on skin pigmentation in virtually every American city. He concluded that skin color was an important, if not the deciding, entity for defining class in the African-American community. Though ancestry, education, manners, morality, occupation, and wealth were significant ingredients for determining class, skin color was paramount, a fact borne out by the "colored aristocracy" which was mostly mulatto.

Though skin color in conjunction with wealth and occupation were indicators of status, another important determinant, social standing, was reinforced through membership in prestigious organizations. Clubs, lodges, and other voluntary associations provided a fertile setting for members to expand their social relationships, promote a cause, or transact business. Most organizations had specific purposes that were apparent in their titles, for example, Free Africa Society, Philadelphia Library Company of Colored Persons, Art and Scientific Association of Philadelphia, and literary and debating societies. Social clubs provided their members with opportunities for relaxation and recreation whether it be keeping abreast with political developments in the reading room, trying their hand at a game of whist, or enjoying a meal with friends in the dining room. Sporting clubs offered vigorous physical activity in the form

of baseball, cricket, or athletics. But even here, at least in the immediate postbellum era, mulattoes held the upper hand. Comprising just one-fifth of Philadelphia's African-American population in the postbellum period, they held
one-half of the African-American organizational memberships and 60 percent
of the leadership posts.[3]

The Pythian Base Ball Club offers a good organizational setting for observing the mulatto-black dichotomy in Philadelphia. Its membership was 70 percent mulatto. Organized in 1866, this "association of gentlemen" took on elite
overtones. New members were elected by the club's membership, but the annual dues of five dollars made it somewhat exclusive, for few below the city's
African-American middle class could join. The Pythians used Liberty Hall for
their meetings and balls. The latter, according to William Carl Bolivar, a
former secretary of the club, "were patronized by our best citizens young and
old, and conducted on a lavish scale." Pythians were, for the most part, comparable to what W.E.B. Du Bois would later call the "aristocracy of the Negro
Population in education, wealth and general social efficiency."[4]

The club's elite African-American composition has been substantiated by a
socioeconomic analysis of its membership. Table 9.1 shows the birthplaces of
the Pythians in comparison with Philadelphia's African-American population.[5] According to the 1870 census, Pennsylvania was the birthplace for no
less than one-half of the city's African Americans. Within the mulatto and
black subdivisions, the Pythian mulattoes approximate the mulatto population

Table 9.1
**Comparison of Birthplace of the Pythians with Philadelphia's African-
American Population**

Place of Birth	Pythians			Philadelphia African Americans*	
	%Black	%Mulatto	All	%Black	%Mulatto
Pennsylvania	75.0	62.9	66.7	50.8	60.6
Mid-Atlantic/ New England	16.7	11.1	12.8	21.0	13.5
South	8.3	25.9	20.5	28.0	25.9
Total N	12	27	39	15,204	5346
	(30.8)	(69.2)		(74.0)	(26.0)

*From Theodore Hershberg and Henry Williams, "Mulattoes and Blacks:
Intragroup Color Differences and Social Stratification in Nineteenth-Century Philadelphia," in *Philadelphia: Work, Space, Family and
Group Experience in the 19th Century* (New York: Oxford University Press,
1981), p. 400

in general, whereas Pythian blacks did not approximate the city's black population. With respect to birthplace, black Pythians were overrepresented in Pennsylvania and underrepresented in the South when compared to the city's black population at large. This disparity is the result of two forces. The small number of blacks in the Pythian Club (12) was not representative of the city's entire black population, and the elite nature of the club tended to attract members from the city's African-American middle and upper classes which had proportionally fewer blacks than mulattoes.

An analysis of the club members' occupations reinforced the Pythians' elite nature. Table 9.2 reveals that 50 percent of them held low white collar positions and another 40 percent worked as artisans, while less than 20 percent of Philadelphia's African Americans in general worked in occupations at those ranks. More than 75 percent of the city's African Americans worked as unskilled laborers. When occupations were broken down further along black-mulatto lines, the discrepancies were amplified. Pythian mulattoes held a disproportional number of artisanal positions. Just one percent of the Pythians worked as laborers. By virtue of their low white collar and artisanal vocations, the Pythians, as a group, had some flexibility in their daily routines to make time for baseball.

Table 9.2

Occupations of Pythians in Comparison with Philadelphia's African-American Population

	Pythians				Philadelphia African-Americans*		
Occupation	%Bl	%Mul	%Unk	All	%B	%M	All
High white collar	0	0	0		0.9	1.3	0.1
Low white collar	22.2	61.5	40.0	50.0	3.8	7.8	4.7
Artisan	55.6	30.8	60.0	40.0	12.4	23.7	15.1
Specified unskilled	11.1	7.7	0	0.8	46.0	46.8	46.2
Unspecified unskilled	11.1	0	0	0.3	33.0	18.5	29.5
Total N	9	26	5	40	3908	1230	5138
	(22.5)	(65.0)	(12.5)		(76.1)	(23.9)	

*From Theodore Hershberg and Henry Williams, "Mulattoes and Blacks: Intragroup Color Differences and Social Stratification in Nineteenth-Century Philadelphia," in *Philadelphia: Work, Space, Family and Group Experience in the 19th Century* (New York: Oxford University Press, 1981), p. 413.

The Pythian Base Ball Club, though not the first African-American organization to play baseball in Philadelphia, was the most successful and prestigious. Founded by political activist Octavius Catto and educator Jacob White
along with David Knight and J. Whipper Purnell, the Pythians quickly grew to
a number which enabled them to field four baseball teams. Led by Catto, "the
brainy captain [who] managed the players under him with consummate skill,"
the Pythians challenged and soon outplayed the Excelsiors, Philadelphia's
first African-American baseball club whose venture into baseball predated the
Pythians by just a few months. As the Pythians began to grow in stature as a
result of their excellent play on the diamond, the best Excelsior players joined
their ranks, leaving the older club destined for extinction. About the same
time, two superb players from West Chester, Abram Brown and William Price,
bolted their local club for the Pythians. Years later, William Carl Bolivar, the
nineteenth-century African-American historian, in a column in the *Tribune*,
referred to Brown as the "Ty Cobb of the Pythians." John Cannon, another
player with exceptional talent, drew raves as the "baseball wonder" from black
and white players alike.[6]

At first the Pythians played the Excelsiors and scrub nines (i.e., players
organized into a team on the spot for the purpose of playing a single game) at
Diamond Cottage, a picnic grove and recreational area located across the
Delaware River in Camden, New Jersey. They also played some games on the
Parade Ground at 11th and Wharton Streets adjacent to the prison. Bolivar
reported that practicing was difficult and often dangerous for the Pythians
who were assaulted by white groups, primarily the Irish, whenever they dared
to venture to the open pastures south of Bainbridge Street. More recently,
Roger Lane, a noted authority on violence in nineteenth-century black Philadelphia, maintained that the Pythians needed four teams to protect themselves from white assailants as they approached the "deadline" on Bainbridge
Street.[7]

The Pythians and Excelsiors played each other and scrub teams until the
Bachelors, an African-American club from Albany, New York, visited Philadelphia in September 1866. The Bachelors had little trouble with either the
Pythians or the Excelsiors as they defeated both clubs handily on the Parade
Ground site. Their visit, however, not only introduced intercity play to Philadelphia's African Americans—the Pythians would soon take on black teams
from Brooklyn, Washington, Harrisburg, and Chicago—but it also created a
festive mood in certain African-American neighborhoods. Visiting teams
stayed in Philadelphia from several days to a week and usually played two or
more games. In between games, the host club entertained the visitors with pic-

nics, lunches, dances, and banquets in which women and children joined the players in the festivities.[8] Thus baseball was part of a larger social atmosphere which brought certain African-American neighborhoods together. It facilitated social intercourse and helped instill a sense of community among those involved. But at the same time it reinforced class consciousness within African-American culture.

Apart from the club members and their families, few African Americans participated in social functions connected with baseball games. Black society, like its white counterpart, was stratified along class lines with skin color serving as a distinguishing stratifier. Because a majority of the Pythians were mulatto who considered themselves "gentlemen" and because aristocrats, whether black or white, tended to avoid socializing with the hoi polloi, few, if any, of the black masses enjoyed the social benefits of the intercity baseball visitations. That is not to say, however, that some of the masses did not attend the baseball games, for Carl Bolivar contended that baseball did "wonders in the way of levelling prejudice" and reported that "everyone was interested, always well-attended."[9]

The Pythians, of course, received equal hospitality when they traveled to distant cities for return games. This so-called "interchange of privileges" was quite comparable to lodge members having the same benefits at out-of-town lodges as they had at their own. This practice confirms DuBois' belief that Philadelphia's light-skinned African Americans were more interested in what their mulatto compatriots were doing in New York City and Washington than in the black masses of their own city.[10]

Regardless of the social implications baseball may have had for Philadelphia's African Americans, the Pythians, by the end of the 1867 season, had established themselves as a force to be reckoned with on the baseball diamond. During that season they lost but one game in eight, and the following year they put together a string of seven victories without a defeat. Catto's organizational skills and John Cannon's pitching and batting contributed immeasurably to their success. Clearly they were peerless among Philadelphia's six other African-American baseball clubs on the field and off. Organizationally sound from the beginning, the Pythians quickly established a reputation for winning which not only attracted the best African-American ballplayers in the Philadelphia region, but also increased revenue through gate receipts and new club memberships. Adequate resources tempered by careful planning and sober spending put the Pythians way out in front on the social scene, too. Their functions attracted the black community's most esteemed citizens. But it was baseball for which the Pythians were best known, and they may have even challenged the Athletics of Philadelphia or the Atlantics of Brooklyn, reputed champions of baseball during this era, for the supremacy of the entire baseball world, but they never had the opportunity to play either one, though they did play against the Olympic Club, a local white team, in 1869 and lost. For the most part, their baseball talent put them in contention for the "Colored Championship of the United States" in 1871 and perhaps on other occasions. They played a series of games for the coveted title against the Mutuals of Washington, D.C.[11]

The Mutuals, undefeated during the two previous seasons, lost the first game to the host Pythians which, for important games such as this, secured the home grounds of the Athletics at 25th and Jefferson Streets. Eight hundred spectators attended the contest. Theodore Bomeiser of the white Eureka Club, and recognized as the best umpire in Philadelphia, served in that capacity. It was a common practice for white baseball players from the Athletics and other local baseball clubs to umpire for the Pythians. The outcome of the entire series is not known, but John Cannon once again led the blue (pants) and white (shirts) clad Pythians to victory in the opening game. Their solid play and pleasant demeanor brought them accolades and favorable publicity. Following a disputed one-run loss to the Mutuals four years earlier, the *Sunday Mercury* praised the Pythians as the club that "stands at the head of all colored organizations hereabouts. [They are a] well-behaved, gentlemanly set of young fellows, and are rapidly winning distinction with the use of the bat."[12]

Although the Pythians experienced little difficulty meeting challenges on the baseball diamond, they could not control events off the field which imposed restrictions upon their civil rights. As the Pythians' reputation in baseball grew, white players, particularly members of the Athletics, began to take notice. In fact, E. Hicks Hayhurst, an officer of the Athletics, encouraged the Pythians to seek admission to the Pennsylvania State Convention of Base Ball Players. Following his advice, the Pythians made application to the Convention at Harrisburg in the fall of 1867. Their effort, however, fell short. Even with Hayhurst as the Convention's newly elected president, the Pythians were doomed. The Convention had already drawn the color line which thwarted Hayhurst's attempts to convince a majority of delegates to support the Pythians' application. Dejectedly, Hayhurst urged the Pythians to withdraw their application in order to avoid the embarrassment of a black ball. At first the Pythians remained steadfast, but ultimately decided to heed Hayhurst's advice when it became apparent they would not be admitted.

A second civil rights and racial incident involved the Pythians' founder, Octavius Catto, who paid with his life. As a political activist, Catto had been deeply involved in equal rights for African Americans ever since emancipation. He was highly visible in movements to integrate the city's street cars, militia, and Franklin Institute. Following the ratification of the Fifteenth Amendment which gave African Americans the right to vote, Catto called upon them to voice their opinions at the ballot box. In Philadelphia, resentment of the African-American vote turned ugly on election day. Violence at the polling places dispersed most of the would be African-American voters. But despite the tense situation in the streets, Catto decided to vote anyway. He was harassed by white antagonists at several locations as he made his way toward his polling place. When his call to the mayor for help fell upon deaf ears, he purchased a gun but had to return home for the bullets. On his way, one of the hecklers, Frank Kelly, called out to him. Catto stopped and turned toward the voice. Kelly, seeing a gun in Catto's hand, fired without hesitation. The bullet struck Catto, killing him instantly.[13]

Catto's assassination devastated the cause of African-American civil rights and may have been the death knell for the Pythians as well. Newspaper coverage of the Pythians after 1871 was sparse; other than a box score in 1872, little else appears in print. By 1874 another local African-American club, the Williams, was challenging the Mutuals of Washington, D.C., for the "Colored Championship of the United States," and in 1876 they were widely recognized as the colored champions. During the mid-1870s, both the Williams and the Mutuals tested their mettle against white baseball teams.

Less is known about the course of African-American baseball in Philadelphia during the 1880s and 1890s because of a decline in press coverage of African-American games which happened to coincide with the increasing presence of Jim Crow. The United States Supreme Court in 1883 overturned the Civil Rights Law of 1875 and legalized segregation with its 1896 decision in Plessy v. Ferguson. In baseball, the color line was officially drawn in 1887 when the International League, a professional minor league, adopted a written statement banning blacks. The major leagues followed suit with their unwritten "gentlemen's agreement" which kept African Americans out of the "national game" until Jackie Robinson opened the door in 1947.[14] Actually, the notion of the gentlemen's agreement dates back to 1867 when the National Association of Base Ball Players agreed to exclude African Americans from their ranks. Nonetheless, the emphasis placed upon the race issue during the 1880s doubtless contributed to reduced press coverage of African-American games. Then, too, African-American players abandoned their teams for a chance at making more money by playing for either mixed-race franchises or barnstorming black teams. Prior to 1887, several professional teams hired black players, but afterward their best hope was a junket on the barnstorming circuit. The case of the Philadelphia Orions was indicative of ballplayers jumping to other teams for higher salaries. The team lost its three best players to the white-owned Cuban Giants operating out of Trenton, New Jersey. Pitcher Shepard Trusty, shortshop Abe Harrison, and second baseman and captain George Williams defected in 1885, the year the Cuban Giants won the colored championship with a record of 105 wins and 24 losses. Two years later, the Philadelphia Pythians, no apparent connection to the Pythian Base Ball Club of two decades earlier, was the city's entry in the League of Colored Baseball Clubs. This nine-team league, consisting of teams along the Atlantic seaboard and the Midwest, was shortlived due chiefly to transportation costs and player defections to local and barnstorming teams.[15]

Concurrent with their venture into baseball, certain African Americans took up cricket, highly popular among Philadelphia's whites during the Antebellum period. In the mid-1860s, Philadelphia had at least three African-American cricket clubs. The Olives and Metamora Clubs were fierce rivals, while a third club, the Diligente, served as a practice team for both of them. Contests between the Olives and Metamoras "waxed furious, and every game had its partisans out in large number to witness their games." They played their matches on a vacant lot behind the Music Academy at 16th and Pine Streets. Members of the more than thirty contemporary white clubs had heard about, if not witnessed, the African-American cricketers; yet they did not challenge them to a match, nor did they invite them to join their clubs. Evidently, the color line had been just as prevalent in cricket as it would become in baseball. Though color was a divisive issue within each sport, baseball was the sport of choice regardless of race. In fact, a number of African-American cricketers wound up playing for the Excelsiors and Pythians, as was the case with Pythian founder Octavius Catto.[16]

African Americans preferred baseball, but within the club setting it offered little recreational opportunities for family members and non-players, except as spectators. As a consequence, Philadelphia's blacks turned to picnics, concerts, balls, and parties for their recreational pleasure. For example, one of the most popular outings for the entire family was the July 1887 picnic at Neshaminy Falls in Montgomery County. African-American churches and Sunday schools organized the affair in which six trains brought an estimated 8,000 people to the resort where they enjoyed the merry-go-round, donkey rides, bathing, and a pick-up game of baseball. While mostly middle and lower class African Americans went to Neshaminy and other nearby sites, the well-to-do journeyed to Saratoga and Cape May to escape the discomfort of the city's summertime heat. Octavius Catto spent part of his summers at Cape May.[17]

For the majority who remained behind, churches were a primary source of recreation and amusement. They sponsored suppers, fairs, and concerts for parishioners. Dance was quite popular among youth, even though it was taboo in some churches. By the later part of the century, the home increasingly became the center of recreation for aristocrats as they took up whist and table games. For the lower elements of African-American society, excursions remained popular, but often drinking and fighting accompanied them. Gambling was common, too, and could be found in pool halls, clubs, private homes, and in the street. Balls and cake-walks enjoyed a more salubrious reputation, but even here drinking and gambling were present.

Highly popular among the city's African-American lower class was boxing. This was no accident for prizefighting "has always drawn its champions and victims from among the poorest and most desperate of ethnic groups." Interracial fighting has had a long history in Philadelphia dating back to the 1840s when Irish and African Americans battled each other on the city's streets. Both groups competed for jobs and territory; eventually blacks replaced the Irish in urban jobs. When prizefighting reached its peak in nineteenth-century Philadelphia a half century later, they also replaced the Irish in the prize ring.[18]

One of the city's most notorious boxers of this era was a middle and lightweight, Walter Edgerton, a.k.a. "de Kentucky Rosebud." He grew up on Lombard Street in the heart of black Philadelphia. A courageous street fighter with quick hands and feet, Rosebud quickly carved out a reputation as the "toughest kid on the block," earning the moniker "Champion of Lombard Street." Rosebud's career peaked in 1895 when a loss to Joe Gans, a lightweight fighter from Baltimore with a national reputation, sent it on a downward spiral. Rosebud interrupted his career's descent with two good performances against George Dixon, "Little Chocolate," the reigning World Bantam and Featherweight Champion; one ended in a draw, the other in a Rosebud loss.[19]

Prior to the Gans fight, Edgerton was a fixture in Philadelphia's boxing spotlight. The previous year was a particularly active one for him. In March 1894, the city of Philadelphia, in an attempt to raise money for the starving poor and unemployed who suffered from the economic depression of 1893, organized the "Bread Fund Carnival." Actually, Heavyweight Champion "Gentleman" Jim Corbett suggested the fund raiser in which sparring exhibitions, wrestling matches, fencing bouts, and weightlifting contests would be held. Prizefighting was banned in Pennsylvania at this time, but boxers and promoters easily skirted the law by calling them scientific sparring exhibitions for which the contestants were not paid. Some of the biggest names in boxing—Corbett, Peter Jackson, the black Australian heavyweight challenger, and George Dixon—agreed to participate. Prior commitments, however, kept Jackson in St. Louis and Corbett in Johnstown, Pennsylvania, where his theater troupe was performing.[20]

Only Dixon among the renowned fighters showed up, and he did so in spite of a respiratory ailment. As it turned out, Dixon was paired with Rosebud for a three-round exhibition. The two had fought in Philadelphia on three previous occasions with each bout ending in a draw. During the second round of the Bread Fund match, Rosebud tried to turn the exhibition into the real thing. Backing away from an advancing Dixon, Rosebud caught him off-guard with an uppercut that knocked "Little Chocolate" off his feet. Dixon took at least fifteen seconds to regain his composure which carried into the rest period between rounds. The Philadelphia *Times* described Edgerton's punch as a "lucky blow" thrown in self-defense. Though Rosebud was a good fighter, he was not in Dixon's class. In fact, Dixon would not have sparred had he not agreed to appear for the charity. Rosebud's followers, of course, were ecstatic with this sudden turn of events, but the *Times* chastised Edgerton for his behavior in the ring. In the first round and most of the second, Rosebud's dancing and evasive tactics produced little excitement. Dixon thought he had to take the initiative, lest the audience be disappointed. His aggressive surge left his chin vulnerable to Rosebud's blow. But then Rosebud made the third round even more farcical than the first two. He literally ran away from "Little Chocolate," but bragged afterward that he could have knocked him out had his manager not told him to go easy on Dixon. Rosebud laid claim to Dixon's title and challenged him to a title fight for $2,500 to $5,000. Dixon's backers immediately called Rosebud's bluff when they entrusted $1,000 in earnest money to the Philadelphia *Times* for a match; Edgerton's camp failed to match it.[21]

In June Rosebud was confronted in his own neighborhood by John Henry Johnson who coveted the "Champion of Lombard Street" title bestowed upon Edgerton. A fracas between the two antagonists broke out in Weaver's Cigar Store. When Johnson charged Rosebud with a pool cue, Edgerton pulled out his pistol and fired, hitting Johnson in the face. Miraculously, the bullet only grazed Johnson, leaving just a superficial wound. Edgerton, however, thought the shot was fatal and fled to Atlantic City where an attempt to find solace in the ocean nearly cost him his life. Escaping this brush with death, Rosebud returned to Philadelphia to resume fighting. He fought in July and October before losing to Australian middleweight Young Griffo. Yielding fifteen pounds to the heavier Griffo, Rosebud took a pounding. Griffo's blows to the head and chest put away Edgerton in the third round. In the face of defeat, one local newspaper, *The Item*, praised Rosebud for his valiant effort.[22]

A contemporary of Edgerton's was Joe Butler, a well-known heavyweight boxer. Butler's reputation grew following his victory over Jim Corbett's sparring partner, Jim Daly, at Coney Island, New York, in the early nineties. In 1894 both agreed to spar each other for the benefit of the Bread Fund. In the exhibition, their evasive tactics and light hitting drew the wrath of the crowd. Butler had fought more aggressively in his other bouts that year, though in two of them authorities arrested him for violating the state's anti-prizefighting statute. In a February bout at Philadelphia's Ariel Athletic Club with Fred Craig, "The Harlem Coffee Cooler," Butler ran into a double whammy; the first by Craig who knocked him out before two minutes of the fight had elapsed, and then by the police for taking part in a prizefight. Craig, a New Yorker, was not detained because Pennsylvania authorities had no jurisdiction over him. Later that year in September, police arrested Butler a second time. They halted his fight with Jack "Bubbles" Davis at the Southwark Athletic Club as soon as he maneuvered his opponent for the knockout. Producing a document that revealed Butler would receive $50 for his work that night, police charged him with prizefighting. The state boxing ban, however, did little to deter Butler. He was back in the ring within a month, knocking out a six-foot-four miner from Mt. Carmel, Pennsylvania.

Butler fought a myriad of opponents during the latter half of the decade, but three of his most prominent and controversial fights occurred in 1897. In June of that year, he endeared himself to San Franciscans when he knocked out Frank Slavin in two minutes of the first round. Then he took on Tom Carey of New York City at the Arena in Philadelphia. Butler wore his opponent down in the third round with a barrage of low blows to which his hometown followers protested. But in spite of their objections, boxing officials allowed the fight to continue. In the fifth round, Butler put away a weakened Carey to a chorus of boos and hisses from the audience. Local fans chided Butler as he made his way from the ring to the dressing room; they cheered as Carey left the ring.

The premier boxing match of the year paired Butler with John Bonner for the Middleweight Championship of Pennsylvania. Bonner won the championship with a knockout in front of 3,000 spectators at the Arena. His wicked right to Butler's jaw in the second round led one reporter to call the fight "one of the fiercest and roughest ever witnessed in this city." Butler's superior height and reach proved no advantage. Not only was Butler stunned by Bonner's fist, but

he was frustrated by the officiating. He accused the referee of unfairly inter-
rupting his attack in the first round just when he was about to knock out
Bonner. Crying foul, Butler called for an immediate rematch. Less than two
weeks later he got his wish. This time an overflow crowd packed the
Arena—possibly the largest up to that time. After an uneventful first round,
Butler went into a tirade in the second. Overcome with emotion, he threw
Bonner to the mat, jumped on him, and began punching the fallen boxer while
he was down. As the referee attempted to break up this melee, Butler threw
punches at him, too. The crowd erupted and threatened Butler, forcing the
police to escort him to safety.[23]

Boxing touched the African-American community in a variety of other
ways, mostly in demeaning form as entertainment for white folks. The Ariel
Athletic Club in 1892 held a prizefighting tournament for blacks in which the
winner's prize was a janitorial job at the club. More demeaning was the
"Colored Gladiators" show in 1899 at the white Oxford Club in the city's
Frankford section. Five African Americans were hired to stage "what was
called 'an old Roman sport,' the 'battle royal' of all against all until a single
'winner' crawled out of the ring." In a few instances, however, African Americans came out on top. Jem Moulton, "The Black Pearl," walked away with a
purse of $85 after defeating two white pugilists in consecutive bouts at Kelly's
Hall on Christian Street. In somewhat of an anomaly, George Dixon received
overwhelming white support in his match against England's Jim Lynch at the
Ariel Athletic Club.[24]

Apart from boxing, horse racing was one of the few avenues of economic
promise for poor African Americans. But by the mid-1890s, Jim Crow laws also
forced them out of this sport, too. Isaac Murphy, America's leading African-
American jockey, had a spectacular, though brief, career during the 1880s
when he earned $15,000 to $20,000 per year, more than than three times the
annual wages of other topflight jockeys of his era. By the 1890s, however, his
career took a downward twist. Though self-inflicted problems associated with
excessive drinking and erratic dieting and fasting binges to make weight took
their toll on his body, social pressures were just as instrumental in hastening
his demise. The white man's entry into the jockey profession in conjunction
with the advent of Jim Crow pushed the African-American jockey aside. During the 1890s, Philadelphia's African-American jockeys experienced a similar
fate. Because there was no flat racing in Philadelphia (the city's two harness
tracks catered to white gentlemen), African-American jockeys had to seek
employment across the river at the track in Gloucester, New Jersey. In the late
nineteenth century, Gloucester, commonly known as the "Sin City of the

Delaware," was a haven for gambling, prostitution, and other illegal activities. But it also had a brighter side as its boardwalk created a carnival atmosphere that provided commercial amusements for the masses. Philadelphians flocked to this center of amusement, particularly on Sundays, when enforcement of the state's blue laws shut down their city's commerce and entertainment. Moralists in both states, viewing the festivities at Gloucester as a threat to the common weal, clamored for reform. In a campaign spearheaded by the *Inquirer*, Philadelphia reformers called upon New Jersey officials to shut down the operation at Gloucester. A combination of events led to Gloucester's demise, ranging from a pugilist's death in the boxing ring in 1893 to the election of new county officials who opposed gambling, to the State Assembly's newly adopted opposition to the race track. Closing the Gloucester track had ominous overtones for black jockeys throughout America, for this move "coincided with the national campaign to bar Afro-Americans from riding thoroughbreds at major races across the country."[25]

Among the other sporting activities which attracted Philadelphia's African Americans during the late nineteenth century were track and field events. Excluded from white athletic clubs that emerged in postbellum America, African Americans organized their own. Running and jumping events, of course, were part of their repertoire, but they frequently sponsored tournaments similar to the one held by the Crescent and Independent Athletic Clubs in 1893. Boxing, wrestling, jumping, kicking, and tug of war games were the featured events. John C. Lewis and William H. Warrick ran track in 1889 and 1890 at the University of Pennsylvania. The latter held the quarter-mile championship; upon graduation he studied medicine and built a successful career as a physician. At the Warren Athletic Club games at Wilmington, Delaware, in the fall of 1892, W. A. Morris won races of 1,000 yards, 880 yards, and one mile. Morris' victories in the three races prompted one reporter to label the Philadelphian "the most graceful distance runner ever seen here." Professional runners, at this time, staged long-distance races for prize money on the pedestrian track. Philadelphia's Frank Hart was one of the few African Americans involved in this passing fad. He set a record at one competition in New York in 1879. The following year, Tommy Huggins, a shoeblack, won a bet worth several hundred dollars when he completed a walk from New York City to Philadelphia in less than twenty-four hours.[26]

The new fad of cycling also had its African-American participants. In 1892 there were at least three African-American bicycle clubs in Philadelphia. The first club, the Ebon, was founded by black policemen on bicycles. The bicycle "cops" were part of the 19th District Bicycle Corp within the city's Police

Department. Some African-American women formed a club of their own, the Stars of Hope, which operated out of the seventh ward on Lombard Street. They were often seen cycling up Chestnut Street with the bicycle cops.

Jim Crow's ugly tentacles reached cycling in 1894 when the League of American Wheelmen barred blacks from its organization. Though their action kept blacks out of League functions, it did not deter them from enjoying the pleasure of the wheel, nor did it prevent them from holding their own races and competitions. In Philadelphia, the Germantown Colored Wheel Club sponsored an open meet for African Americans in October of 1898. The featured event in this first annual tourney was a 5-mile pursuit race in which Peter French of the Magnolia Club defeated Alexander Daniels, the Germantown champ. Five other races filled the docket, each having at least three heats, which kept the large turnout entertained throughout the day. All of the races were filled with excitement. That, combined with no accidents or injuries, made for a successful meet.

The previous June, Major Taylor, the African-American bicyclist whose racing victories brought him distinction as the fastest rider in America, flashed his form in the Quaker City. He won national championship races in the 1/3- and 2-mile races at the city's Tioga Racetrack, and later that same day he won a third race at the Woodside Track. He complimented Philadelphia audiences for being well-versed in bicycle racing.[27]

CONCLUSION

What started out in the last third of the nineteenth century as a great promise of freedom with the ratification of the Thirteenth (freedom), Fourteenth (citizenship), and Fifteenth (voting rights) Amendments to the Constitution of the United States turned to disillusionment and despair by the century's end. The discrepancies between rhetoric, even when appended to a document as protective as the U.S. Constitution, and the reality of day-to-day living, clearly evident in all aspects of life, were highly visible in the institution of sport. Just three years after Appomattox, the color barrier sprung up quickly when the Convention of Pennsylvania State Base Ball Players denied the Pythians admission to its organization. The state convention mimicked the action taken by the National Association of Base Ball Players in 1867. These exclusionary measures forced African-American baseball teams to play, for the most part, among themselves. When in the 1880s professional teams instituted the color line, intraracial play led to separate leagues with segregated play. By the 1890s the color line extended to virtually every other sport. Jim Crow barred African-American cyclists from the League of American Wheelman in 1894 and forced African-American jockeys out of horseracing by the middle of the

1890s. In boxing, African Americans fared somewhat better, though in the heavyweight division white titleholders refused to fight black challengers.

But boxing was a double-edged sword for African Americans. While some fighters received praise and adulation for their stellar performances in the ring, others were the objects of ridicule and derision. For every George Dixon and Joe Gans—renowned boxers with national reputations—there were hundreds of others whose only purpose in the ring was to entertain white audiences. One case in point was the Oxford Athletic Club's black slugfest which pitted five African Americans against one another in a free-for-all as the century drew to a close. Two black Philadelphians of this era—Walter Edgerton, "de Kentucky Rosebud," and Joe Butler—had boxing careers that vacillated between admiration and contempt. As skillful boxers, they were entertaining and enjoyable to watch, but when they on occasion resorted to unethical tactics inside the ring or criminal behavior on the outside, they bore the brunt of severe criticism. Both had been successful street fighters whose success in their neighborhoods propelled them into the prize ring. In the streets survival was the only objective; rules or decorum were anathema. Literally, the fittest survived by calling upon their own resources and ingenuity. While Rosebud's and Butler's illegal actions either inside or outside the ring cannot be condoned or even justified, one can at least recognize the source of their behavior.

More important than the boxing issue, however, is the question of postbellum sport and its role and meaning for African Americans during that period. On the positive side, sport, baseball in particular during the sixties and seventies, brought segments of the African-American community together. It fostered a degree of pride among the inhabitants and opened the way for the exchange of ideas between African Americans in different cities. Whether or not baseball was also a divisive force among African Americans who were excluded from their own clubs or teams, either wittingly or unwittingly, has not yet been determined. The downside of baseball, of course, was the color barrier which inaugurated the extension of racial segregation into sport. This practice doubtless held African Americans back in the sporting arena and deprived them of economic benefits enjoyed by their white counterparts.

The cloud of segregation, inherently discriminatory and racist, played on the dignity of African Americans. As second-class citizens, the majority of African Americans were forced into subservient roles. Sport, as a component of American culture, reinforced this process. Its negative impact on African Americans is clearly visible and easily documented. But in the throes of segregation, sport (and recreation) could be useful to African Americans. As a diversion, it gave them a brief reprieve from the onerous discrimination they faced in their daily lives. Escaping into the fantasy world of sport, some would argue, took their minds off their troubles, replenished their energy, and renewed their drive to fight for the rights and freedom denied them by the onset of Jim Crow. Sport alone was not their salvation; it could not by itself rectify society's ills. But, nevertheless, it offered them temporary asylum from the burden of segregation and in this small way helped African Americans cope with life in nineteenth-century America.

Bo Jackson, Michael Jordan, and Mike Tyson—three highly talented African-American athletes of the present day—are well known not only for their athletic prowess but for commercial endorsements that fill our television screens and newsprint. They represent America's gradual recognition, though not total acceptance, of black athletes. Their celebrity status with its lucrative benefits is one indication that this country's glorification of athletic superstars has reached certain African Americans. But this was hardly the case a generation ago, and even less so a century ago when Philadelphia had its share of superlative African-American athletes. Octavius Catto, John Cannon, Jefferson Cavens, Robert Adger, Joe Butler, and Walter Edgerton, "de Kentucky Rosebud," were the Jacksons, Jordans, and Tysons of the nineteenth century. Their success in sport brought them local acclaim within the African-American community which in due time spread to the city's white communities. For some, most notably Butler and Rosebud, reputations extended beyond Philadelphia's environs. In no case, however, did nineteenth-century African-American athletes receive the acceptance, recognition, and economic remuneration they deserved.

NOTES

This project was supported by William Paterson College Research Development Award for the 1990–91 academic year.

1. Theodore Hershberg et al., "A Tale of Three Cities: Blacks, Immigrants, and Opportunity in Philadelphia, 1850–1880, 1930, 1970," in *Philadelphia, Work, Space, Family and Group Experience in the 19th Century*, ed. Theodore Hershberg (New York: Oxford University Press, 1981), pp. 464–65, 469–70.

2. Theodore Hershberg and Henry Williams, "Mulattoes and Blacks: Intragroup Color Differences and Social Stratification in Nineteenth-Century Pennsylvania," in *Philadelphia*, p. 425.

3. Willard B. Gatewood, *Aristocrats of Color: The Black Elite, 1880–1970* (Bloomington: Indiana University Press, 1990), pp. 55, 61, 152–53, 190, 101, 210–15; Hershberg and Williams, "Mulattoes and Blacks," p. 425.

4. Laura Weinstock, "The Pythian Base Ball Club: A Study of a Black Elite Organization and Its Implication for Social Structure in Nineteenth-Century Philadelphia," unpublished manuscript, Philadelphia Social History Project, 1972. Philadelphia *Tribune*, November 16, 1912; W.E.B. Du Bois, *The Philadelphia Negro* (Boston: Ginn,

1899; repr. Millwood, N.Y.: Kraus-Thomson Organization Ltd., 1973), p. 316. See pp. 316–18 of his *Philadelphia Negro* for more of his views on this issue.

5. Socioeconoimic data on the Pythians was gathered from the Census Population Manuscripts, U.S. Bureau of the Census, 1870.

6. Philadelphia *Tribune*, August 24, 1912.

7. Philadelphia *Tribune*, May 3, 1913; Roger Lane, *William Dorsey's Philadelphia and Ours: The Past and Future of the Black City in America* (New York: Oxford University Press, 1992), p. 522.

8. See Gatewood, *Aristocrats of Color*, p. 107; Leon Gardiner Collection, Box 8G, Historical Society of Pennsylvania (hereafter HSP), Philadelphia, Pennsylvania; Philadelphia *Tribune*, August 24, 1912; Harry A. Reed, "Not by Protest Alone: Afro-American Activists and the Pythian Baseball Club of Philadelphia, 1867–1869," *Western Journal of Black Studies* 9 (Fall 1985): 148–49.

9. Gardiner Collection, Box 8G, HSP; Philadelphia *Tribune*, August 24, 1912; Gatewood, *Aristocrats of Color*, p. 190; DuBois, *Philadelphia Negro*, pp. 317–20.

10. Gatewood, *Aristocrats of Color*, pp. 100, 107; DuBois, *Philadelphia Negro*, pp. 317–20.

11. The other six African-American clubs in Philadelphia at this time were the Aldridge, Excelsior, Liberty, L'Ouverture, Resolute, and Rouen. Gardiner Collection, Box 8G, HSP; *Sunday Mercury* (Philadelphia), August 26, 1871; George B. Kirsch, *The Creation of American Team Sports* (Urbana: University of Illinois Press, 1989), p 166. The Olympics defeated the Pythians by a 44–23 score.

12. *Sunday Mercury* (Philadelphia), August 6, 1871; August 27, 1871; July 23, 1867.

13. Gardiner Collection, Box 8G, HSP; Reed, "Not by Protest Alone," pp. 146–47; Harry C. Silcox, "Nineteenth Century Philadelphia Black Militant: Octavius V. Catto (1839–1871)," *Pennsylvania History* 44 (January 1977): 68–76.

14. *Sunday Mercury*, August 23, 1874; August 27, 1876; Arthur R. Ashe, Jr., *A Hard Road to Glory: A History of African-American Athletes, 1619–1918* (New York: Warner Books: 1988), p. 72; Jerry Malloy, "Out at Home, Baseball Draws the Color Line, 1887," *The National Pastime: A Review of Baseball History* (1983), pp. 24–27.

15. New York *Age*, September 15, 1888; Trenton *Times*, May 10, 1886; Malloy, "Out at Home," pp. 18–20; Ashe, *Hard Road to Glory*, p. 74.

16. Philadelphia *Tribune*, May 3, 1913; Silcox, "Octavius V. Catto," p. 66.

17. Gardiner Collection, Box 8G, HSP; Philadelphia *Times*, July 12, 1887. DuBois, *Philadelphia Negro*, pp. 319–20. Lane, *William Dorsey's Philadelphia*, pp. 28–29.

18. Ibid.

19. William Dorsey Collection, Scrapbook no. 243, Cheyney State University, Cheyney, Pennsylvania; Lane, *William Dorsey's Philadelphia*, p. 521.

20. See David K. Wiggins, "Peter Jackson and the Elusive Heavyweight Championship: A Black Athlete's Struggle against the Late Nineteenth Century Color Line," *Journal of Sport History* 12 (Summer 1985): 143–68.

21. Philadelphia *Times*, March 23, 1894, March 26, 1894, March 29, 1894; Philadelphia *Press*, March 22, 1894.

22. Lane, *William Dorsey's Philadelphia*, p. 521; Dorsey Collection, Scrapbook no. 243; *The Item* (Philadelphia), July 29, 1894; December 6, 1894.

23. Dorsey Collection, Scrapbook no. 243; *The Item*, February 22, 1894; October 25, 1894. June 2, 1897; September 2, 1897; November 5, 1897; 12 November 1897.

24. Lane, *William Dorsey's Philadelphia*, pp. 29–30, 520; Philadelphia *Times*, February 5, 1899; Dorsey Collection, Scrapboook no. 243; *The Item* (Philadelphia), March 9, 1890.

25. Lane, *William Dorsey's Philadelphia*, 519; Ashe, *Hard Road to Glory*, pp. 47–48 For a superb synopsis and analysis of Murphy's career, see David K. Wiggins, "Isaac Murphy: Black Hero in Nineteenth Century America Sport, 1861–1896," *Canadian Journal of History of Sport and Physical Education* 10 (May 1979): 15–32. Roger Lane, *Roots of Violence in Black Philadelphia 1860–1900* (Cambridge, Mass.: Harvard University Press, 1986), pp. 117–18.

26. Dorsey Collection, Broadside; Dale A. Somers, *The Rise of Sport in New Orleans, 1850–1900* (Baton Rouge: Louisiana State University Press, 1972), pp. 241–42. New York *Age*, May 18, 1889, May 24, 1890, September 28, 1889; Lane, *William Dorsey's Philadelphia*, pp. 30–31, 523. Dorsey Collection, Philadelphia *Record*, 8 May 1880.

27. Dorsey Collection, Scrapbook no. 243, unidentified newspaper, May 6, 1894; Lane, *William Dorsey's Philadelphia*, pp. 524–25. Philadelphia *Press*, October 7, 1898; Philadelphia *Times*, October 7, 1898; Marshall W. "Major" Taylor, *The Fastest Bicycle Rider in the World* (Freeport, N.Y.: Books for Libraries Press, 1971), pp. 54, 230.

10

Sport and the Americanization of Ethnic Women in Chicago

Gerald R. Gems

Sociologists and historians began their examination of ethnic groups in Chicago as early as the 1890s. The diverse population, almost 80 percent of which was foreign-born at that time, provided fertile ground for such research. Many of these early works portrayed the city as a patchwork of ethnic neighborhoods. Such enclaves provided a ready supply of workers for the dynamic growth of Chicago's industrial plants, but they also proved an obstacle to the social reformers who sought a more homogeneous culture. The reformers' efforts were particularly frustrated by ethnic leisure practices, especially those that emanated from the social, fraternal, and athletic clubs designed to maintain ethnic nationalism.

Previous studies of such nationalistic groups have focused upon male members and have, for the most part, been limited to the German Turner movement. Other ethnic groups, particularly those from eastern Europe, remain relatively unstudied. The role of women within such organizations is largely unknown and is often assumed to be a passive one which followed the dictates of male leadership. Ethnic women, even more isolated within the ethnic enclaves than their working husbands, remained segregated from the mainstream culture. It was, however, largely through leisure that ethnic women reached some accommodation with American society and a measure of relief from male domination in other areas of their life.[1]

A CLASH OF CULTURES

After the 1865 flow of European immigrants to Chicago, which had begun before the Civil War, the city sprawled outward in a ramshackle fashion, its development fueled by German and Scandinavian craftsmen and an unskilled Irish labor force. By 1880 Chicago had become the nation's third largest city with a population of over a half million, as newer immigrants from eastern Europe settled in the city. Many of them settled in their own enclaves, where they re-created their village life within the expanding urban center. Most of the Bohemians ended up living in the two wards that comprised the Pilsen District in the southwest part of the city, and almost eight out of every ten Poles resided in two wards to the northwest.[2]

This distinct residential pattern was tied to socioeconomic status and the shared values of particular groups. Native-born white Chicagoans and other English-speaking peoples, the Irish excepted, owned the vast majority of the city's wealth; they were financiers, commercial entrepreneurs, and industrialists. These men, led by Potter Palmer, built large mansions along an exclusive strip of land on the near south side of the city. There they planned, played, and displayed in the ostentatious manner befitting and reinforcing their social positions. A burgeoning middle class—also of native-born and other English-speaking peoples—held an increasing number of white collar jobs and chose to reside in the outlying suburban areas, such as Hyde Park to the south or Riverside to the west. They were sufficiently removed from the laboring classes and urban squalor, yet able to commute to work by rail.[3]

For many of these middle class social climbers, the opportunities present in Chicago during the mid-nineteenth century made the American dream attainable. For immigrant groups the promise of America meant religious or political freedom and economic opportunity, but not the denial of their ethnic cultures. They continued to pursue such traditional lifestyles within their ethnic enclaves, much to the chagrin of Nativists.

Polish communities revolved around their parishes, fifteen of which began in the nineteenth century. Residents of the Polish neighborhoods segregated themselves from the mainstream culture; and, in clerical matters, Poles even opposed German and Irish prelates, whom they viewed as too secular and Anglicized. By the end of the century St. Stanislaus Kostka had become the world's largest congregation, with 40,000–50,000 parishioners. By 1890 five large, decentralized Polish enclaves had taken shape around Chicago's industrial complexes. Some of these areas where shared with Germans, Bohemians, and later, Lithuanians, all of whom had been old world neighbors and antagonists. The Bohemians, like the Germans, had fled from the upheavals of 1848 and in the aftermath of the Italian-Austrian War of the 1860s. After the Civil War, Bohemians numbered 45,000, and most of them were Catholics. A few were Protestants, and another minority were non-religious, "free-thinkers" who espoused atheism and socialism.[4]

Residential patterns of the various ethnic groups fostered clannishness, and the reliance of many of them on religious leaders for direction limited their perspectives on American life. In such neighborhoods, small ethnic businesses served the needs of residents and provided limited access to information about the outside world. Social activities often revolved around churches or fraternal associations. The ethnic neighborhoods also spawned athletic clubs that preserved old world cultural values and lifestyles. Among these were the Czech Sokols, or "Falcons," which organized in Chicago in 1866, a year after the introduction of the Sokol movement in St. Louis. Dr. Miroslav Tyrs, a Bohemian patriot opposed to Austrian oppression, founded the organization in 1862. Tyrs was influenced by the classical ideals of the Greeks, but he modeled his organization after the nationalistic German Turners.[5]

Poles, Slavs, Serbs, and Lithuanians would all organize their own Falcon groups in succeeding years; and by 1879 Chicago had become the center of the National Sokol Union, which had 120 clubs in the United States. All valued individual and collective strength through physical exercise, primarily gymnastics for nationalistic purposes. Dances, picnics, choral groups, and sporting activities provided solidarity and fund-raising ventures for the European patriots. Such communal leisure practices also provided a mutual support network within the city.[6]

An early study of the Czech community stated that "almost every Bohemian man and woman belongs to some society. Unlike other Slavonic nations, Boehmian women have many organizations. Among the younger women the gymnastics societies, known as 'Sokolky' are best organized. Women, like men, separate their social from their religious life and have organizations of free-thinkers and Catholics."[7] The non-religious "free-thinkers" had already established thirty-five Sokols and seven cycling clubs by the turn of the century. Such ethnic associations posed a particular problem for Nativists who sought greater cultural cohesion and a cooperative and efficient workforce to serve the industrial economy.

The processes of urbanization and industrialization affected other American communities at uneven rates, but eastern towns and cities were able to address the accompanying problems and issues inherent in social and economic change over an extended period of time. In Chicago the transformation from a frontier community to an industrial metropolis was largely condensed in a single generation. Wage labor caused many to question the nature of equality and freedom in America. The questions were answered with emotion and intensity, and the responses included class warfare as natives, ethnics, employers, and employees tried to make sense of their rapidly changing lives. Caught within this social vortex, women struggled with conflicting values of tradition and progress. Wage labor marked a departure from the domestic sphere. Discretionary income and leisure pursuits allowed for even greater emancipation.[8]

THE MOVEMENT FOR CLASS EMANCIPATION

Ethnic social-athletic organizations often spearheaded the assault on the industrial system. Radical groups held their meetings at the Turner and Sokol halls, and heavily armed ethnics posed a particular concern to employers. The Bohemian Sharpshooters, a workers' militia, had maintained useful skills by holding regular shooting matches throughout the war years. The Sharpshooters alarmed employers, as did the German Turners who responded to authoritarian measures by forming the Lehr und Wer Verein, another quasi-military organization, in 1875. Various strains of socialist philosophy defined the class struggle more clearly for a growing number of workers, including women.[9]

At least eleven German Turner officers, the Scandinavian Turners, and Bohemian Sokol members participated in the International Working People's Association. Women, who had formed their own Working Women's Union in 1878, with Alzina Parsons Stevens as president, also joined. The Bohemian women of Chicago had already organized themselves as early as 1870, and the women of St. Louis founded the first women's Sokol in America in 1876.[10]

The women and ethnic groups within the movement often shared their leisure time in dances, masquerade balls, picnics, drama productions, athletic competitions and in choral groups which served as fund raisers for socialist causes. The gymnastic activities of the ethnic sport associations complemented the militaristic shows of strength by the rifle companies. Such cultural forms were antithetical to the value systems of the dominant native culture. Leisure practices organized on a communal basis and designed to support socialist activities presented a direct challenge to the capitalists and reinforced the old world customs. A survey of *The Alarm*, a socialist paper, showed ads for five socialist dances held in November of 1884 alone, and the period from 1884–86 averaged at least two per month. The twenty-six gymnastic groups held one or two festivals per month in addition to the dances. Picnics celebrated both American patriotism and European socialist holidays and drew thousands of participants. Such affairs regaled the new-founded freedom of expression found in America, but they also confronted the lack of freedom in the workplace and the increasing attempts to control workers' leisure time. An 1878 affair raised $7,000 from the estimated 15,000–30,000 people in attendance. By 1888 some Sokols had adopted the militaristic khaki uniforms with the Garibaldi red shirt customary to the European nationalists. They also adopted the communal slogan "neither profit nor glory."[11]

The fund-raising leisure activities of the socialist groups enabled them to spread their message through ethnic papers and garner new members, thereby increasing their strength. In the fall of 1878 the Socialist Party was able to elect a state senator and three state representatives, including Leo Meilbek from the Czech district. Other radical groups turned to the ballot in ever-increasing numbers, particularly after their suppression following the armed conflicts of the Haymarket Massacre and the Pullman Strike. The stigma of anarchy and the cooperation of the Populist movement of the 1890s brought such groups even closer to the mainstream. Women, too, questioned their role within the movement and sought a more active participation in effecting their own destiny.[12]

THE MOVEMENT TOWARD GENDER EMANCIPATION

As the fragmentation of the labor movement took place, the ethnic social-athletic associations that had been integral members of the socialist movement turned increasingly to nationalistic efforts to maintain their European traditions. Others allied with the Populist movement that included the middle class reformers. Women, too, came to expect freedom from the repressive conditions and male domination found in Europe. Women split with the Socialists over their more passive role in the movement and the suffrage issue. Bozena Kosman, later a Sokol director, became an active suffragette, and the Lithuanian Women's Alliance continued to support the Socialist cause. Other women increasingly sought support for their causes from within their own ranks, and many formed their own labor unions. Bohemian feminists published their own paper in Chicago, with a circulation of over 6,000. Campaigns for equality brought greater contact with like-minded native Americans.

The church, too, perceived a threat from the Socialists and the free-thinkers in 1890. The clergy also showed concern over the rising trend toward female autonomy that might upset traditional family values. Reverend Stephen Furdek founded the Slovak Catholic Union and the Women's Catholic Union in Cleveland to counter the atheists of the Pittsburgh-based National Slovak Society. In Chicago, Polish women had organized for religious purposes as early as 1871. Clergy, fearful of urban temptations, began to organize the leisure time of their parishioners as well. Reverend Joseph Ziemba of St. Stanislaus founded a sports club in 1883, and the parish Society of Virgins, founded with fifteen members in 1874, had 1,500 adherents who took the pledge of celibacy by 1917. Such organizations proved beneficial in material matters, too, as priests channeled fund-raising efforts into the parish coffers.[13]

Sporting practices of such groups also provided more social contact between natives and ethnics, once the latter adopted some of the American sport forms. German and Irish men appeared on baseball diamonds in the post war years, and eastern Europeans followed suit in the 1890s. By that time both native and ethnic businessmen competed in bowling leagues, while other immigrants contended for prizes in billiard tournaments and track meets. Most ethnics, however, and women in particular, clung to the fraternal and gymnastic associations that still nourished social and nationalistic aims. Before women could seek greater independence in the larger society they first had to succeed within their own. Annual picnics, used as fund raisers for such ventures, featured women in gymnastic exhibitions and races for both girls and women. By 1909 the American Turnerfest drew 25,000 spectators to Lawndale Park in Chicago to watch Jennie Billas, Georgie Hydle, and Mamie Frada compete alongside the men.[14]

Better educated than all other immigrant groups, Czech women already enjoyed a large measure of independence. Urban, mostly middle class Czech women had long been involved in the Sokol activities, such as gymnastics, lectures, and the libraries that reinforced their European traditions. In 1890 the Czech women of St. Louis initiated their own gymnastic classes, and the Sokol Ladies Gymnastic Association was founded in Milwaukee the same year. Chicagoans founded three additional women's clubs and a Czech school within the next few years.[15] In 1891 Chicago Czechs formed a cycling club as well. Within a decade the women also took up fencing. In each of these ventures the Czech women matched the contemporary efforts of their native sisters as they led the way for other eastern Europeans to follow.

By 1892 Polish women in the city organized their own Falcon society for the purpose of practicing gymnastics, despite the protests of their husbands, who advocated a more traditional domestic role. A Polish cyclists' club soon followed. By 1898 the Polish Women's Alliance sought greater independence in their lives under the leadership of Stefania Chmielinska. But two priests at St. Stanislaus Kostka Parish formed a women's group under clerical control to maintain their focus on Catholicism and nationalism. By 1907 the group numbered 388 members and had more than $2,000 in its treasury. The following year a Catholic Gymnastic Union Sokol was organized to secure leisure practices within the religious sphere. The leisure world of most working class women continued to revolve around the church, shopping, and visits among friends within the ethnic enclave.

The desire to retain traditional lifestyles challenged the progressive notion of a homogeneous society, and conflict erupted over educational issues. Most ethnics sent their children to church-related schools to avoid the Protestant influences of the public educational system. The parochial school system provided separate yet parallel organizational structures that allowed ethnics to protect and preserve their religious differences. By 1890 Catholics had established sixty-two elementary schools with 31,053 students in the city, another 1,571 in the suburbs, and 1,348 in Catholic high schools. Under Archbishop Feehan, administrator of the Chicago Archdiocese from 1880 to 1902, ethnic parishes grew and prospered. By 1900 each of the 520 Polish Falcon units in the United States had their roots in the parish halls. The widespread parochial school system fostered not only Catholicism but cultural pluralism, rather than the cohesion sought by the reform groups.[16]

Progressive reformers worked hard to address the glaring inequities of the social-industrial system and the concomitant health concerns of urban ghettoes at the turn of the century. Social reform provided women with an active role in fomenting change, yet social moves still required them to labor within the prescribed boundaries and values of the Victorian image of womanhood by providing moral guidance and female nurturance. Nevertheless, ethnic women, particularly Czechs, were quick to challenge the male hierarchy. When denied complete equality by the men, they struck out on their own. By 1910 the women's groups gained recognition as full members of the Slovak Gymnastic Union, and Marie Simek was elected second vice-president of the organization. The Czech women stood in stark contrast to the other immigrant groups, whose efforts failed to transcend religious strictures.[17]

AN ACCOMMODATION OF CULTURES

Native reformers, too, became enamored with sport and its possibilities for producing social change. With much non-work time among people who, for the most part, did not speak English, play and games figured prominently in their "Americanization" programs. Progressive reformers formed a number of social agencies, enlisted commercial sponsorship, and invoked the powers of the city government to deliver play spaces to the ethnic masses throughout the city. In these public spaces natives, ethnics, and various religious agencies shared facilities and gave an international flavor to operational and governance structures. The joint efforts masked different motives, however; and, combined with ethnic, class, and religious values, they denied any one group the realization of its goals. Park and playground administrators believed that the community centers, such as parks and playgrounds, might re-create, at least approximately, the rural values and social relations of the past. Competitive games might also foster physical and social development, as well as obedience to authority and allow immigrant children to interpret the American culture for their parents.

Some of the centers were allowed local autonomy in their management and programming, and Mary Sakowska campaigned for the five parks of the West Side to be utilized as Polish Community Centers, where Janina Dunin and Jadwiga Krassowska-Stopawa served as teachers. Contributions from business organizations and women's clubs allowed many schools to be utilized as community centers and playgrounds. Public schools initiated interscholastic soccer play for boys in 1908, and the Amateur Athletic Federation followed with a girl's soccer program by 1914. Two years later the city was managing seventy-three small parks, seventy playgrounds, sixty-three of which were in schoolyards, three beaches, and four public pools. Supervisors and trained instructors at such sites organized competitive American sports and games to inculcate particular values, and introduced athletic efficiency tests to address some of the health concerns produced by life in the industrial city.[18]

Playground administrators were pleased that 31 percent of the boys and girls had passed the athletic efficiency tests by mid-decade, well above the 13 percent when they introduced the tests in 1911. The supervisors offered the athletic activities as alternatives to the customary leisure practices of the working class which often took place in saloons and dance halls. The debate over leisure time and its use was an ongoing one emanating from the labor struggle and the opposing values of employers and employees.

The temperance wars that were an aspect of this debate followed not only class but ethnic and religious lines as well. Evangelical Protestants, the dominant powers in the Progressive Party, Swedish Lutherans, and the conservative Catholic Paulist order favored prohibition, citing alcohol as the root of disease, crime, vice, and poverty. The prohibitionists represented a distinct minority, however. Most Catholics, Lutherans, and Episcopalians, all of whom used wine in their religious rituals, and the overwhelming majority of laborers, to whom beer or the saloon were a way of life, opposed abstinence.

Company reprisals and middle class crusades upset workers, who judged leisure time as their own. On May 26, 1906, a parade of 80,000 ethnics, consisting of Germans, Bohemians, Poles, Hungarians, Danes, and Norwegians, demonstrated against a prohibition law. In that same year 1,087 ethnic organizations allied in the United Societies for local self-government under the leadership of a Czech politician, Anton Cermak, to oppose the Anti-Saloon League. In 1910 Cermak, as alderman, studied alternative means of income for the city and concluded that, without the revenue derived from taxes on liquor sales, Chicago would go bankrupt.[19]

The economics of the situation probably meant little to the masses, who continued to pursue their traditional leisure pastimes as well as the newer commercialized entertainments. In 1913 the Lithuanian newspaper *Lietuva* complained that the young no longer attended the ethnic schools because they spent too much time in saloons and pool rooms. The assessment was probably correct. Chicago had one saloon for every 335 residents and an unknown number of unlicensed "blind pigs," some of them operated by women. By 1900 Illinois stood as one of the leading brewery and distillery states, a part of an industry that ranked fifth nationally in invested capital by 1915. The United Breweries of Chicago allied with ethnic groups to present a formidable lobby against the evangelical crusade. The United Societies required aldermen to sign an anti-prohibition pledge in order to gain the support of ethnic voting blocs. Consequently, in 1914 a coalition of the Anti-Saloon League, the Law and Order League, and churches failed to win their prohibition campaign, garnering only 90,000 of the required 171,000 signatures. By 1916 the few Catholic temperance societies reported "greatly diminished numbers," and temperance speakers were no longer welcome in Catholic churches, although they continued their Sunday harangues from Protestant pulpits.[20]

Despite the inability of the various groups to stem the flow of alcohol, Catholics and other conservative ethnic groups agreed with the need to reduce vice and gambling, and such support may have encouraged other actions by the reformers. Middle class social agencies, such as the Juvenile Protection League, founded by the Chicago Women's Club in 1906, and the Immigrant Protective League, established by Hull House workers in 1908, united their opposition to commercial dance halls and cabarets. They believed not only that the dancing was lewd but that such places served as haunts for white slave traders, who sold unknowing or drunken girls into lives of prostitution.[21]

Commercialized leisure afforded new and exciting experiences for the ethnic youths and young adults mired in the drudgery of industrial work, however. Dancing in particular apparently held great fascination for many young people. A 1913 study found that 75 percent of the females between sixteen and twenty-four years of age attended dances, and men danced between two and seven times each week. Various groups tried to restrict, or restrain, the most offensive dancing forms. In the largely Bohemian town of Cicero, the town council prohibited the tango and other "disorderly" dances, and no dances were allowed without a police permit. Some churches did hold dances as fund raisers, but there, too, proper decorum was expected to be followed.

Sporting endeavors proved more agreeable to the social reformers, clergy, and commercial interests, who saw them as a more wholesome leisure alternative. Middle class sponsors, promoters, or managers, who shared some of the commercial values of the native merchants, often brought the ethnic athletic clubs and their fans into contact with the mainstream culture. The Polish owner of the bowling alleys at Ashland and Milwaukee Avenues sponsored a team in 1906, and by 1913 an eight-team men's league and a women's team had joined in the competition. George M. Rozczynialski became a national bowling champ and later was elected alderman. Other aldermen, many of whom were also tavern owners, sponsored bowling teams, just as Anton Cermak had done among the Czechs. Casimir Wronski, born in Poland in 1888, was a real estate speculator and owner of the Romeo Recreation Rooms. He promoted and hosted newspaper, industrial league, and state bowling association tournaments. He also sponsored baseball, volleyball, rowing, skating, swimming, hockey, and fishing clubs.

Numerous other Polish politicians held park district positions. Among them, William Fuka, owner of a clothing store, sponsored an array of teams, including an interstate football champion, a baseball contingent, and basketball squads for both boys and girls. He also sponsored several bowling leagues, a softball team, and an athletic club that included a ladies' auxiliary. In return, all team members were expected to shop exclusively at his store. By 1926 the Polish director at Pulaski Park had organized a swimming meet for local boys and girls. The athletic programs of the parks and those of the middle class sponsors proved attractive to ethnic youth. Immigrant children increasingly favored the American sport forms over the gymnastic practices of their parents.[22]

The Sokol groups also competed against natives and other ethnics in gymnastics and track and field. The Chicago set of 1909 featured a team from Czechoslovakia as a demonstration of homeland ties. Just a year later, however, the Pilsen Sokol, a perennial power in gymnastics, joined the Amateur Athletic Federation and the International Gymnastics Union. The All-Slavic Meet of 1913 included Slovaks, Bohemians, Poles, Lithuanians, and Ukrainians in competition for both men and women. In 1914 the American Sports Club, dedicated to developing an interest in all sports, solicited the Sokols as members for their gymnastic prowess. American competitions provided a stage to showcase ethnic pride, but also brought the Europeans into the native structure and a bit closer to the mainstream.[23]

AMERICANIZATION AND THE
REASSERTION OF MALE DOMINANCE

World War I ruptured many European ties, and the achievement of independence in the Polish and Czech homelands led many to a greater degree of assimilation. For Nativists, the war provided an opportunity to counteract the ethnic influences. An indication of the things to come occurred when Congress required immigrants to pass a literacy test early in 1917. Four years later, Congress imposed a limit on the number of émigrés, equal to 3 percent of the ethnic groups in the 1910 census.[24]

Nativist opposition to ethnic culture and influence extended well beyond the matter of demography. Reductions in the numbers of immigrants had their parallel in the educational system, where earlier ethnic curricular themes were displaced. Administrative "reforms" carried over to the extracurricular program. When the Public Schools Athletic League became subsumed by the Bureau of Physical Education in 1920, it made its intentions clear:

The purposes and aims of the league are to promote and provide for American sports and games among the students of the Chicago public schools . . . and to make a wider use of the splendid park and playground system of the city of Chicago.[25]

In addition to the American sports and games offered in the parks and playgrounds, ethnic girls who attended the public schools could participate in volleyball leagues or in an extensive intramural program that included captain ball, volleyball, track and field, softball, swimming, golf, tennis, and field hockey. Physical education became an integral means of assimilating ethnic youth, and such activities were conducted throughout the school day, as well as after school. The program, run in conjunction with the parks, was extensive. One hundred fifty-five schools competed in basketball and two hundred in baseball. Girls fielded fifty-seven volleyball teams, while newspapers helped to sponsor swimming, track, and skating meets for both boys and girls.[26]

The American sports and games of the schools, parks, and playgrounds proved attractive to ethnic youth. Park records indicated a continually rising rate of attendance and participation, and neighborhood groups clamored for more recreational facilities than the city could possibly provide. As youth adopted the American practices, the ethnic clubs, which were denied the steady flow of European recruits by the restrictive immigration laws of the 1920s, lost their appeal.

At the same time, native middle class athletic clubs induced some of the best ethnic and working class athletes to compete for them with offers of membership, sponsorship in international events, use of outstanding facilities, and tutelage under professional coaches. Both men and women benefited from such sponsorship. The Illinois Athletic Club enrolled Johnny Weismuller, a local swimming champion, in 1922. He soon achieved fame as an Olympic hero in 1924 and as a Hollywood movie star thereafter. Sybil Bauer, another protégé of the Illinois Athletic Club, held nine swimming records by 1922,

even surpassing the men's mark in the backstroke. The *New York Times* specu-
lated that "the discussion prior to the 1924 Olympics was whether Bauer would
swim against women or men. So remarkable is her speed that she may be
allowed to swim against the men contestants at the Olympic games in Paris."[27]

The initial women's Olympic gymnastic team of 1928 featured two more
Chicagoans, Anci Vackova and Bozena Cibulkova. Both were products of the
Czech Sokol Clubs. Albina Osipowich also added two gold medals in swim-
ming for the Americans. Many other Czech and Polish girls competed for
AAU track championships that might provide membership on the Olympic
team. Such promising athletes were conscripted as early as their high school
years. Betty Robinson earned fame as a sixteen-year old world champion.
Annette Rogers, who ran for the Illinois Catholic Women's Club track team as
a fourteen-year-old, won a gold medal at the 1932 Olympics. The Illinois
Women's Athletic Club had at least three world record holders on its track
team that won two successive national titles. Ethnic and working class athletes
helped the elite clubs achieve their goals as they vied with intra-city rivals for
athletic and social status. Recruitment of working class athletes also enhanced
the perception of sport as a meritocracy.[28]

Ethnic athletes dominated the local competition as well. The women of the
Jewish People's Institute vied for the Central AAU basketball championships
as early as 1927, and German, Jewish, Italian, and Irish girls swam for the
Amateur Athletic Federation titles, while Poles, Swedes, and Germans raced
for the ice skating honors. Polish girls from Eckhardt Park captured the junior
volleyball title, while three Lithuanian women contributed to the victory in the
senior division by the end of the decade. Such programs drove other ethnics to
seek affiliation with mainstream groups in order to safeguard their own interests. For some ethnics the Amateur Athletic Union offered a program consistent with their own ideology. This was particularly true for the Scandinavians
who disliked professionalism in sport. For others, such as the Turners, Falcons,
or Sokols who often swept the gymnastic laurels in major competitions, sport
fostered ethnic pride, and the AAU provided a showcase to display it.[29]

The Amateur Athletic Union held jurisdiction over the American athletic
competitions in which the Turners, Sokols, and Falcons engaged. By the 1930s
the AAU controlled amateur competition in track, basketball, boxing, gymnastics, handball, swimming, wrestling, weightlifting, volleyball, softball, and ice
hockey. Participation in the best and biggest events required AAU affiliation,
and the major ethnic clubs had all become members before World War II. The
Sokols continued their international excursions, however, and the American
women won the team gymnastic title at Prague in 1929, but they continued to

drift toward Americanization. By 1930 more than 40 percent of the Sokol membership was American-born.[30]

Middle class white, native, Protestant athletic clubs composed the charter membership of the Midwest branch of the AAU, and ethnic groups who aspired to compete at the highest levels were enticed to accept the native leadership. An AAU official explained that, even though "Turners and Sokols have their own 'closed' championship, they must win an AAU championship to be on the Olympic team."[31] In return, the AAU acknowledged the significance of the ethnic organizations by adopting the Turner gymnastics program of individual and apparatus events. By the 1930s Mildred Prchal, a Sokol instructor who had been trained in ballet, introduced rhythmic gymnastics as an alternative to the formal calisthenics. Governing boards remained dominated by males, however, and women continued to find their greatest opportunities for leadership within the ethnic framework. Despite the native influences, ethnic clubs continued to operate within parallel spheres. In 1932 the Czech-American women traveled to Prague to participate in the World Slet IX, where Chicagoans garnered second and fourth places in the women's 60-yard swimming race and won the volleyball competition. The movement away from the gymnastic emphasis became even more evident the following year when the American slet was held at Chicago. Girls and women of Czech, Russian, Polish, Yugoslav, and Urkrainian descent met at Soldier Field to compete in track and field, tennis, swimming and diving, volleyball, and basketball.[32]

Whereas middle class women had brought a sense of moral balance to the reform movements, working class women actively participated in the transition to commercialized leisure and sporting practices. For women, sporting activities promised new outlets, if not the economic mobility enjoyed by many male athletes. As women entered the workforce in ever-increasing numbers, employers began to organize women's teams in bowling and track after 1900. Baseball, softball, basketball, and tennis soon followed. A dislike for the formal gymnastic routines of scholastic physical training programs led younger women to seek more competitive games and athletic pastimes. Native physical educators, however, denounced the competitive male model as inappropriate for women and introduced the concept of play-days in girls' interscholastic programs in the 1920s. School girls unable to find competitive opportunities in the schools could still be accommodated on industrial teams, ethnic athletic clubs, the Catholic Youth Organization (CYO), and in the Chicago parks, where they engaged in at least thirteen competitive activities by the onset of World War II.[33]

That women had such competitive inclinations so decried by the physical educators and medical professionals is evident by the widespread activity and success of Chicago's women's teams. High school girls engaged in interscholastic competition well before the war, having started basketball play as early as 1895. Chicagoans were prominent in the founding of the Women's International Bowling Congress in 1916, although women's tournaments had been conducted since 1900. By 1920 they were offering more than $2,000 in prize money at the national tournament. During the 1920s, Chicago women won six national bowling championships and another national championship in basketball. Chicagoans held national and world records in swimming and track and field and were among the first women's Olympic team members. The Jewish People's Institute coordinated with the *Daily News* in inaugurating the annual women's Olympic track meet, and it acted as sponsor for the Post Office meet. The Western Electric Company also showcased women's track events, including a 60-yard dash for women with more than twenty-five years of service. The annual track meet drew more than 10,000 spectators on its twentieth anniversary in 1930 to watch Pauline Tomich capture three events, while Georgiana Bilek and Adele Rozhon won individual titles. Marian Kabachinski, Mildred Badtke, Anna Polcik, Amelia Kosilo, and Lillian Ciosek had won honors in the girls division of the Central AAU meet the year before.[34]

Industrial activities increased throughout the 1920s, as the large utility companies, steel producers, and department stores fielded golf, tennis, riflery, and ice hockey teams for the men. Women's teams competed in softball, basketball, volleyball, bowling, track, swimming, and tennis. Some industrial organizers supported sport as a democratizing agent that would ameliorate class distinctions by associating shop men or women with middle class office personnel in a common purpose. Eva Skrzydlewski exemplified the possibilities. After a successful career on the Western Electric baseball, basketball, and track teams, she was selected as an official of the eight-team company baseball league for women in 1931.[35]

Despite such intentions and the extensive nature of sport programs, oppositional groups countered with movements of their own in an attempt to create class consciousness, or at least to maintain labor solidarity. Radicals found enough support to organize a Communist sports program based on European models and designed to attract women and black workers. Chicago hosted the track and gymnastics competition of the Communist Labor Sports Union in 1927 and the International Workers' Olympics in 1931 and 1932. German athletic clubs published the *Arbeiter-Sport in Amerika* (Proletarian Sports in America) from 1927 to 1932, and an association of fifteen workers' clubs formed the Arbeiterkultur und Sportkartel in Chicago in 1931. The Czech Socialists competed in the Labor Olympiad held in Cleveland in 1936. Still, the attempt to resurrect the radical culture of the nineteenth century proved fruitless.[36]

Workers chose to work within the system and continued to support the institutions that proposed greater class and religious cohesion. The more moderate labor unions, the CYO, and the B'nai B'rith also built expensive facilities and sponsored competitive teams in competition with those of the corporate sponsors. The Chicago Association of Street, Electric Railway and Motor Coach Employees of America managed to construct a building with provisions for bowling and billiards at a cost of more than $1,000,000. The union also sponsored a number of bowling teams. The Amalgamated Clothing Workers, with more than 16,000 members, had their own gym, handball courts, exercise room, wrestling and boxing facilities, bowling alleys, and billiard tables. The union sponsored both men's and women's teams in softball, bowling, basketball, and volleyball. For many, the union halls became the clubhouse and social center.[37] Particularly during the Depression, the union replaced the political machine as a job provider. In so doing, the unions intended to strengthen their base and extend the scope of their organization by cultivating a labor tradition and a labor class consciousness. The Amalgamated and Clothing Textile Workers proclaimed that "its cultural program was centered on the objective of achieving the intellectual and emotional cohesion of the members . . . to unify the minds and hearts."[38] Sport was the most popular means of unification, with 5,000 members engaged in some form of activity. Other activities numbered between 500 and 3,500, but none matched sport in popularity.[39]

Bowling was particularly important for women in the industrial settings; in fact, it even surpassed softball among industrial recreation offerings. Similar to the Italian game of bocce ball and after suffering a decline during World War I, the sport made a dramatic resurgence in the 1920s. More than 10,000 women entered the *Evening American's* women's tournament by the end of the decade, and Marie Polacki, Mary Wilovsky, Lillian Ziemsa, and Angeline Blazewicz emerged among the divisional leaders who competed for cash and jewelry. By 1938 there were 900 bowling leagues, 9,000 teams and 500,000 bowlers in the city, with thirty-five churches providing bowling alleys. Both men and women enjoyed the sport, and tournaments could be held throughout the year. The Polish National Alliance supported sixty men's teams in ten leagues and another sixteen women's teams in four leagues. In 1939 the Public Schools Athletic League adopted bowling for interscholastic play.[40]

THE AMALGAMATION OF CULTURES

The proliferation in sporting activity accommodated the various ethnic, class, and religious interests; but with the increased leisure time enforced by the Depression, the city admitted that it was unable to accommodate the over-whelming number of requests for baseball, basketball, and softball facilities. Along with bowling and boxing for men, these sports formed the basis of working class and ethnic participation in the sporting culture. The working class groups conducted that participation in accordance with their own values, focusing primarily on power sports that required a demonstration of physical prowess and on activities that fostered communal solidarity and opportunities for gambling.

However, as exercises in quelling labor discontent and improving social relations, industrial recreation programs produced only limited success. Employers still perceived work and leisure as intertwined and attempted to inculcate work values into their employees' non-work lives. A government study found that office girls and shopworkers continued to forego each other's company. For others the European competitions still held attractions. Fifty-three Americans traveled to Prague to join the 30,000 European women and 31,000 girls in front of a million spectators at the Tenth World Slet in 1939. Such sporting activities helped women to break the traditional domestic bonds, but particular structures only reinforced the social status quo.

One agency, perhaps more than any other, that managed to bring ethnics closer to the American mainstream, as it reinforced masculine authority, was the Catholic Youth Organization. The CYO capitalized on already existing Catholic athletic structures, such as the Knights of Columbus tournaments and the Catholic Schools Athletics League, and allied itself with the native middle class media and the public park districts to promote its programs throughout the archdiocese. World War I witnessed both the birth of an American Catholicism and the CYO, whose rise coincided with and contributed to the decline in ethnicity. The accession of George Mundelein to the archbish-opric in 1916 marked the beginning of both phenomena.[41]

During the war Mundelein had each parish in the city create a Holy Name Society to coordinate religious functions, social programs, and athletic activi-ties. The program took on greater organization when Father Bernard J. Sheil inherited the task. Sheil incorporated most of the parishes in Chicago and the five surrounding counties into an athletic network that featured regular com-petitions and major events in coordination with native co-sponsors. Catholic organizations sponsored such events as the National Catholic Interscholastic Basketball Tournament, held at Loyola University after 1923. It served as a parallel to Amos Alonzo Stagg's national tournament, held at the University of Chicago since 1918. The Knights of Columbus continued to offer local and national sponsorship for athletic events. More important, the CYO encouraged the transition from private to public sporting practices by using public facilities, which would bring the ethnics closer to the mainstream.[42]

Sheil, a controversial figure like his mentor, was closer to the people. The incorporation of the Catholic Youth Organization in 1932 and funding from the Chicago *Tribune* Charities, the Knights of Columbus, and other groups brought even greater expansion to its programs. Vacation schools operated in conjunction with the park district, utilizing the public facilities for parochial programs. The agency provided social services as well as athletic programs in baseball, football, basketball, softball, volleyball, tennis, swimming, cycling, table tennis, boxing, track, horseshoes, marbles, ice skating, billiards, bowling, swimming, cross country, hockey, and golf in more than 60 percent of its parishes.[43]

With such expansion in programs, women, and Catholics in general, readily mixed with the mainstream culture in their leisure pursuits. Although many affairs were still conducted in the native tongue, members of fraternal clubs sometimes used English to communicate, especially when sports competition involved other ethnics or Americans. As early as 1922, when the American Catholic Sokols sent a team to compete in the slet in Czechoslovakia, they presented the American flag. The immigration laws curtailed the flow of European recruits into the ethnic clubs, and American-born youth lost the facility to communicate in their ancestral tongues, forcing ethnic publications to turn reluctantly to English. Organizers printed slet programs in Czech until 1937, and teams from Czechoslovakia continued to compete, but the Americanization of the event was evident by 1941. The Chicago slet drew 4,000 participants and 60,000 spectators, but it included competition in volleyball, basketball, and tennis, in addition to the customary gymnastics.[44]

The dilution of ethnicity became noticeable in other ways among the Czechs and other groups as well. Ethnic newspapers, such as the *Bohemian Review*, the organ of the Czech National Association, began publication in English. The Italian *Vita Nuova* followed suit in 1925, and the Polish Roman Catholic Union began using English in its journal "to attract youth" in 1929. The German athletic clubs published the *Arbeiter-Sport in Amerika* in both German and English after 1927. Moreover, even as they continued to foster the traditional gymnastic groups, the Turners also adopted such American sports as basketball as a concession to younger members.[45]

A preference for American sports, especially among young ethnic Americans, rose sharply during the 1920s. In 1927 the Polish newspaper *Dziennik Zjednoczenia* advocated rowing, hockey, tennis, volleyball, and basketball to improve the health and appearance of girls. The Polish National Alliance included 320 locals, whose members included one-seventh of all Poles residing in the city. The PNA fielded twenty baseball teams in two leagues, and twenty softball teams were organized into three leagues, as were its twenty-three basketball teams. Even the more strident nationalists, such as the Polish Roman Catholic Union, initiated its own baseball league, and others had founded the Midwest Slovak Catholic Baseball League. At Holy Trinity High School, a Polish institution, boys and girls founded an athletic association to bowl and play basketball and baseball. By the end of the decade its women's basketball team competed with that of the Jewish People's Institute and the native Illinois Women's Athletic Club for the city crown. The Poles also created a Commission of Sports and Youth to finance its athletic clubs in 1929. In addition to a baseball league, bowling and basketball received greater attention within the organization. By 1934 a Chicago team had won a national Sokol basketball championship.

Other groups shared the interest in the native games. Lithuanians also became enamored with basketball, sending a team to the national Catholic tournament in 1930 and exporting the game to the homeland on a YMCA mission the same year. The West Side Sportmen's Association, a club of 150 composed almost entirely of Italians, had been fielding basketball teams since 1927. In 1930 a Slovak won the *Daily News* golf tournament, and Lithuanians founded their own golfers association within three years. By 1936 the Lithuanian newspaper *Jaunimas* sponsored a basketball league. As early as 1931 the Sports Congress of Germans, Poles, Hungarians, and other ethnic groups had convened at Soldier Field, under the auspices of the Chicago *Tribune*.[46]

The "Americanization" programs of the companies, parks, playgrounds, and churches taught the English language to many immigrants and introduced them to the American sport forms. These same programs offered women new sporting opportunities which fulfilled a number of functions. For both native and ethnic women, sport provided escape from the drudgery of work, as well as camaraderie and "bonding" such as that ascribed to the male sporting fraternity. The women claimed that such associations bound them together in a common purpose and engendered lifelong friends. Most important, sporting practices, particularly power sports, such as track, basketball, and softball, allowed women to encroach upon the male domain. Leisure practices and entry into the labor force thus helped to partially dismantle the wall of male hegemony. A solid base, however, remained intact.[47]

Women were less than uniform in their efforts. Although leisure practices allowed them to challenge patriarchy, their struggle was hampered by particular class and religious constraints. Polish women, mostly of peasant stock, deferred to male leadership in their social and athletic clubs, particularly when clergy assumed their traditional roles of leadership. Middle class ethnic women, more educated and self-assured in their status, were also tentative in their approach. Czech women, perhaps because of the greater number of non-religious free-thinkers, assumed active responsibility for change. They served ethnic athletic organizations as officers, administrators, and trustees. They authored books and directed their own efforts. Such ethnic leaders, more attuned to the middle class value system, increasingly led their followers into the American mainstream as federal immigration laws and the Second World War denied them their European lifelines. Ethnic class, religious, and gender differences were supplanted by mobilization efforts as the war approached. Political and racial issues superseded feminism thereafter.[48]

While ethnic clubs originally espoused nationalism and the retention of European customs and traditions, their structure and programs that emphasized order and discipline were also consistent with the industrial model. Ethnic youth who were not members of the fraternal clubs were even more easily swayed by the American sports and games that they learned in the parks, playgrounds, and schools. With the alliance of religious, commercial, and public agencies, patriarchy reestablished itself. Within such structures Americanized women continued to struggle for their athletic rights, visibility, and opportunity.

NOTES

1. Royal Melendy, "The Saloon in Chicago," *American Journal of Sociology* 6 (November 1900): 289–306; 6 (January 1901): 433–64; Josefa Hempel Zeman, "The Bohemian People of Chicago," in *Hull House Maps and Papers*, ed. Richard T. Ely (1895; repr., New York: Thomas Y. Crowell, 1970); Henry Metzner, *History of the American Turners* (1911, rev. ed. Rochester: National Council of American Turners, 1974). An exception is Mari Jo Buhle, *Women and American Socialism, 1870–1920* (Urbana: University of Illinois Press, 1981).

2. Arthur Todd, *Chicago Recreation Survey* 1 (1937): 14; Bruce C. Nelson, "Culture and Conspiracy" (Ph.D. diss., Northern Illinois University, 1985), pp. 28–30.

3. Thorstein Veblen, *Theory of the Leisure Class* (repr. New York: Macmillan, 1989); Richard Sennett, *Families against the City: Middle Class Homes of Industrial Chicago, 1872–1890* (Cambridge, Mass.: Harvard University Press, 1970) regarding the concerns of those who continued to reside within the city. Helen Lefkowitz Horowitz, *Culture and the City* (Lexington: University Presses of Kentucky, 1976) attests to the exclusive and interlocking social network that helped to establish and reinforce the social structure of Chicago. Paul F. Cressey, "The Succession of Cultural Groups in the City of Chicago" (Ph.D. diss., University of Chicago, 1930); David Ward, *Cities and Immigrants: A Geography of Change in Nineteenth Century America* (New York: Oxford University Press, 1971), pp. 133–34, 142.

4. Victor Greene, *For God and Country: The Rise of Polish and Lithuanian Ethnic Consciousness in America, 1860–1910* (Madison: State Historical Society of Wisconsin, 1975), pp. 1–17; Zeman, "The Bohemian People of Chicago," pp. 115–28.

5. Cressey, "Succession of Cultural Groups," pp. 91–92, states that both Poles and Czechs were even more heavily concentrated in ethnic enclaves in 1920 than they had been in 1898. Jarka Jelinek and Jaroslav Zmrhal, *Sokol, Educational and Physical Culture Association* (Chicago: American Sokol Union, 1944), p. 21; American Sokol Organization, *Centennial of the Sokols in America, 1865–1965* (Chicago: National Slet Committee, 1965), n.p.

6. Frank Dobbs, (Ferry, N.Y.: Oceana Publishing, 1973). Renkiewicz, ed., *The Poles in America*, pp. 6–7, 11 places the beginning of the U.S. Movement as late as 1893. Jelinek and Zmrhal, *Sokol*, p. 47, established the date of introduction for the Polish Falcons in Chicago as 1887; while *Dziennik Zjednoczenia*, March 21, 1928, a Polish language daily, sets the date almost a decade earlier in 1878.

7. Zeman, "The Bohemian People of Chicago," p. 122.

8. Hartmut Keil and John B. Jentz, eds., *German Workers in Industrial Chicago*, 1850–1910 (DeKalb: Northern Illinois University Press, 1983).

9. David J. Hogan, *Class and Reform: School and Society in Chicago, 1880–1930* (Philadelphia: University of Pennsylvania Press, 1985), p. 7; Keil and Jentz, eds., *German Workers*, pp. 210, 213; Pierce, *History of Chicago*, vol. 3 p. 243; Nelson, "Culture and Conspiracy," p. 110.

10. Daniel Rodgers, *The Work Ethic in Industrial America* (Princeton: Princeton University Press, 1978), p. 158; Nelson, "Culture and Conspiracy," pp. 101, 135–38, 171–72, 222–24, 258; Buhle, *Women and American Socialism*, p. 22. *Fiftieth Anniversary of the Slovak Gymnastic Union, 1896–1946,* n.p.; American Sokol Organization, *Centennial of the Sokols in America,* n.p.

11. Buhle, *Women and American Socialism*, p. xiii. *Fiftieth Anniversary of the Slovak Gymnastic Union,* n.p.

12. Buhle, *Women and American Socialism*, pp. 110–17, 170–71, 308; Vlasta Vras, ed., *Panorama: Historical Review of Czechs and Slovaks in the United States of America* (Cicero: Czechoslovak National Council of America, 1970), p. 33; Pierce, *History of Chicago*, vol. 3, p. 254.

13. Buhle, *Women and American Socialism*, p. 301; Daniel D. Droba, *Czech and Slovak Leaders in Metropolitan Chicago* (Chicago: Slavonic Club of the University of Chicago, 1934), p. 220; *Fiftieth Anniversary of the Slovak Gymnastic Union Sokol,* n.p.; Sister M. Andrea, "The Societies of St. Stanislaus Kostka, Parish, Chicago," *Polish-American Studies* 9 (January–June, 1952): 27–37; Joseph Parot, *Polish Catholics in Chicago, 1850–1920* (DeKalb: Northern Illinois University Press, 1981), p. 224. *St. Augustine's Parish Golden Jubilee Program and Chronological History, 1886–1936* (Chicago, 1936), pp. 51, 57, 93.

14. Broadside for Turner Picnic, July 27, 1890, at the Chicago Historical Society, Chicago *Tribune*, July 15, 1900, also featured women's races in the nineteenth Annual Caledonian Picnic. American Sokol Organization, *Centennial of the Sokols in America,* n.p.; Chicago *Examiner*, August 28, 1909.

15. George J. Svejda, "The Czechoslovak Immigration to the United States," in Vras, ed., *Panorama*, p. 7, indicates that more than 98 percent of Czech immigrants were literate. American Sokol Organization, *Centennial*, n.p.; *Pamatnik, 1904* (Chicago: Tiskem Narodni Tiskarny), p. 115.

16. *Svornost*, May 20, 1891; *Zgoda*, August 14, 1892, *Dziennik Chicagoski*, October 14, 1892; W.P.A., Foreign Language Press Survey (FLPS), 1942; Oral History of Chicago Polonia, Composite tape, side one, Chicago History Society; *Diamond Jubilee, Immaculate Conception B.V.M. Parish, 1882* (Chicago: 1957), p. 154; Renkiewicz, *The Poles in America*, pp. 13, 62; Robert Slayton, *Back of the Yards* (Chicago: University of Chicago Press, 1986), pp. 80–81; Jelinek and Zmrhal, *Sokol*, p. 47. Joseph Parot, *Polish Catholics in Chicago, 1858–1920*, p. 225; *St. Adalbert: A Tribute to 100 Years of Service, 1874–1974* (n.p.); Hogan, *Class and Reform*, pp. 125–27; Pierce, *History of Chicago*, vol. 3, p. 389, estimates the 1890 figure at 38,000.

17. *Fiftieth Anniversary of the Slovak Gymnastic Union Sokol*, n.p.

18. *Report of the South Parks Commissioners, 1908–1909*, pp. 110–11, 115–16. Mary McDowell, "The Struggle in the Family Life," *Charities* (December 3, 1904), in *The Ordeal of Assimilation*, ed. Feldstein and Costello, pp. 196–97; Amateur Athletic Federation, *Rule and Year Book* (1914), pp. 97–99; City of Chicago, *Annual Report of the Committee on Parks, Playgrounds and Beaches, 1916* (Chicago: Bernard and Miller), pp. 5, 7, 10. Shoop, *Report of Social Centers*, pp. 19–20, 22, 33–6, 40–41; D. M. Krzywonos, ed., *The Poles of Chicago* (Chicago: Polish Pageant, 1937), p. 135.

19. *Annual Report* (1916), p. 34. James H. Timberlake, *Prohibition and the Progressive Movement, 1900–1920* (Cambridge, Mass.: Harvard University Press, 1963), pp. 2, 5–6, 40; Klaus Ensslen and Heinz Ickstadt, "German Working Class Culture in Chicago: Continuity and Change in the Decade from 1900–1910," in *German Workers*, ed. Keil and Jentz, pp. 236–52; Hogan, *Class and Reform*, pp. 76–77; *Denni Hlasatel*, February 28, 1910 (FLPS).

20. *Lietuva*, November 7, 1913 (FLPS); Kingsdale, "The Poor Man's Club," 473; Timberlake, *Prohibition and the Progressive Movement*, pp. 102–4, 138, 150. Rev. Thomas L. Harmon, *Church of the Annunciation, Parish History, 1866–1916* (Chicago: D. B. Hansen & Sns, 1916), p. 25, on the "greatly diminished numbers."

21. "Protection of Immigrant Girls on Arrival at Interior Points," from *First Annual Report of the Immigrants' Protective League of Chicago*, pp. 13–18, in *The Ordeal of Assimilation*, ed. Feldstein and Costello, pp. 86–91; Department of Public Works, *Social Service Directory* (City of Chicago, 1915), pp. 14–15.

22. *St. Augustine's Parish Golden Jubilee Program and Chronological History, 1886–1936* (Chicago: 1936), pp. 63–64, 90–61. Janice Rieff Webster, "Domestication and Americanization: Scandinavian Women in Seattle, 1888–1900," *Journal of Urban History* 3 (May 1978): 275–80. The 1913 survey is cited in Slayton, *Back of the Yards*, pp. 61–62; Krzywonos, ed., *The Poles of Chicago*, pp. 147, 256; Slayton, *Back of the Yards*, p. 59: *Dziennik Zwiazkowy*, August 2, 1926 (FLPS).

23. *Dziennik Zjednoczenia*, May 23, 1913; *Denni Hlasatel*, January 11, 1914 (FLPS).

24. John Higham, *Send These to Me: Immigrants in Urban America* (Baltimore: Johns Hopkins University Press, 1984), p. 52; Rev. Anthony F. LoGatto, *The Italians in*

America, 1492–1972 (Dobbs Ferry, N.Y.: Oceana, 1972), pp. 14–15; Renkiewicz, *The Poles in America*, p. 22.

25. E. C. Delaporte, "Administration and Control of Athletics in the Public Schools," *American Physical Education Review* (March 1922): 100–102.

26. Chicago Public School Athletic League files, 1920.

27. New York *Times*, March 9, 1924.

28. W. A. Cameron, *Chicago Athletic Association Annual Report*, 1908, p. 6. *Sokol Americky*, November 15, 1927; Don Maxwell, ed., *Chicago Tribune Sports Almanac* (1929), p. 194. On Rogers, see Paula Welch, "'32 Track and Field's Annette Rogers," *The Olympian* 10 (February 1984): 12–14; Chicago *Evening American*, July 3, 1930; July 4, 1930. Five of the nine team members were still students.

29. *Chicago Tribune, Sports Almanac* (1927), pp. 211, 295, 335, 341; *Amateur Athletic Federation Handbook* (1929–30), pp. 28–31, 37, 49, 61–68; Chicago *Tribune*, September 15, 1930, p. 15. Harry Sundby-Hansen, ed., *Norwegian Immigrant Contributions to American's Making* (New York: R & E Research Assoc., 1921), pp. 163, 165 for opposition to the professionalization of winter sports.

30. Roy E. Moore, "Gymnastics over the Years," *AAU Golden Anniversary Book*, pp. 12, 60; Charles A. Dean, "The AAU in the Midwest," *AAU Golden Anniversary Book*, p. 18; *Fiftieth Anniversary*, n.p.

31. Todd, *Chicago Recreation Survey* 3 (1938): 117–18.

32. *Golden Anniversary Book, Amateur Athletic Union of the United States, 1888–1938* (AAU: 1938), p. 43; American Sokol Organization, *Centennial*, n.p. *Dejiny: Jednoty Sokol Havlicek-Tyrs, 1911–21* (Chicago: Tiskem Ceske; Tiskarny, 1921); Conversation with Lillian Chorbat, curator of Museum of the Czechoslovak Society of America, and a student of Prchal, January 31, 1990; Jarka Jelinek, *Telocvicna Hlidka* (Chicago: n.d.), p. 56; *Sokol Americky*, July 15, 1933.

33. Schaper, "Industrial Recreation for Women," *American Physical Education Review* 27 (March 1922): pp. 103–13.

34. Chicago *Tribune*, March 25, 1920, on girls' high school basketball. Women's International Bowling Congress, *WIBC History: A Story of 50 Years of Progress, 1916–17; 1966–67* (WIBC: 1967), pp. 4, 9, 11–12; *Reform Advocate* 71 (March 20, 1926): 207; Bernice Amanda Miller, "Growing Need for Physical Recreation among Employed Women," *Journal of Health and Physical Education* 1 (December 1930): 3–8, 43–45. *Chicago Tribune, Sports Almanac* (1927), p. 225; Evans, "The Status of American Women in Sport," pp. 118–19; Chicago *Tribune*, July 4, 1930; July 5, 1930; September 3, 1930; September 14, 1930, on track. See Chicago *Tribune*, January 15, 1930; *Diamond Jubilee Book of St. Aloyisius, 1884–1959* (Chicago: n.p.; 1959), p. 50; *St. Bridget's Church, 1850–1975* (Chicago: Kurash Press, 1975), n.p.; and *Lietuva*, December 11, 1914 (FLPS), on gymnastics.

35. Schaper, "Industrial Recreation for Women," pp. 103–13; *Chicago Tribune*, April 3, 1930; July 1, 1930; July 13, 1930; September 3, 1930. *The Hawthorne Microphone*, December 31, 1928; Chicago *Tribune*, September 14, 1930; July 5, 1931.

36. Sam Darcy, *The Challenge of Youth* (Chicago: Young Workers Communist League, 1926): n.p.; Schaper, "Industrial Recreation for Women," p. 109. Mark Naison, "Righties and Lefties: The Communist Party and Sports during the Great Depression,"

Radical America 13 (July–August 1979): 47–59; Official Program, *First Workers Olympiad of America*, July 3–5, 1936, pp. 8, 10, 55; Dirk Hoerder and Christiane Harzig, eds., *The Immigrant Labor Press in North America* (Westport, Conn.: Greenwood Press, 1987), vol. 3, pp. 331, 390. Vras, ed., *Panorama*, p. 89; Official Program, *First Workers' Olympiad of America*, July 3–5, 1936.

37. Todd, *Chicago Recreation Survey* 3 (1938): 153. Richard C. Wade, "The Enduring Chicago Machine," *Chicago History* 16 (Spring 1986): 5–19; Amalgamated Clothing and Textile Workers Union, "Why Cultural Activity," 1940, pp. 5–7.

38. Amalgamated Clothing and Textile Workers Union, "Why Cultural Activity," p. 6.

39. Todd, *Chicago Recreation Survey* 3 (1938): 150–51.

40. Chicago *American*, March 1, 1929; Public Schools Athletic League, bowling file, 1939–59; *National High School Bowler's Bulletin* 1 (May 15, 1939): 4.

41. Schaper, "Industrial Recreation for Women," p. 109; Jelinek, *Sokol*, pp. 39, 58, 63; Edward R. Kantowicz, "Cardinal Mundelein of Chicago and the Shaping of Twentieth Century American Catholicism," *Journal of American History* 68 (June 1981): 52–68.

42. On Stagg's tournament, Axel Bundgaard, "The World's Greatest Interscholastic," unpublished manuscript. *Chicago Tribune, Sports Almanac* (1927), pp. 206, 213, 226. Chicago *Daily Journal*, January 10, 1925; Chicago *American*, January 10, 1925; *Sandara*, March 21, 1930 (FLPS). *Diamond Jubilee of Immaculate Conception B.V.M. Parish, 1882* (Chicago: 1957), pp. 40–41, 45, 49; *Sacred Heart, 1910–1985* (n.p.), p. 42; St. Wenceslaus Church, *Silver Jubilee, 1912–1937* (Chicago: 1937), p. 19; St. Augustine's *Golden Jubilee*, pp. 224, 227, 280.

43. Archdiocese of Chicago, *Manual for Leaders: CYO Vacation Schools* (Chicago: Catholic Youth Organization, n.d.), pp. 10–11; program, *Testimonial Celebration in Honor of Bishop Bernard J. Sheil*, May 15, 1941.

44. *Denni Hlasatel*, January 30, 1921; May 15, 1922; June 25, 1992; July 11, 1922; July 17, 1922. For other track and gymnastic activities, see *Denni Hlasatel*, September 27, 1906; April 16, 1911; May 23, 1912; January 27, 1913; May 10, 1915; October 12, 1918; May 21, 1920; August 31, 1920; March 30, 1922; May 7, 1922. *Denni Hlasatel*, May 3, 1917; August 23, 1915.

45. *Dziennik Zjednoczenia*, April 27, 1929; *Denni Hlasatel*, February 11, 1917, May 13, 1917; *Vita Nuova* (April 1925); *Dziennik Zjednoczenia*, July 9, 1927; *Bulletin of the Italian American National Union* (April 1925); Hoerder and Harzig, eds., *The Immigrant Labor Press in North America*, vol. 3, pp. 331, 389.

46. *Dziennik Zjednoczenia*, March 8, 1930; April 27, 1929; January 16, 1929; September 14, 1927; July 9, 1927 (FLPS) states that the PRCU bowling league was organized in 1926. *Osadne Hlasy*, January 3, 1930 (FLPS). Chicago *American*, March 5 and 6, 1929; March 7, 1929, on women's basketball championship. *Osadne Hlasy*, August 22, 1930; April 13, 1934 (FLPS); *Sandara*, March 21, 1930 (FLPS); Chicago *Tribune*, April 6, 1930, part 2:2. *Record Book of the Lithuanian Colfers Association* (n.p., n.d.) listed 165 members; *Jaunimas*, December 25, 1936; *Otthon*, June 31, 1931; *Interest*, November 1934 (FLPS).

47. Chicago *Tribune*, April 5, 1910; September 4, 1910.

48. Jennifer Hargreaves, ed., *Sport, Culture and Ideology* (London: Routledge and Kegan Paul, 1982), pp. 12–13.

11

Radical Immigrants and the Workers' Sports Federation of Canada, 1924–37

Bruce Kidd

In Michael Ondaatje's novel about the construction of public works in depression-ravaged Toronto, *In the Skin of a Lion*, the protagonist remembers a night when as a young farm boy in eastern Ontario he had been drawn out into the cold by

> lightning within the trees by the river. . . . The ice shone with light. It seemed for a moment that he had stumbled on a coven, or one of those strange druidic rituals. . . . But even to the boy, deep in the woods after midnight, this was obviously benign. Something joyous. A gift. There were about ten men skating, part of a game. One chased the others and as soon as someone was touched he became the chaser. Each man held in one hand a sheaf of cattails and the tops of these were on fire. This is what lit the ice and had blinked through the trees.
>
> They raced, swerved, fell and rolled on the ice to avoid each other but never let go of the rushes. When they collided sparks fell onto the ice and onto their dark clothes.
>
> It was not just the pleasure of skating. They could have done that during the day. This was against the night. The hard ice was so certain, they could leap into the air and crash down and it would hold them. Their lanterns replaced with new rushes which let them go further past boundaries, speed! romance!
>
> To the boy growing into his twelfth year, having lived all his life on that farm where day was work and night was rest, nothing would be the same.

Years later, while working and living with immigrants, he realized that the magical, midnight skaters of his childhood had been Finns.[1]

Though a work of fiction, Ondaatje's sketch of the athletic exuberance of Finnish-Canadian workers is based on interviews and archival photos. He could well have been describing their real-life passion for the out-of-doors, their seemingly endless energy, and their ability to transform almost any setting into an arena of athletic drama. The haunting imagery of the bewitching hour is appropriate too, not only because as working men (and women) they had little time during "normal" hours for leisure pursuits and often ran, swam, skied, and competed late into the night. Like many other immigrants to Canada in the early years of this century, the Finns pursued these activities in their own clubs, outside the middle class, staunchly pro-British organizations which created and conducted the mainstream sports of Euro-Canadian society.[2] While some gave their ethnocultural organizations a religious character, the Finns and other radical immigrants created a socialist federation, the Workers' Sports Association of Canada, which explicitly contested the bourgeois stamp of establishment sports. Yet their rich experience remains a dark, mysterious corner of Canadian sports history. To be sure, Canadian historians have considered the dominant institutions' response to immigrants, especially the efforts of YMCAs, churches, settlement houses, and schools to accelerate their assimilation through sports and physical education.[3] Others have described the remarkable successes of immigrant athletes on established teams and leagues.[4] But there was another view of this process. As Robert Harney writes:

If many historians see in sport an effective narrative about the good that follows from equality of opportunity, meritocracy, and assimilation, few of them have comprehended as well the obverse story as it would have been emplotted and told by an immigrant narrator. For although willingness to accept a world in which one's children were under the sway of strange adults in the schoolyard or playground rather than contributing to the family economy and submitting to parental discipline and flexibility enough to tolerate the secularization of the sabbath by sports-crazy kids, may have varied from one family to another, almost all would have written the narrative as a tragedy of values and ways lost. . . . Many immigrant parents and most immigrant religious and ethnocultural leaders [saw sports] as a threat to group solidarity, a process of deprivation which meant the loss of ethnoculture, parental control, esteem between generations, and sometimes salvation itself.[5]

In contrast to the receiver society's perspective, this study takes the immigrants' experience as its starting point. The purpose is to bring to light the sporting experience of the radical Finns, Ukrainians, Czechs, Jews, and others who formed the backbone of the workers' sports movement during the interwar years. These groups sought to continue favored activities first learned in their homelands as a way of maintaining contact with those they had left behind, establishing support networks in their new surroundings, preserving language and history, and passing along their traditions to their children. In the small company towns of the resource hinterland, where the middle class was largely absent, they provided the only opportunities available.

But the radical immigrants also saw sports as integral to the task of mounting a "total culture" of opposition to the harsh capitalism in which they lived and creating the beginnings of a new society. Those who lived and worked in cities worried about the numbers of working people joining middle class and corporate associations to play sports and being drawn into the capitalist leisure market as consumers of spectacles and other sports-related commodities. In response, the movement tried to organize class-centered and controlled athletic activity in a way that transcended ethnocultural rivalries. Their publications offered a critique of dominant institutions and practices and an alternative vision of what might be. Unlike other sportspersons of the day, they campaigned politically for their causes—usually against the International Olympic Committee's Olympic Games and for increased state spending on sport and recreation. Why they did so, what they tried, and how well they succeeded will be the subject of this paper.

THE EUROPEAN PRECEDENT

The origins of workers' sports, as an explicitly class-conscious movement, must be traced to Europe. Toward the end of the nineteenth century, European socialist groups and trade unions formed gymnastics and sporting associations, usually as an alternative to upper class clubs from which they were excluded, but occasionally as a cover for otherwise illegal political activity. By 1913 there were sufficient numbers and interest for five national associations to form an international federation, first known as the Lucerne Sports International (after the site of its successful postwar conference) and subsequently as the Socialist Workers' Sports International (SWSI). The SWSI and its member federations were noted for their attempts to improve the quality of working class recreation by providing technical assistance and agitating for improved public facilities and physical education.[6]

The SWSI's crowning achievement was the Workers' Olympics, which it staged in Prague in 1921, Frankfurt am Main in 1925, Vienna in 1931, and Antwerp in 1937. (There were winter games, too, in Schreiberhau, Germany in 1925, Muraaushlag, Austria in 1931, and Johannisbas, Czechoslovakia in 1937.) The Vienna Games were perhaps the most successful athletic festival ever held. 76,245 athletes from 23 countries competed in 220 events in fifteen sports (including "military sport" and motorcycling). In addition, there was a children's sport festival, a fitness biathlon (run-and-swim) for tourists and citizens, artistic displays, dramatic performances, fireworks, and mass exercises. On opening day an estimated 250,000 watched 100,000 men and women parade to the new stadium constructed by the socialist Viennese government; 65,000 spectators watched the soccer finals and 12,000 the cycling finals.[7]

The Workers' Olympics differed significantly from the better-known International Olympic Committee (IOC) Games of the same period. The SWSI made a much more concerted effort to foster international solidarity. After the First World War, the IOC allowed the Belgian and French governments to bar athletes from the "aggressor nations" of Germany and Austria from the 1920 Antwerp and 1924 Paris Games. In response, the SWSI held its 1925 Olympics in Germany under the slogan "No more war." The centerpiece of the opening ceremonies was a mass artistic and gymnastic display symbolizing working class solidarity. Athletes marched and competed as part of national teams, but national flags and anthems were replaced by red flags and revolutionary hymns like "The Internationale." Compared to the IOC's stiff performance standard for entry, the SWSI invited both the record holder and the novice and set no limit on the size of teams. In Vienna, for example, 36,600 worker-athletes were entered by the host Austrian federation, 29,054 by the Germans. Unlike the staunchly patriarchal IOC, the SWSI actively encouraged female participation. Some 25,000 women competed in Vienna. A year later at the IOC's Los Angeles Games, only 107 of the 1,408 competitors were female.[8]

Despite these successes, the movement could not often boast of unity. After the formation of the Communist International in 1921, a minority of workers' sports organizations broke away to form the Red Sport International (RSI). Whereas the SWSI was primarily concerned with conditions *in sport*, the RSI "wanted to build a sport international that was a political instrument of the class struggle; it was not interested in developing a sports system for workers' in a capitalist world."[9] Although physical culturalists in the Soviet Union hotly debated the proper goal of sport and physical activity for the working class,[10] these discussions rarely filtered through to the deliberations and pronouncements of the RSI. Initially, the RSI sought to win adherents by infiltrating SWSI clubs and pushing its own line, without formally affiliating as an organization. When the SWSI, understandably, did not invite the RSI to the Frankfurt Olympics, the RSI tried to stage counterdemonstrations. Only after relations broke down completely did RSI begin to organize events of its own, beginning with the "counter-Olympic" World Spartiakiade in Moscow in 1928.[11] These maneuvers were conducted within the lurches of Comintern policy, which was continually redrafted in response to the internal struggles and foreign policy debates of the Soviet Union. It was not until the Comintern entered the "common front" phase in late 1934—after Hitler had destroyed workers' sports in Germany—and a number of national associations began to push for unity that the two internationals began to patch up their differences. They jointly sponsored the ill-fated "Peoples' Olympics" of Barcelona in 1936, and Soviet athletes competed in the SWSI's Antwerp Games of 1937, but they were never able to agree upon a basis for fusion.

TRANSPLANTING THE MOVEMENT TO CANADA

The ambition of workers' sports was brought to Canada by two intercon-
nected social networks, radical Finnish immigrants and the Communist Party
of Canada. Finnish immigration began in the late 1880s. Some sought to
escape Czarist conscription and repression, others to obtain the farm land
promised by the federal government and railway recruiters or simply for
adventure. By the First World War, 17 percent of all Finnish emigrants were
living in Canada. After the Civil War in Finland, the flow resumed. While most
were described as "farmers" on their immigration cards—even political refugees like Finland's first prime minister, Social Democrat Oskari Tokoi!—very
few ever settled on homesteads. The land they were given was usually unsuit-
able for agriculture, or they lacked the capital and the commitment to make a
go of it. Most ended up as wage laborers in the mines and lumber camps of the
resource hinterlands of northern Ontario and British Columbia, or as trades-
persons in the cities. There they quickly developed a reputation for labor
radicalism.

Many of them had been socialists or active in the cooperative movement in
Finland, so it was hardly surprising that they formed similar organizations to
combat difficult economic conditions, racial prejudice, exploitative employers,
and a repressive state in Canada. Finnish forestry workers played a leading
role in organizing the Lumber Workers Industrial Union of Canada and the
Finnish Socialist Organization of Canada, later renamed the Finnish Organization of Canada (FOC). They also made common cause with Canadian socialists, and became active in the Socialist Party of Canada, the Social Democratic
Party of Canada, and the Communist Party of Canada, formed in 1922.[12]
Although such activity led to their removal from the federal government's
"preferred immigrants" list in 1919, they continued to come in large numbers
throughout the 1920s, many to escape the persecution of left-wingers which
followed the Civil War.[13]

The Finns always seemed to possess a larger-than-life *joie de vivre,* and in
the nineteenth century, despite—or perhaps because of—their inclusion in
the Russian Empire where the highly organized and rule-bound approach to
game contests we call sport today was virtually unknown, they were quick to
adopt it. From the very beginnings of international competition, they entered
distinct Finnish teams and they excelled in both the SWSI and IOC Olympics.[14] (Some like to boast that they "ran their way onto the map of the
world!") The enthusiasm for sport seems to have been shared by men and
women of all classes and political perspectives. In Canada, wherever they
settled in numbers, they created a rich social and cultural life for themselves,

usually in their community halls or *haali*. They ran educational meetings and camps for their children, published and discussed their own newspapers, novels, and political literature, wrote and performed their own plays, and listened and danced to their own choral groups and orchestras. They also formed sports clubs. By 1910 there were clubs in Toronto, Cobalt, Copper Cliff, Garson Mine, Port Arthur, and Sellwood, with heroic names like Endeavor (*Yritys*), Frolicking brothers and sisters (*Kisa Veljet—Kisa Siskot*), Energy (*Tarmo*), and Hard Blow (*Isku*). Their boundless energy bubbles up during interviews, and it jumps off photographs and out of minute books.

The Finns were prepared to compete against all comers. In 1920 one Toronto Yritys wrestler, Enok Lopponen, represented Canada in the IOC's Olympics in Antwerp. In northern Ontario and British Columbia, they frequently staged "dual meets" and games with athletes from nearby native reserves. But after the creation of a Workers' Sports League (TUL) in Finland in 1919, and the growing Young Communist League interest in a sports movement, both of which were followed through the Finnish-language press,[15] they created an exclusively workers' federation. In 1924 the clubs in the Sudbury area formed the Central Ontario Gymnastics and Sports Federation. A year later the northern and northwestern Ontario clubs joined, and the new association was renamed the Finnish Workers' Sports Association of Canada (FWSAC). Its objectives were "to raise the physical, intellectual, and cultural level of workers by promoting an interest in physical activity; and to further the country's militant labour movement."[16] The FWSAC was closely associated with, but never formally affiliated to, the FOC. The first secretary was Hannes Sula, a former Finnish champion in the 100 meters, who had been a fierce Red partisan during the Civil War. He was also the editor of *Vapaus*, the FOC's daily newspaper.[17]

The favored Finnish activities were track and field and gymnastics in the summer, "classical" or Greco-Roman wrestling (which they liked because of its spectacular over-the-head throws) and cross-country skiing in the winter. Even if they only had a small clearing or a corduroy road, they tried to race, throw the javelin, and perform mass drill. In many communities, they blasted rock and cleared trees and stumps to level out athletic fields and running tracks (usually 300 or 400 meters and always metric), and they built *haali* which could serve as gymnasiums. They built most of their own equipment, including track and field implements, wrestling mats, gymnastic apparatus, and skis. They competed intensely in track and field, and they were always conscious of their own records. (In 1933, at the peak of membership, Finnish-Canadian athletes held *all* of the WSAC's senior men's records.)

Most WSAC competitions were held at Finnish grounds, such as Toronto Yritys' Camp Tarmola (in the Don Valley until 1927, and then near Woodbridge). While they did not compete in gymnastics, each year a central committee determined a set of routines to be practiced by individual clubs. These would then be performed en masse at the annual summer festival (called the *liittojuhla*). In the winter, skiing was a way of life for many ("you skied to the outhouse, you skied to work and the grocery"), but they raced, too—for "sweaters and socks, not that useless bourgeois stuff, cups and medals," as one participant remembered. In the mining districts, they practiced at night with the aid of their miners' lamps. Girls and women were encouraged to participate in everything but wrestling. Most practice sessions, competitions, and festivals ended with the sauna.[18]

The Finns often traveled long distances to engage in these events, even if it meant hopping freight cars ("the slide-door pullman") or bundling up in open trucks. Several Toronto participants told me about traveling to Sudbury in winter in an open truck to compete in a wrestling meet. In the collection of Montreal's *Jousi* ("Cross-bow") Athletic Club, a photo shows twenty-two men and women from the Toronto Yritys Club who had ridden there in a small truck for a track meet. While there are mattresses laid out on the truck bed, there is almost no room for sitting. One other annual trek is noteworthy. During the 1930s, when many were unemployed with lots of time on their hands, the clubs around Sudbury and Timmins would each stage a ski race. One week, the men from Sudbury would ski to Timmins, a distance of some 240 kilometers, stopping at lumber camps along the way, race, and then return. Two weeks later, the Timmins men would do the same in the opposite direction. By comparison, the longest ski race in Canada today, the Canadian Ski Marathon from Lachine to Ottawa, is a mere(!) 160 kilometers.

The Finns' political focus was sharpened by parallel developments in the socialist world. In the early 1920s, the youth wing of the fledgling Communist Party of Canada sought to implement the instructions of the Comintern and the Young Communist International (YCI) to create sports clubs on the RSI model. "Sport," the Young Communist League (YCL) told its members, is

an essential part of League work. Baseball should be the most popular, but hikes and runs and boxing and swimming can all be added. But these sports must be turned from commercial antagonistic games into "Red Sports." . . . They are recruiting agencies because they are beneficial to League membership at large and develop a feeling of comradeship and vitality.[19]

The League hoped the WSAs would help win sympathetic and uncommitted non-party members to the cause.

The YCLers quickly took up the challenge. In 1925 soccer teams were started in Montreal, Toronto, and Winnipeg (the latter called the "Hammer and Sickle Club"), and smaller centers such as Oshawa, Renfrew, Kirkland Lake, Lethbridge, Sylvan Lake (the "Red Hope Club"), and Drumheller reported field days, team games, boxing clubs, swimming parties, picnics, and "tramps" or hikes. By 1926 WSAs were established in 17 centers. The Toronto WSA operated a seven-team softball league, with two teams of cigar makers, one of jewelers, one from the Earlscourt Labour Party, and three WSA teams. The Montreal WSA fielded senior and junior soccer and basketball leagues and attracted a large following. "You didn't have to be a communist to go to Fletcher's Field on a Saturday afternoon and cheer for the WSA," one participant has remembered.[20] During the 1930s the Toronto and Montreal WSA soccer teams played each other on an annual basis, and these games attracted crowds as large as 5,000. (Montreal usually won.) Games were followed by speeches, songs, a collection, and an invitation to the WSA dance in the evening.

The WSAs encouraged a diversity of activity, but the staple was the mass drills, acrobatics, and stunts of gymnastics. The great majority of WSA members were eastern European immigrants for whom these were familiar, if not favorite, activities. Gymnastics could be practiced almost anywhere, in backyards, community halls, and parks. Routines could be set to music and combined with choral and theatrical performances in movement "concerts" of great appeal.[21] In Toronto, a Jewish Workers' Sports Club held competitions in the "Olympic" events, but elsewhere gymnastics were pursued for mass exercise and display. Usually an entire group would participate in sequences of carefully coordinated field or floor exercises, while smaller groups and individuals would perfect statue posing, and apparatus, tumbling, and acrobatic stunts: hand and head balancing; teeter, trapeze, and trampoline twists and spins; and sometimes juggling. The most frequently performed routine was the multiperson pyramid, which the YCL encouraged because it was believed to depict the importance of working class solidarity during the class struggle. Clubs also sought to develop comedy routines for their regular "concerts."[22]

During the 1930s, the Winnipeg WSA developed gymnastics to such a level that many of its members subsequently made careers for themselves as circus and nightclub performers. The driving forces were Walter Kaczor and his younger brother, Fred. They came from a left-wing family, had been members of the YCL, and their older brother Mike had been a circus acrobat. Although Walter had competed in gymnastics for the YMCA, he was disillusioned by that organization's "failure to do anything for anybody who wasn't a star," and he wanted to create a more accessible club. In 1931, with $100 in savings from his job at the Canadian Pacific Railway:

he bought and cleaned all the remaining equipment from a defunct Y on Selkirk Street and set up shop in a room we rented above a store. In no time at all, we had so many members that we had to get our own hall. We found an old ballroom on Dufferin Street, with a beautiful hardwood floor, a stage and a balcony, and a kitchen in the basement. It cost $60 a month in the winter, $40 in the summer so we paid the rent by holding dances every Sunday, charging 10 cents admission, five cents for checking. We usually made enough to hire a live band. At first, some gangs and then the cops gave us trouble, but we got 20 of our most muscular gymnasts to put on a show at intermission and then serve as bouncers and that seemed to intimidate them.[23]

Club membership was 25 cents a month—free for the unemployed and their children—and it gave admission to all activities and a subscription to the mimeographed newsletter, "The Universal Sportlite." As the membership grew—by the late 1930s it averaged 500—the Kazcors developed their own leadership training program and recruited sympathizers with professional skills to help with administration.

The Winnipeg WSA offered twice-weekly classes in weight training, bodybuilding, boxing, wrestling, swimming, table tennis, snowshoeing, and skiing; it conducted summer camps for children; and it fielded teams in basketball, volleyball, and softball ("never hockey—it was already well organized"). It was best known, however, for gymnastics. Almost every week, its top squad traveled to small towns in Manitoba, northwestern Ontario, and North Dakota, staging displays. ("These were farming communities," Fred Kazor has recalled, "they always wanted to feed us, and most of our kids were always hungry. Sometimes they ate so much they had trouble performing.") Twice a year, the club staged a choral and gymnastics festival in the 1,000-seat Winnipeg Auditorium.

In urban clubs, radical Ukrainian immigrants and their children usually provided most of the members. Ukrainian immigration to Canada began in the 1890s, increased dramatically in the decade prior to World War I, and quickened again after the war. Most immigrants had been peasants in the overpopulated western Ukraine, and they went straight to the prairies where they struggled with the soil, the railroads, the bugs, and the banks to eke out a living on their homesteads. Despite constant Anglo-Saxon chauvinism, they were politically conservative. Later they would support the movement for an independent Ukraine and agitate against the Soviet Union. But a few ended up in cities and the industrial projects in the resource hinterlands and worked as unskilled or semi-skilled laborers. These became the radicals who joined or formed trade unions, supported socialist political struggles, and created cultural organizations to provide resources and a social basis for this activity. The first of these, the Taras Shevchenko Society, was formed in Winnipeg in 1904 with a membership of 400. The establishment of the Soviet Union inspired many more, and by 1924 there were enough to establish a national federation, the Ukrainian Labour Farmer Temple Association (ULFTA).[24]

Unlike the Finns, the Ukrainians did not have a strong sports tradition of their own. While their community halls and summer camp grounds could be used for gymnastics and other forms of athletics, they rarely did so. Dave Kashtan, the WSAC national secretary in the early 1930s, has argued that many of the Ukrainian-Canadian members would never have taken up sport if it were not for the WSAs.[25] While the Ukrainian members rarely entered the track and field and other competitions, they were outstanding gymnasts. Many of them became very successful leaders and instructors. Other WSA members came from British, Czech, Hungarian, and Jewish backgrounds. In order to minimize divided ethnocultural loyalties, the WSAs signed up members directly, even if they were also members of affiliates like the ULFTA (whose facilities the clubs often used). The only exceptions to this practice were the Finns, whose clubs had been formed well before the WSAs came into being.

Both the FWSAC and the YCL wanted to create a national body that could inspire working people and link up with the European movement. The first attempt in 1927 failed when no club outside Toronto was able to send a representative to the founding convention. But the leaders persisted, and the Workers' Sports Association of Canada was created a year later. Twenty clubs joined directly, and the ULFTA, the twenty-club FWSAC, and the Canadian Party of Labour became affiliates.[26] The national committee began to organize leadership training and regional and national events.[27] In 1929 the WSAC joined the RSI. In 1932 the Finnish clubs agreed to dissolve the FWSAC and join directly, enabling the WSAC to claim a total membership of 4,000 in fifty clubs from New Waterford, Nova Scotia, to Ladysmith, B.C.[28] In 1933 membership was 5,000.[29] Although turnover was high, the organization had a presence in many communities, no mean accomplishment.

AGAINST "BOSSES' SPORTS"

The YCL's approach to sport was heavily influenced by its reading of Marxist-Leninist theory and its directives from the YCI. During the 1920s and early 1930s its primary concern was advancing the possibilities for revolutionary change. This was especially the case after 1927, when the CI leadership came to believe that the capitalist world was entering a prolonged crisis.[30] The WSAs were repeatedly admonished to win other workers away from "bosses'" or "bourgeois" sports organizations, and to turn them from "sport for sport's sake" to physical activity with a revolutionary purpose. "Sports is the stronghold of the bourgeoisie so far as the youth is concerned," the YCL decided in its 1925 convention. "Our sport must have no other object than the attacking of that stronghold and the capture of it, if possible."[31]

The League tried to break bourgeois ideological hegemony in sports by demonstrating the class character of mainstream sports in speeches during WSA events and articles in the party press:

To many workers, sports are still neutral, in other words they claim that sports have nothing to do with the class struggle, merely being a beneficial method of bettering one's physical self, developing the spirit of fair play and so on ad infinitum. This is certainly false.

The bosses today use sports as a means of drawing the workers away from the class struggle, they use it as a means of drawing the workers into the cadets, preparing them for future wars, to combat the radicalism of the workers, for increasing productivity, and so on.[32]

It also sought to discredit the organizations it regarded as competitors: the YMCA and YMHA, the Boy Scouts, and the Amateur Athletic Union (AAU). The YMCA was repeatedly "exposed" for its "despicable role in suppressing workers in India, China, Korea, etc."[33] and in North America, for strike-breaking[34] and masking the fundamental antagonisms of class relations. The Boy Scouts, "future White Guards," were picketed for their militaristic exercises and their loyalty to British imperialism.[35] WSAs demonstrated against AAU championships and the British Empire Games, held their summer events under "counter-Olympic" banners, and sent athletes to the RSI's Spartiakiades and the ill-fated Barcelona "People's Olympics" in 1936.[36] In the face of the growing industrial recreation movement, they tried to organize oppositional factory leagues.[37] They marched for the unemployed, passed the hat for jailed union and political leaders, and guarded the podium during political rallies. "The fascists never entered the North End (of Winnipeg) as long as the WSA was around," one communist boasted.[38]

Instead of "bosses' sport," the YCL espoused a militantly partisan movement which would play a leading role in not only union organizing and strikes, but other mass struggles. All recreational activity, it argued, ought to have a direct relationship to the needs of class struggle. Games, picnics, and children's camps were to be organized around collective tasks and the legends and aspirations of communism. The polemic against "sport for sport's sake" constantly reminded members that these activities had an ultimate, external purpose. "Recreations are serious work," N. Gollam explained in *The Worker*:

even if the work is done in an atmosphere of laughter and frolic, social activities tie those who belong to the League in that closer comradeship that comes from common understanding. They keep the youth in contact with the work that is being done for the union of all the militant youth into one organization for the great task that lies before the workers of the world.[39]

The best example of what was necessary was to be found in the Soviet Union. The WSAs were repeatedly told that Soviet athletes "vied with each other in raising production"[40] and trained for the defense of the revolution. In 1930, for example, a relay of cross-country skiers assisted the Red Army in its offensive against "Chinese bandits" along the Manchurian border. *The Young Worker* reported:

This was no mere "endurance test" as we see in capitalist sports. This was no crazed effort to break a "record." The Soviet sportsmen have given the lie to the empty slogan of "sport for sport's sake"! In all their campaigns, they have taken their full share as the physically most perfect specimens of the Russian working class in the construction of socialism. The working sportsmen of Canada must take their full share also in the struggles of the Canadian working class.[41]

Not surprisingly, few WSA members viewed their participation with quite the same revolutionary ardor. Most clubs struggled just to keep going. In 1927 in Drumheller, the WSA had to close when local businessmen refused to rent it enough space.[42] Clubs lost members because workers moved to find work, or they sought the better equipment and coaching provided by the Y and the AAU. Other needs were knowledgeable leaders, rule books, uniforms, and funds for travel. In these circumstances, club secretaries demanded practical help, not words. "We must maintain a proper balance between propaganda and serious athletics," the Alberta secretary advised. "A successful team should give us all the propaganda we care for."[43] On the few occasions it chose to acknowledge these criticisms, the national WSA committee responded by urging more YCLers to become involved, but to no avail.

Even the best clubs resented the criticisms of "sport for sport's sake." Most members were sympathetic to left-wing causes, but their chief motivation in joining the WSA was to participate in physical activity. They were not eager to drop what they were doing for the unlikely projects the YCL wanted—trying to win members away from the YMCA or leafleting plant gates in an attempt to establish factory leagues. "I guess I was primarily interested in what they called 'sport for sport's sake'," Emmanuel Orlick, once the director of the London WSA and a national training school for WSA leaders, has recalled:

I shared some of their criticisms of the Y—I was upset that it wouldn't lower its membership fees for the unemployed, for example—so I helped them form the London WSA (actually we called it the London Unemployed League). But I had no intention of publicly discrediting the Y or running a campaign against it—I was working there at the time and I got a room at the Y for the League to use. I was always prepared to defend the WSA in public, but I wanted a career in physical education, and it didn't look like the WSA had anything like that in mind. They wanted me to do everything myself.[44]

Although Orlick would remain a thorn in the side of the "bourgeois sports organizations" for the rest of his life,[45] he "eventually lost interest in the WSA and left." The Kaczors never left—in fact, in 1935 Fred traveled to Toronto to become national organizer—but they have said much the same. As their reputation grew, they continued to be critical of the sports establishment, and they lobbied for improved public programs, but they abhorred the idea that the athletes they coached were regarded as defense corps by the party. They welcomed the invitations to perform and parade because they gave them something to train for, not because they advanced the class struggle. "Most athletes—even the political ones—came to the gym because they wanted to work out," Walter Kaczor said. "They didn't want to discuss the political questions there."

Of course, the YCL had other worries and responsibilities. "I was once walking down St. Lawrence Avenue [in Montreal] posting notices for the Spartakiad campaign," Dave Kashtan, national WSA secretary from 1930 to 1932, has remembered:

I came across 200 French-Canadian ladies who had just walked off the job because the foreman had just fired somebody. So I spoke to them briefly and led them back to our office. They needed someone to negotiate for them, find strike support, places for people to live because they didn't have any money, and so on. It was two weeks before I even looked at the Spartakiad posters again.[46]

In addition to sports and union organizing, Kashtan and the few other full-time organizers were also responsible for contributing to the party journals, establishing youth centers, and conducting political education. Most of them had very little previous experience in sport. During the early 1930s, several of them, including Kashtan and his brother Bill, the national secretary, were arrested (for "sedition" and "vagrancy" respectfully) and jailed. Dave Kashtan's imprisonment came shortly after he had agreed to start a WSA sports magazine. It was never printed. Several WSAs were victims of the same repression—clubs in Toronto, Oshawa, Lachine, and Vancouver reported events that were canceled or broken up by the police.[47] There was also the time-consuming struggle to maintain "life and love." ("During the first two years of our marriage, we were evicted fourteen times," Kashtan remembers.) Yet even if the YCL leaders had the time, there is little indication they would have addressed the practical needs of the WSAs. Their annual resolutions stressed the instrumental importance of political work. Little effort was ever made to pool the talents and experience of the different clubs to strengthen the WSAC *as a sports movement.*

ETHNOCULTURAL TENSIONS

The YCL's failure to address the WSAs' sports-related needs eventually cost it the strongest section, the Finnish clubs. After the WSAC was founded, the YCL began to press the Finnish members to give up their separate identity. This demand took two forms, both stemming from Comintern directives. The WSAC sought to "liquidate" the FWSAC in the interests of building a "unified" national organization.[48] The Finns were also urged to take up "mass Canadian games" and throw their considerable organizational skills into recruiting English-speaking workers. "We do not wish to be too critical of the Finnish Workers' Sports, which form the vanguard of our movement," *The Young Worker* wrote during the midst of this campaign, "but there is a strong need for augmenting these individual sports with popular group sports such as hockey, basketball, football and baseball, which will more readily interest the broad strata of workers in mines, factories, and farms."[49] Initially, in 1932, the FWSAC agreed to dissolve. The Finnish clubs became direct members of the District associations. Yet five years later they reestablished their own national organization, the Finnish-Canadian Amateur Sports Federation, and ended all formal ties with the WSAC.

Other scholars have stressed the ethnic divisions in the working class. Within the communist movement, they were so strong that they ultimately defeated the CPC's campaign to create a membership undifferentiated by language.[50] They also contributed to the ultimate breakup of the WSAC. In 1932 the Finns' strenuous objections forced it to abandon the "Canadianizing" campaign. While they put out the welcome mat for athletes from other communities, they were impatient with the other groups' relative lack of competitiveness and felt much more comfortable with just their own clubs. There was another factor, too. Many of the Finnish sportspersons felt uneasy with the political line of the WSA. This must have been difficult for English-Canadian leaders like Kashtan to read, for the Finnish sports leaders shared the CPC's revolutionary goals and openly campaigned for them. The FWSAC restricted membership to trade unionists and those associated with the FOC. Some clubs bitterly opposed competition with anybody else. One participant recounted a family which had been "run out of Beaver Lake because the father had traveled through Amsterdam to watch the bourgeois Olympics (of 1928) on his way back from Finland."[51] A number of the Finnish members volunteered for Soviet Karelia and the Spanish Civil War. Yet they were not prepared to reduce every aspect of participation to an instance of class struggle. Many of them liked to run or ski or wrestle better than anything else. They were also heavily influenced by the social democratic traditions of the SWSI. The few communists who remained in Finland after the Civil War did not form their own sports organization, but stayed as a faction within TUL and competed in the Workers' Olympics. They continually pushed for the fusion of the two internationals. The Finns in Canada avidly read the extensive TUL sports press, and occasionally brought over TUL instructors and athletes to conduct clinics and stage exhibitions. They, too, believed in a measure of "sport for sport's sake."

The split was precipitated by the WSA's frequent lack of organization. By 1935, although Kashtan had been replaced by the Finnish athlete Jim Turner (Terho Tuori), the Finns became convinced that

the WSAC was going nowhere. It couldn't in reality fulfill the organization's goals. Meetings were never called, debts grew, and the level of activity declined. The district executives seemed neither interested nor capable of organizing any ongoing events. Only the Finnish clubs were paying dues. There were forty Finnish clubs with 2,000 members, men were idle because of the depression, and we had nothing to do.[52]

At the urging of Toronto Yritys, the Finns pushed for a more active national executive and created a technical committee, composed entirely of their own members, to coordinate their own events. But the frustrations continued. A year later the technical committee complained that "the (national) executive has for a long time been totally incapable of directing affairs and it has apparently gone to sleep." After another year of unfulfilled promises, the Finnish members decided to reestablish their own association. They continued to invite the other clubs to their events, but they gave up on the national movement.[53]

After the Finns departed, the WSAC wound up its affairs. (The RSI ceased to function about the same time.) But individual clubs continued, and some like the Winnipeg WSA (renamed the "Universal Athletic Club" after the CPC's 1935 turn to the "united front") grew stronger than ever. It became so well known as a training center for recreation leaders that the Manitoba government hired senior members to conduct its own leaders' courses.[54] In 1940 the RCMP seized the facilities of organizations sympathetic to the CPC, including the FOC and ULFTA, and much of the remaining activity came to a halt (though after the Soviet Union was recognized as an ally, many WSA leaders became fitness instructors in the army.) After the war, the FCASF and some gymnastic clubs affiliated with the ULFTA (renamed the Association of United Ukrainian Canadians in 1946) resumed. A few aging clubs continue to this day. But most members' children are happy to participate in "Canadian" sports in mainstream organizations. While workers' sports organizations still flourish in Austria, Finland, and France and there is still an international—le Comité Sportif International du Travail—they have little contact with Canada.

Despite its ultimate failure, the WSA still merits our attention. However stridently it presented its views, it represented the only sustained attempt by a sector of the Canadian working class to criticize and challenge bourgeois hegemony in the field of sports. Only in the last two decades have the questions it raised been taken up again, this time by professional scholars.[55] More important, the WSA provided many immigrants with recreational opportunities they otherwise might not have had, in an environment which not only respected but affirmed their non-British heritage. Participants still remember their years in the WSAs with gratitude and fondness. Despite the brief campaign for "Canadian sports," the WSAs gave practical encouragement to several continental European athletic traditions, notably gymnastics and nordic skiing. During the interwar years, the AAU excluded all but naturalized citizens from its major events and discouraged the development of competitive gymnastics because it was "ethnic."[56] Canada did not send a gymnastics team to the Olympics until 1956. Ironically, it was two former WSA leaders, Fred Kazor and Em Orlick, who sparked this interest. In the existing histories of Canadian skiing, no mention is made of the Finns, despite their incredible feats of endurance.

NOTES

1. Michael Ondaatje, *In the Skin of a Lion* (Toronto: McClelland and Stewart, 1987), pp. 20–22.

2. See Alan Metcalfe, *Canada Learns To Play* (Toronto: McClelland and Stewart, 1987). Of course, the term "British" covers a wide variety of influences; see also Gerald Redmond, *The Sporting Scots of Nineteenth Century Canada* (Rutherford, N.J.: Fairleigh Dickinson University Press, 1982).

3. Carl Berger, *The Sense of Power* (Toronto: University of Toronto Press, 1970), L. M. McKee, "'Nature's Medicine': The Physical Education and Outdoor Recreation Programs in Toronto Volunteer Youth Groups," in *Proceedings of the 5th Canadian Symposium on the History of Sport and Physical Education*, ed. B. Kidd (Toronto: School of Physical and Health Education, University of Toronto, 1982), pp. 128–39; and Morris Mott, "One Solution to the Urban Crisis: Manly Sports and Winnipeggers, 1900–1914," *Urban History Review* 12 (1983), pp. 57–70.

4. A. V. Spada, *The Italians in Canada* (Montreal: Riviera, 1969), pp. 167–70; and Gerald Redmond, *Sport and Ethnic Groups in Canada* (Calgary: Canadian Association for Health, Physical Education and Recreation, 1978), pp. 66–75.

5. "Homo Ludens and Ethnicity," *Polyphony* 7 (1985), p. 2.

6. Comité Sportif International du Travail, *50 ans de sport ouvrier international* (Brussels: CSIT, 1963); Robert F. Wheeler, "Organized Sport and Organized Labor: The

Workers' Sports Movement," *Journal of Contemporary History* 13 (1978): 252–65; and *Der internationale Arbeitersport*, ed. James Riordan and Arnd Kruger (Cologne: Pahl Rugenstein, 1985).

7. James Riordan, "The Workers' Olympics," in *The Five-Ring Circus*, ed. Tomlinson and Whannel (London: Pluto, 1984), pp. 98–112; and souvenirs and clippings in the British Library of Political and Economic Science, George Elvin Papers.

8. Erich Kamper, *Encyclopedia of the Olympic Games* (New York: McGraw Hill, 1972), p. 297.

9. David S. Steinberg, "Sport under Two Flags: The Relations between the Red Sport International and the Socialist Workers' Sport International, 1920–1939" (Ph.D. diss., University of Wisconsin, 1979), p. 44.

10. James Riordan, *Sport in Soviet Society* (Cambridge: Cambridge University Press, 1977), pp. 82–152.

11. This term was first applied to an athletic festival by Czech communists in 1921. See G. A. Carr, "The Spartakiad: Its Approach and Modification from the Mass Displays of the Sokol," *Canadian Journal of History of Sport* 18 (1987), pp. 86–96.

12. For a history of these earlier parties, see Martin Robin, *Radical Politics and Canadian Labour* (Kingston: Centre for Industrial Relations, Queen's University, 1968) and A. Ross McCormack, *Reformers, Rebels, and Revolutionaries: The Western Canadian Radical Movement 1899–1919* (Toronto: University of Toronto Press, 1977). For the CPC, see Ivan Avakumovic, *The Communist Party of Canada* (Toronto: McClelland and Stewart, 1965); William Rodney, *Soldiers of the International: A History of the Communist Party of Canada 1919–1929* (Toronto: University of Toronto Press, 1965); Norman Penner, *The Canadian Left* (Scarborough: Prentice-Hall, 1977); and Gerry van Hauten, *Canada's Party of Socialism: History of the Communist Party of Canada* (Toronto: Progress, 1982).

13. For Finnish immigration and settlement, see Varpu Lindstrom-Best, "The Impact of Canadian Immigration Policy on Finnish Immigration, 1890–1978," *Siirtolaisuus Migration* 8 (1981): 5–15; idem, ed., "Finns in Ontario," *Polyphony* 3 (1981); idem, *The Finnish Immigrant Community of Toronto 1887–1913* (Toronto: Multicultural History Society of Ontario, 1979); idem, *The Finns in Canada* (Ottawa: Canadian Historical Association, 1985); and Donald Wilson, "Ethnicity and Cultural Retention: Finns in Canada, 1890–1920," *Review Journal of Philosophy and Social Science* 2 (1977): 217–35. For accounts of their politics, see Auvo Kostianinen, *The Forging of Finnish-American Communism, 1917–1924* (Turku: Migration Institute, 1978); Edward W. Laine, "Finnish Canadian Radicalism and Canadian Politics: The First Forty Years," in *Ethnicity, Power and Politics*, ed. Jorgen Dahlie and Tissa Fernando (Toronto: Methuen, 1981), pp. 94–112.

14. See Seppo Hentila, *Suomen Tyolais Urheilen Historia* (Hameenlinna: Arvi A. Karito Oy, 1982, 1984, 1988); and "Finland and Olympism," *Olympic Review* 103–4 (1976): 252–72.

15. Toronto Yritys raised money to support both TUL's founding and its sending a team to the 1921 Workers' Olympics in Prague.

16. Hannes Sula, Paavo Vaurio, and Jim Tester, "The Federation through the Years," in *Sports Pioneers: A History of the Finnish-Canadian Amateur Sports Federation 1906–1986*, ed. Jim Tester (Sudbury: Alerts Historical Committee, 1986), p. 7.

17. Tester, ed., *Sports Pioneers*; H. Sula, "Urheilu ja canadan suomalainen jarjesto," in *Canadan Suomalainen Jarjesto 25 vuotta* (Sudbury: Vapaus, 1936), and Finnish Canadian Amateur Sports Federation, *Canadan Suomalaisten Urheilukurja* (Sudbury: Vapaus, 1965).

18. *Sports Pioneers*; and interviews with Max Ilomaki, Alex Hunnakko, Helen Tarvainen, William Heikkila, and others.

19. Archives of Ontario, *Young Worker*, February 28, 1925.

20. Interview with Dave Kashtan, October 6, 1981.

21. *The Young Worker*, December 1927.

22. This material has been taken from interviews with Fred and Walter Kaczor (Fred later changed his surname to Kazor), Em Orlick, Ilomaki, Hunnakko, and others. For the YCL's view, see Archives of Ontario, *The Worker*, April 28, 1928.

23. Interview with Fred Kazor, June 27, 1977. (Kazor dropped the "c" from his name during World War II.) See also, "The Story of a Man," *Universal Sportlite*, January 1, 1939, pp. 4, 9.

24. Anthony Bilecki, William Repka, and Mitch Sago, *Friends in Need* (Winnipeg: Workers' Benevolent Association of Canada, 1972); John Kolasky, *The Shattered Illusion* (Toronto: Peter Martin, 1979), and O. W. Gerus and J. E. Rea, *The Ukrainians in Canada* (Ottawa: Canadian Historical Association, 1985).

25. Interview with David Kashtan, May 26, 1987.

26. *Young Worker*, May 1928. Hannes Sula always claimed the initiative for the WSAC. See his "Urheilu ja canadan suomalainen," pp. 155–56. I am grateful to Varpu Lindstrom-Best for translating this and other Finnish documents.

27. *The Worker*, February 2, 1929.

28. *The Worker*, October 1, 1932.

29. *Young Worker*, July 19, 1933. This figure was the largest ever claimed by the WSAC.

30. Fernando Claudin, *The Communist Movement: From Comintern to Cominform* (Harmondsworth: Penguin, 1975) and E. H. Carr, *The Twilight of the Comintern* (New York: Pantheon, 1982). During this period the CPC took few positions independent of the CI.

31. *Young Worker*, July 1925.

32. *Young Worker*, November 1929.

33. *Young Worker*, June 15, 1931.

34. *The Worker*, January 12, 1924.

35. *The Worker*, May 24, 1924. Scholars have taken a similar view; see John Springhall, *Youth, Empire and Society* (London: Croom Helm, 1977).

36. Bruce Kidd, "Canadian Opposition to the 1936 Olympics," *Canadian Journal of History of Sport and Physical Education* 9 (1978): 20–40.

37. Communist Party of Canada Headquarters Records, *Party Organizer*, May 1931, pp. 24–25.

38. Interview with Andrew Bileski, who held elected office for many years in Winnipeg.

39. *The Worker*, August 29, 1923.

40. *The Worker*, October 28, 1928.

41. *Young Worker*, June 1930.

42. *Young Worker*, February 1928.

43. *Young Worker*, October 1926.

44. Interview with Orlick.

45. Sheila I. Salmela and John H. Salmela, "Emmanuel Orlick: Canada's Gymnastic Pioneer" (paper delivered at the Département d'éducation physique, Université de Montreal).

46. Interview October 6, 1981.

47. The police stopped a boxing tournament in Toronto (*Young Worker*, May 19, 1931) and seized schedules, membership lists, and equipment in a raid on the Vancouver WSA (*Young Worker*, December 17, 1932).

48. *Young Worker*, May 1930.

49. *Young Worker*, April 20, 1931.

50. Avakumovic, *Communist Party*, pp. 35–38; Kolasky, *Shattered Illusion*, pp. 1–26; and Donald Avery, "Ethnic Loyalties and the Proletarian Revolution: A Case Study of Communist Political Activity in Winnipeg, 1923–36," in Dahlie and Fernando, eds., *Ethnicity*, pp. 68–93.

51. Interview with Kirsti Niilsen.

52. Interview with Hunnako. See also Sula, "Urheilu ja canadan suomalainen jarjesto," pp. 155–57.

53. *Tester, Sports Pioneers*, p. 11. Archives of Ontario, *The Clarion*, August 3, 1937.

54. National Archives of Canada, interview between Stuart Davidson and George Nick.

55. Jean Harvey and Hart Cantelon, eds., *Not Just a Game: Essays in Canadian Sport Sociology* (Ottawa: University of Ottawa Press, 1988).

56. National Archives of Canada, Amateur Athletic Union of Canada, Minutes of the 1936 Annual General Meeting; and interview with Orlick.

12

Sport and Social Mobility among African-American and Hispanic Athletes

Merrill J. Melnick and Donald Sabo

An important component of the promotional ideology of sport is the notion that success in athletics can, and often does, lead to career success away from the court, field, or diamond. Conventional wisdom holds that the lessons learned in the crucible of athletic competition prepare athletes to meet the vicissitudes of the workplace. As stated in *Dun and Bradstreet Reports*, "the professional athlete's discipline, competitiveness, team-playing ability, and expectation of success can mold him into a top-flight business executive."[1] Evidence for the assumed linkage between athletic participation and success in later life often takes the form of personal testimonies, anecdotal data, or "Where are they now?" surveys. For example, among the forty-four former members of an outstanding 1963 University of Pittsburgh football team, there are fifteen dentists, three physicians, a chiropractor, six educators, five engineers, three lawyers, four corporate executives, a banker, two NFL assistant coaches, a college coach, two stockbrokers, and a bookmaker.[2]

Sport sociologists have been generally skeptical about the purported social mobility benefits that are believed to accrue through athletic participation. As Jay Coakley writes, "involvement in top-level competitive sport has not been found to be systematically linked to social mobility in subsequent careers."[3] While many sport sociologists generally adhere to this view, others are of the opinion that, in varying circumstances, athletic participation does contribute to the athlete's social advancement, and this is particularly so for racial and ethnic minorities.

The fact is, social scientific understanding of the relationship between athletic participation and social mobility is muddled by the limited amount of systematic research to date as well as its methodological limitations. In a review of the related research, Jomills Braddock noted that generalizations about sport-induced mobility are hampered by the absence of studies using longitudinal data and by a failure to adequately scrutinize racial and ethnic variations.[4] The interrelationship between athletic participation and social mobility is further blurred by the fact that most of the research to date has focused on males, not females, and has failed to take gender into theoretical or empirical account.[5] In fact, few studies have focused on African-American males, and research on the athletic experiences of women of color is extremely rare. Finally, it must also be remembered that "sport" is no institutional monolith but, rather, extremely variegated. Sport researchers have divided their energies in a piecemeal fashion in order to study the linkages between athletic participation and mobility in specific institutional settings such as high school athletics, intercollegiate athletics, Olympic athletics, and professional athletics.

In this chapter, we explore the nexus between athletic participation and social mobility among African-American and Hispanic athletes. Our major objectives are to (1) review the previous research on mobility patterns among African-American and Hispanic athletes, and (2) evaluate the extent to which the research lends theoretical understanding to patterns of race and ethnic relations within the sport institution as well as the larger society.

Three major questions are considered. First, do the athletic experiences of minority athletes translate into social mobility in later occupational or professional life? Second, to what extent have African-American and Hispanic athletes experienced social mobility within the institution of sport? For example, have qualified minority athletes been able to secure positions as coaches, managers, or athletic directors? And finally, what types of theoretical generalizations are warranted given the existing sport-related research literature on race relations and social mobility?

THE SPORT AND MOBILITY DEBATE

Debates about whether athletic participation promotes or inhibits upward social mobility among minorities can be categorized conceptually in a number of different ways. First, proponents of *assimilationist theories* generally argue that harsh economic conditions motivate low-status racial and ethnic groups to use sport to secure upward mobility. As a minority group becomes more assimilated into the larger opportunity system, the impetus for sport involvement wanes and participation decreases. Assimilationist theories tend to deemphasize cultural conflict and either tacitly or openly endorse a pluralist conception of an American society that provides advancement opportunities for those who embrace the core value system and work hard to succeed.[6]

A second and contrasting point of view is offered by the proponents of *exploitation theories*, who assert that race relations in sport, as in other institutions, tend to reflect and reproduce inequalities within the larger political economy.[7] They argue that the assimilationist position is seriously flawed given the racist nature of sport and the lack of economic progress made by African Americans over the past forty years. Using a variety of materialist theoretical frameworks for guidance, they believe that the exploitation of racial minorities in sports is an extension of the macro-level disadvantages imposed by politically and economically advantaged whites. On this point, Harry Edwards has observed that blacks pursuing a sports career must recognize the fact that "sport inevitably recapitulates society and that, therefore, it would be impossible for a substantially racist society to have a substantially nonracist sports institution as it would be for a chicken to lay a duck egg."[8] Paul Hoch argues that racism in sports derives from the capitalist system of production, and Harry Edwards contends that African American athletes are nothing more than twentieth century gladiators for affluent white America.[9]

In recent years, a third perspective, arguably more critical and theoretically informed than the other two, has emerged with respect to the analysis of race relations in sport and society. For a growing number of sport sociologists, the study of gender, race, ethnic, and class inequalities has become the central focus of attention. The proverbial "waters of sport sociological theory" have become stirred by a provocative and sometimes bewildering array of theoretical positions ranging from feminist theories, cultural studies theory, Foucaultian discourse theory, postmodernist analysis, hegemony theory, critical theory, and post-structuralism. Informed by the theoretical promise of these newer theoretical visions, Susan Birrell has suggested that analysts of racial relations in sports abandon the traditional assimilationist-versus-exploitationist conceptual frameworks altogether. Instead, she calls for the development of critical analyses that generally use cultural studies approaches "to conceive of race as a culturally produced marker of a particular relationship of power, to see racial identity as contested, and to ask how racial relations are produced and reproduced through sport."[10]

The strengths and weaknesses of the assimilationist and exploitationist positions, as well as the merits of more critical theoretical approaches, can be partly assessed by evaluating the research literature presently available. Since the greatest amount of sociological research on the athletic participation-social mobility issue has been quantitative, we examine these studies first.

A REVIEW OF THE QUANTITATIVE
RESEARCH FINDINGS

Since the 1970s, sociological research on the race and mobility issue in sport has used mainly quantitative research methods. A standard approach has been to analyze basic descriptive statistics that served as simple indicators of social mobility: for example, number of minority athletes on intercollegiate or professional teams, college graduation rates, or percentages of racial and ethnic minorities who hold coaching or athletic administrative positions. This type of univariate analysis has occasionally been buttressed by bivariate analyses that uncovered patterns of differential treatment of minorities within selected sports, for example, segregation by playing position or the "stacking" phenomenon in baseball or football. And finally, researchers have conducted cross-sectional and longitudinal surveys to identify and assess differential patterns of mobility across racial and ethnic subgroups, for example, intra- and intergenerational studies. The literature review below organizes the relevant research under four distinct institutional domains: interscholastic, intercollegiate, Olympic Games competition, and professional sports.

Interscholastic Athletic Competition

High school athletic programs are a major characterizing feature in American secondary education, and yet the short- and long-term social, educational, and economic consequences for participants are not fully understood. Over the last three decades, most sport researchers have focused on white male athletes and, to a much lesser extent, white females.[11] Only a handful of studies have examined the effects of high school athletic participation on African-American youth; again, most have focused on males. Even fewer studies have dealt with Hispanic youth. The paucity of research contrasts sharply with the fact that one in three persons living in the United States will be a member of a racial or ethnic minority group by the year 2000, and that one-quarter of all high school athletes are African American and Hispanic.[12]

African-American Athletes: Studies of the short-term effects of high school athletic participation on African-American youth present a confusing mélange of disparate findings. Athletic participation seems to have a *positive* effect on self-esteem and competitive orientation, and *mixed* effects on grades and encouragement to attend college from parents, teachers, and peers.[13] Athletic participation appears to exert no effect on membership in leading crowds and choice of high school program.[14]

Merrill Melnick and associates found that high school athletic participation by *some* African-American males was positively related to self-reported popularity, greater involvement in extracurricular and community activities, higher grades and achievement test scores, and lower dropout rates. These positive findings were strongly mediated by school location, that is, whether the student-athlete attended an urban, suburban, or rural high school.[15] For African-American female athletes, *positive* findings have been reported for competitive orientation, self-reported popularity, and extracurricular involvement.[16] *Mixed* effects have been noted regarding encouragement to attend college from parents, teachers, and peers.[17]

A number of studies have explored the extent to which African-American youth derive post-secondary mobility gains from their former participation in high school sports. The findings are generally mixed. Some studies of African-American males have found that high school athletic participation contributed to higher educational aspirations, college enrollment, college graduation, and adult earnings.[18] No clear relationship between athletic participation and number of years of post-secondary education has been found.[19]

Among African-American females, no clearcut associations have been found between high school athletic participation, educational aspirations, and number of years devoted to post-secondary education.[20] Other studies have uncovered *negative* relationships between high school athletic participation and post-secondary educational attainment, occupational expectations and achievement, and adult earnings.[21]

Hispanic Athletes: The short-term, indirect mobility impacts of high school athletic participation among Hispanic youth have only recently been addressed. Among Hispanic males, Merrill Melnick and associates found significant relationships between athletic participation and self-reported popularity (in urban and suburban schools), greater extracurricular involvement (in rural schools), and lower dropout rates (in suburban schools). Among Hispanic females who attended rural high schools, athletic participation was significantly associated with higher grades, better performance on standardized tests, and a lower dropout rate.[22]

Research studies that gauge the post-secondary mobility gains of Hispanic athletes are scant. Using descriptive statistics, Eldon Snyder and Elmer Spreitzer found that, in general, a higher percentage of Hispanic male high school athletes went to college than their nonathlete counterparts.[23] After conducting multiple regression analyses that included systematic controls for intervening variables, Merrill Melnick and associates found that high school athletic participation was positively related to college attendance only for Hispanic males who attended urban schools; no significant relationships issued among student-athletes attending suburban and rural schools. Interestingly, previous athletic participation was *negatively* related to the educational aspirations of Hispanic males who attended rural schools. And finally, athletic participation exerted no influence on post-secondary occupational mobility (as measured by job status and occupational aspiration).[24]

In the only published study to date on Hispanic female athletes, Merrill Melnick and associates discovered that athletic participation was significantly and positively related to college attendance two and four years after high school. However, athletic participation was unrelated to post-secondary occupational mobility for Hispanic females who entered the labor force after high school.[25]

Summary: While some positive associations between high school athletic participation and short-term mobility measures have been found among African-American youth, the achievement of positive post-secondary educational and occupational mobility gains appears to be much more problematic. Among African-American *females*, not only are the short-term mobility gains derived from athletic participation less impressive than for Caucasian females, but there is evidence that high school sports involvement is related to a lower likelihood of attending college, achieving occupational mobility, and securing adult earnings. The paucity of studies of the sport/mobility nexus among Hispanics calls for cautious inferences. Preliminary findings suggest, however, that among some Hispanic athletes, depending on gender and school location, athletic participation is positively related to popularity, extracurricular involvement, grades, lower dropout rates, and college attendance.

Clearly, the post-secondary educational and mobility patterns of high school minority athletes appear to be highly differentiated by gender, race/ethnicity, and school location. Generally speaking, high school athletic participation is probably best understood as a *means* to social and academic ends *during* the high school years rather than a guarantee of upward social mobility afterwards. Jay Coakley describes the synergy between athletic participation and mobility in this way: "Much of the connection between sport participation and upward social mobility depends on educational achievement. General career success has little to do with sport participation unless participation is combined with higher education and some independent proof of personal abilities."[26] To assign more social mobility influence to high school athletics than this is to run the risk of overestimating and exaggerating its real and potential benefits.

Intercollegiate Athletic Competition

Does intercollegiate athletic participation facilitate upward social mobility among minorities? The most obvious, short-term measure of upward mobility among college students is whether they earn a degree or not. A recent survey by the *Chronicle of Higher Education* found that Division I student-athletes graduated at higher rates than their non-athletic peers.[27] Table 12.1 compares the graduation rates of scholarship athletes and all full-time students who were freshmen in 1983–84 and received a degree within six years. On one hand, the data speak well for intercollegiate sport in that scholarship athletes are more likely to graduate than non-athletes. On the other hand, since the graduation rates for Caucasian athletes (both female and male) are higher than for African-American athletes, whites would appear to be especially advantaged by intercollegiate athletic participation. Yet no inferences in this regard can be made because these descriptive data do not speak specifically to the mobility impacts of athletic programs per se. The comparatively higher graduation rates of Caucasian athletes, for example, may be due to racial differences in high school academic preparation which, in turn, can be linked to variations in socioeconomic status. Or, as regards gender, it is known that female scholarship athletes are better academically prepared for college than their male counterparts.[28]

Only a handful of sport researchers have examined the relationship between intercollegiate athletic participation and social mobility *after* college. John Loy's study of the intergenerational and intragenerational social mobility of more than 1,000 former UCLA male varsity athletes found considerable evidence of upward social mobility, especially for athletes who came from the lowest socioeconomic strata.[29] On the other hand, Paul Dubois found no impacts of intercollegiate athletic participation on post-college occupational

Table 12.1

Comparison of Graduation Rates between Scholarship Athletes and all Full-time Students by Race and Gender

	Black Females	Black Males	White Females	White Males
Full-time Students				
Graduated:	34%	28%	57%	54%
Failed to Graduate:	66%	72%	43%	46%
Scholarship Athletes				
Graduated:	43%	33%	65%	54%
Failed to Graduate:	57%	67%	35%	46%

*Graduation rates for entering freshmen in 1983 and 1984.
Reported in the *Chronicle of Higher Education*, July 22, 1992.

prestige and earnings among former male athletes.[30] Similarly, Allen Sack and Robert Thiel compared the post-college social mobility of former Notre Dame football players and students who were not varsity athletes and found that the athletes were no more mobile than their non-athlete counterparts.[31] Unfortunately, none of the above studies examined variations in social mobility according to race, ethnicity, and gender.

In one of the few social mobility studies to consider the race and ethnicity of college athletes, Paul Dubois found no significant differences in post-college occupational prestige and earnings between athletes and non-athletes who were members of the same racial or ethnic minority groups.[32] On the other hand, James Brown and Harold Green investigated the intergenerational and intragenerational mobility of former athletes who graduated from four state-supported universities in Indiana over a seven-year period and found that African-American athletes surpassed Caucasian athletes in upward intergenerational mobility as measured by occupational prestige and earnings. African-American athletes also experienced greater increases than Caucasian athletes in intragenerational mobility based on a comparison of post-college, first- and last-reported occupations. This was especially true for former football and basketball players.[33] None of these studies focused on women athletes.

The Business of College Sports: Like Xerox Corporation or Bank of America, many intercollegiate athletic organizations are structured and run like businesses. As such they operate as competitive hierarchies in which status and reward are differentially allocated. When upward mobility in intercollegiate sports is conceptualized in this larger, institutional context, it is clear that African-American and Hispanic men, Caucasian women, and women of color are woefully underrepresented in coaching and athletic administrative positions. A recent *USA TODAY* survey of 63 Division I athletic programs determined that minorities were very much underrepresented in key positions in the athletic departments. Out of a total of 3,083 positions, only 384 or 12.5% were held by blacks, Hispanics, American Indians, or Asians.[34] Also instructive is the fact that since 1981 there have not been more than four black head football coaches at predominantly white schools in any one season. For the 1992 season, there was not a single black head coach at the 107 Division I-A schools.[35] Despite the fact that there were 17 new head coaching positions that needed to be filled, none went to the 163 assistant coaches of color at these institutions.[36]

Vivian Acosta and Linda Carpenter have documented a similar pattern of underrepresentation of Caucasian women and women of color in coaching and athletic administrative roles. For example, in 1992, 32% of NCAA Division I schools had *no* women positioned in their administrative structures; only

16.8% of women's programs were administrated by a female head; and only 48% of the coaches of *women's* teams were females (compared to 90% in 1972).[37] It should be added that most of these positions, inside and outside of women's sports, go to Caucasian men. For example, NCAA athletic directors hired 17 new head coaches in fall of 1991, "but none went to the 163 assistant coaches of color at the then 106 I-a schools."[38]

What is pertinent for our discussion of mobility is that between 1972 and 1992, a historical period in which the participation of women and racial/ethnic minorities in intercollegiate athletics accelerated at unprecedented rates, it was Caucasian men who assumed the vast majority of coaching and athletic administrative positions. Indeed, women coaches and administrators actually lost most of the status gains they had garnered up until 1972. An obvious implication for young minority student-athletes who aspire to careers in the business of intercollegiate sports is that opportunities are very limited.

Summary: It is impossible at this time to make sound inferences about the mobility impacts of intercollegiate athletic participation among African-American and Hispanic student-athletes. There are simply too few studies to allow for generalizations. The handful of studies that do exist either present mixed findings, fail to consider gender, or employ research designs that do not allow for the systematic, statistical analysis of longitudinal relationships. And finally, available descriptive data on opportunities for mobility *within* the business of college sports yield the conclusion that upward mobility for women and minorities has been the exception rather than the rule.

Olympic Athletic Participation

George Eisen and Diana Turner conducted the only study that looked at the intergenerational and intragenerational social mobility of former American Olympic athletes. Although racial and ethnic differences were not considered, their findings remain instructive. Comparisons between athletes' first and present employment revealed considerable upward mobility. This was matched by the athletes' own positive self-perceptions of their status advancement. Former athletes were found to have achieved significantly greater occupational prestige than their parents, though the researchers caution that these gains were largely mediated by higher educational attainment. Unfortunately, no data were presented for the social mobility of former Olympic athletes who are members of racial and ethnic minority groups.[39]

Participation in Professional Sports

African-Americans, who constitute 12% of the American population, are statistically overrepresented in professional football (62%), baseball (17%), basketball (75%), and boxing (70%). The same can be said for Hispanic males in professional baseball (14%) and boxing (unknown). African-American women predominate in professional track and field. Because professional athletes in these fields are paid extraordinarily well and receive considerable media attention, it is understandable if an aura of success surrounds minority athletes who participate in professional sports. Becoming a successful professional athlete translates directly into immediate upward social mobility when measured by salary and celebrity status. Consider the fact that, whereas the median salary for a person age 25–34 with four or more years of college was $29,773 in 1990, the *minimum* starting and average salaries in the National Basketball Association, major league baseball, and the National Football League are $130,000/$1.04 million, $109,000/$1 million, and $50,000/$422,000 respectively. In the context of this chapter, therefore, it is useful to examine the extent that men and women of color attain mobility *in* or *through* professional sports.

Success in Professional Sports: Generally speaking, the probability of African-Americans and Hispanics to derive upward mobility gains from a professional sports career is extremely low. There are probably no more than 3,000 athletes altogether participating in major league baseball, NBA, the NFL, and professional boxing. Specifically, there are only 737 jobs in major league baseball, 345 jobs in the NBA, and 1,400 jobs in the NFL. It is these three professional sports in addition to boxing where African-Americans and Hispanics have had their greatest successes. Obviously, women are excluded from these activities.

Putting aside racial and ethnic considerations for the moment, the statistical probabilities of *any male* becoming a professional athlete are extraordinarily low. For example, the percentage of players who will make it from high school sports to the NFL, major league baseball, and the NBA are 0.14%, 0.06%, and 0.18% respectively.[40] The NCAA has determined that the odds against a high school senior basketball player making an NBA team as a rookie are 2,344 to 1 and, for making an NFL team, 1,233 to 1.[41] The percentage of *college* seniors who make it as rookies in professional football (150 rookies), basketball (50 rookies), and baseball (80 rookies) every year are 1.1%, 1.4%, and 1.4%, respectively.

With respect to men of color, Wilbert Leonard and Jonathan Reyman calculated the odds of a 20–39-year-old African-American male playing in the NFL at 1:47,600, an 18–39-year-old playing major league baseball at 1:333,000, and a 20–39-year-old playing in the NBA at 1:153,800.[42] For Hispanic males in the same age cohorts, the respective odds are 1:2,500,000 in the NFL,

1:500,000 in major league baseball, and 1:33,300,000 in the NBA. Indeed, there are probably no more than 1,200 African-American and 150 Hispanic males playing professional sports in the United States today.

The relative absence of professional opportunities for outstanding female team sport athletes in the United States renders any discussion of social mobility through sport somewhat moot. For highly skilled athletes in volleyball and basketball, some opportunities do exist in European professional leagues. Lucrative professional careers are also possible in golf and tennis, but only for the few. The recent emergence of professional track and field has also created some opportunities for women of color, both in the United States and Europe.

Mobility through Professional Sports: While conventional wisdom advises that a professional sports career is a guarantor for social advancement, for every "rags to riches" success story, one can identify just as many "riches to rags" stories. Barry McPherson and associates observe that "many athletes often lose any social and economic gains they made during their playing careers after they retire."[43] For far too many minority male athletes, physical injuries and/or diminished abilities often cut them down at a relatively early age. Without any marketable skills or a formal education to fall back on, the final scenario is all too familiar for the truly unfortunate ones: substance abuse, irregular employment, downward mobility, and sometimes prison. Harry Edwards makes the point well: "Blacks in sport . . . function in a semi-caste system relegated as they are to the least powerful, least secure, most expendable and most exploited population in the sports institution—that of the athlete."[44]

Mobility in the Professional Sport Industry: Though racial and ethnic minorities are statistically overrepresented among professional athletes, they are very much underrepresented among coaches, managers, and front office staff.[45] Richard Lapchick and Jeffery Brown found that for 1991–92 African Americans were 7% (2/27) of NBA head coaches, 7% (3/28) of NFL head coaches (in 1991), and 11% (3/28) of major league baseball managers (in 1992). In 1991–92, African-Americans comprised 14% of NBA front office personnel, 8% of NFL front office personnel, and in 1992, 9% of major league baseball management and support staff (7% were of Hispanic ancestry). Given the high percentages of racial and ethnic minority athletes in these sports, minority representation in non-athletic positions is obviously very low. Despite this, Lapchick and Brown conclude that racial minorities made small but significant gains in the late 1980s, especially when compared to the social and economic setbacks that many African-Americans experienced in the wider economy.[46]

Reliable data on women's participation in front office positions in professional sports is virtually nonexistent. It is likely that women have probably made small gains in the burgeoning professional sport industry in marketing, management, advertising, and public relations. It is also likely that women of color have made far fewer gains than their Caucasian counterparts. Clearly, the opportunity systems in the professional sport industry continued to be dominated by white males during the 1980s.

Summary: The high visibility of racial and ethnic minorities in the sports media has led to the false conclusion by some that sport is an effective vehicle for upward social mobility of minority athletes. Michael Jordan soars across cereal box covers and television screens. Florence Griffith Joyner and Jackie Joyner-Kersee appear on the cover of *Sports Illustrated*, and Americans assume that sports provide an automatic gateway to social advancement for minorities. The facts are, however, that only a relative few ever become professional athletes. Indeed, only 1 in 10 intercollegiate athletic scholarships go to African-American males. Off-the-field opportunities within the sport institution are especially limited. While there has been an incipient trend during the latter 1980s toward greater inclusion of racial and ethnic minorities in coaching and management positions in professional football, basketball, and baseball, the actual total number of minorities working in these positions is probably no more than 450.

IMPLICATIONS AND LIMITATIONS
OF THE RESEARCH

Considerable theoretical debate surrounds the question of whether athletic participation accelerates upward social mobility among people of color in the United States. Some argue that sport "has become a treadmill to oblivion rather than the elevator to wealth and glory it was believed to be."[47] Others are just as quick to argue that sport is a powerful resource for minority athletes, an effective vehicle for upward social mobility. And finally, a third position holds that the purported mobility benefits gleaned from athletic participation are entirely illusory; that is, no real mobility benefits are produced for anyone—whites, blacks, or Hispanics. The earlier review of the quantitative research literature showed that *none* of these views adequately explains the complex ways that athletic participation influences the mobility struggles of African-Americans and Hispanics.

To begin with, the thesis that athletic participation *actively* contributes to downward mobility among minorities has received little empirical corroboration. For example, involvement in high school athletics is generally unrelated to *occupational* mobility, though, among African-American females attending urban schools, some negative effects have been documented. Recent NCAA data show that African-American athletes have higher graduation rates than their same-race, non-athletic counterparts. And finally, data gathered by the Center for the Study of Sport in Society show slight but gradual increases in African-American and Hispanic occupancy of coaching, administrative, and front office positions in the NFL, NBA and major league baseball.[48]

In contrast, some research findings point toward a positive synergy between athletic participation and educational mobility for some racial and ethnic minorities. For example, Hispanic female high school athletes, particularly those who attend rural schools, improve their academic standing while in high school, graduate, and attend college in greater numbers than their non-athletic peers. High school athletic participation is also related to lower dropout rates among African-American males in rural schools and Hispanic males and females in rural and suburban schools. At issue, therefore, is not the traditional dichotomistic question: Does athletic participation result in either upward mobility or exploitation for racial and ethnic minorities? Rather, the review of the race-and-mobility research literature suggests a more nuanced line of inquiry: What kinds of institutional processes facilitate upward mobility among minority athletes and what kinds of processes impede mobility?

The inability of quantitative researchers to provide better insights into the relationship between race and mobility is, in part, grounded in the conceptualization of athletic participation as a single and primary explanatory variable. It makes better theoretical sense to see athletic participation as a catalyst for social and educational changes which, in turn, may or may not translate into mobility gains for some minorities, depending on variations in gender, social class, and school location. In other words, too much theoretical emphasis has been placed on the independent effects of athletic participation on mobility rather than conceptualizing sport involvement in synergistic relation to a wider array of variables and processes that are known to influence race relations and mobility outcomes. Ironically, this *theoretical* tendency to regard athletic participation in monolithic, causal terms is due, in part, to a *methodological* and *statistical* reliance on univariate and bivariate analyses. In the future, quantitative researchers will need to employ multifactorial research designs and multivariate statistical analyses in order to grapple better with the large array of variables and processes that surround the race-mobility nexus.

CONCLUSION: HOW TO THEORIZE BETTER AND RESEARCH THE RACE AND MOBILITY ISSUE IN SPORT?

Three types of research approaches to understanding race and gender relations in sport have been recently identified: (1) "categoric research" focuses on race or gender differences owed to biology or socialization; (2) "distributive research" analyzes the unequal allocation of rewards, resources, or opportunities in systems of structural inequality; (3) "relational analyses" regard race and gender relations as socially, historically, and culturally constructed processes that affirm the advantages of dominant groups. The bulk of previous quantitative research on race, sport, and mobility is best characterized as distributive research. Its strength has been to expose inequalities in sport and to identify differential patterns of mobility among and between racial and ethnic groups. However, these studies have *not* been able to explicate the intricate and complex processes that: (1) inspire and motivate individuals, (2) influence perceptions and relationships between racial and ethnic groups, and (3) reproduce or challenge the complex of structured race relations organized around dominance and subordination.[49]

In short, previous research has subsidized and perpetuated the "assimilation versus exploitation" debate, but it has prevented sport researchers from more fully exploring how power relations between racial and ethnic groups are constituted and challenged in and through sport.[50] Toward this end, more relational research is needed and, consonant with Susan Birrell's call for critical analyses of race relations in sport, a growing number of ethnographers and social historians have begun to illuminate the myriad processes of domination and subordination inherent in racial and ethnic struggles for upward mobility.[51]

Loïc Wacquant's participant observation study of boxers in a ghetto gym in Stoneland, Chicago, for example, illustrates the physical and emotional struggles of black males to distinguish themselves from street culture through disciplined, successful competition in and outside the ring. He contextualizes the individual aspirations, values, and experiences of these boxers against the historical transformation of Stoneland, from a prosperous white neighborhood at the end of World War II to a predominantly black, impoverished, and dilapidated ghetto. The fighters, who mostly come from working class not underclass backgrounds, perceive boxing "as a skilled trade, highly regarded by their immediate entourage, and with potential for big earnings."[52] While Wacquant's analysis lends credence to the economic argument of ethnic succession, he also shows that a lack of financial resources was less likely to fuel a young man's boxing aspirations than basic working class values of self-discipline and hard work.

Mark Grey's ethnographic study of sport and ethnic relations in a southwestern Kansas high school reveals how the interplay among ethnicity, social class background, coaches' values and practices, administrative decisions, and the structure of athletic programs themselves influenced the status gains of Hispanic and Asian-American students. Grey challenges James Coleman's contention that interscholastic athletic programs democratize the student body while providing mobility opportunities for athletes from lower socioeconomic backgrounds. He found that, while it was true that *some* minority student-athletes reaped recognition and upward mobility from their participation, the cultural emphasis on sport as a chief vehicle for achieving status in the school community served to isolate the majority of ethnic immigrants, many of whom could not culturally relate to "American" sports. In short, the structural and cultural processes which attended school athletic programs were constituted in ways that mainly enhanced an elitist structure dominated by elite groups of Caucasians.[53]

A third example of the way in which sport reproduces race relations is provided by anthropologist Douglas Foley's critical studies of high school football in a small south Texas farming/ranching community. The community contains a large Mexican-American population. Not only did Foley find evidence to support the work of critical sport theorists who maintain that ruling elites employ popular cultural practices like mass sports rituals to create an ideological hegemony, but perhaps even more important, he discovered that sport scenes also become sites for ethnic resistance to ruling class hegemony. For example, many Mexicanos voiced strong protests when "the Anglos enacted the homecoming football ceremony in a way that marginalized them."[54] Other examples of ethnic resistance to the football ritual included the times when Mexicano players sat together in the back of the bus on away-trips, when Mexicano players verbally challenged their Anglo coaches over the assignment of high status playing positions to Anglo players, and the non-conformist actions of the "vatos" (cool dudes), a number of Mexicano males who formed themselves into anti-school, anti-sport peer groups. For them, "fighting, smoking pot, and chasing females were far better sport than huffing and puffing around for 'some fucking coach.'"[55] Despite the fact that the powerful and popular football ritual helped reproduce the class and racial domination of white male elites, this detailed microethnographic study reveals how human agency and autonomy can combine to resist hegemonic forces within a sport setting.

SUMMARY

Do some minority college athletes who are talented and lucky enough to succeed in professional sports experience upward social mobility? Of course. Are some minority high school athletes who never thought of getting a college education able to improve themselves socially and economically as a result of earning an athletic scholarship? To be sure. And what about the thousands of minority high school athletes who, although not good enough to play at the college level or the "Big Leagues," still experience positive social, educational, and career mobility gains as a result of their athletic participation, for example, improved self-esteem, graduation from high school, higher educational aspirations, and college attendance? There can be little argument that many minority athletes have been able to translate their athletic experiences, whether it be at the high school, college, or professional level, into a better standard of living for themselves.

Having recognized the impact of athletic participation as a catalyst for upward mobility, we must also face up to the cold, harsh reality that for many socially and economically disadvantaged minority athletes, sport, regardless of the competitive level, has had little or no impact on their life chances. In some cases, unfortunately, sport has probably contributed, either directly or indirectly, to even greater despair, frustration, and failure. Nowhere is this more tragically reflected than in the graduation rates of black athletes at some Division I schools. For example, for all black athletes at the University of Georgia, from 1969 to 1986, the graduation rate was 15%. Only 10.5% of black basketball players at Memphis State University graduated between 1973 and 1986. As one African-American athletic director bitterly notes, "There have been a lot of $40,000 homes built for coaches and administrators on the backs of black athletes who didn't get anything in return except a lot of courses in eligibility."[56]

The assimilationist argument that American sport has facilitated the upward mobility of countless minorities appears to be only a half-truth at best given that researchers have documented a variety of racial injustices in sport including: racial stereotyping, the presence of higher entry-level performance standards for minorities, salary inequities and racial quotas at the professional level, and limited opportunities for advancement into off-the-field work roles such as umpire, general manager, head coach, or athletic administrator.

While exploitation theorists can certainly draw support for their position from these findings, what seems lacking in their critique of the sport-mobility nexus is a fuller understanding of the diverse processes and forces that inform race relations in an Anglocentric and androcentric society. Their analyses have been mired in a mechanistic, sociological determinism that has impeded scrutiny of resistance practices and institutional pressures for change. They have also failed to recognize sites where athletic participation does produce positive mobility gains for minorities. We have also argued that the relationship between athletic participation and social mobility cannot be fully comprehended by quantitative methods and univariate or bivariate statistical analyses. We have tried to show the contributions of ethnographic and historical studies for understanding the sport-mobility nexus, particularly as regards the development of critical theories of race relations and sport. We are not, however, advocating the abandonment of quantitative research methods. Just as there are quantitative studies that oversimplify or obfuscate the processes of domination and subordination that inform race relations in sport, there are ethnographic studies of sport that ignore issues of power and inequality.[57] Like quantitative research, qualitative research is a tool and not an escape route from the epistemological quandaries faced by twentieth-century social scientists.

What is needed is a better understanding of how sport contributes to the construction of racial and ethnic relations, as well as the ways that these processes either facilitate or inhibit social mobility. In addition, if race is to be treated as a social construct rather than a biological given, "our analysis of racial relations and sport must move beyond the treatment of race as a descriptive variable and address ideological questions about the production of race relations and the specific forms such relations take in particular times."[58]

Unfortunately, the research to date as well as our adherence to assimilationist versus exploitationist argument have conjoined to narrow discourse on the subject to a consideration of important but nevertheless isolated phenomena, for example, college graduation rates of Division I black athletes, number of black head coaches in the NFL, etc. This approach is not likely to help us answer the more crucial question, "What is the part of sport in the construction of racial relations, and how do dominant forms of sport continue to reproduce particular configurations of racial relations?"[59] More generally, what impact have highly successful African-American and Hispanic athletes had on the social and economic advancement of their reference groups? Has the outstanding success of African-American athletes like Evander Hollyfield, Michael Jordan, Kirby Puckett, and Warren Moon positively impacted on the life chances of blacks in general? Have their obvious mobility gains been paralleled by similar gains by other blacks? And what about the emerging presence of Hispanic athletes on the American sports scene? What impact have such highly successful athletes as José Canseco, Ruben Sierra, Dennis Martinez, and Hector Comacho had on their constituent populations?

Would it not be a cruel irony if we eventually discovered, through the critical analyses previously called for, that while sport has contributed to the social advancement of some individual minorities or some racial or ethnic subgroups, its *net effect* has been to consolidate and ensure Anglocentric and androcentric privilege. It remains to be seen whether the extraordinary material rewards that white elites have heaped on a handful of superstar, minority athletes in professional and intercollegiate sports was a price only too willingly paid in order to maintain racial hegemony and an ideology of racial exploitation. Perhaps even more ironic is the worsening fiscal crisis faced by American high school sports. While the empirical evidence shows that interscholastic athletic participation does offer social and educational advantages to some racial and ethnic groups, dwindling financial resources are forcing administrators to "redefine the role of sports in the education system and, too often, sports are being eliminated in the attempt to balance budgets."[60] It may be that two over-arching and interrelated patterns of racial relations have configured in American sport during the last thirty years. First, while the greatest amount of fiscal and cultural capital has been poured into intercollegiate and professional athletics, only a disproportionately small number of racial and ethnic minorities benefit from their athletic participation. Second, while youth and inter-scholastic athletic programs attract a large number of racial and ethnic participants and produce some mobility benefits for participants, the cultural and fiscal foundations for maintaining these programs have been eroded. If our appraisal of these trends is historically accurate, the power of sport to facilitate upward social mobility and to heal a nation divided by race and ethnicity will remain in question.

NOTES

1. "Do Athletes Make Good Business Executives?" *Dun and Bradstreet Reports* (July–August 1976): 4–7.

2. "Alumni Roll Call," *Sports Illustrated* (December 5, 1983): 9.

3. Jay J. Coakley, *Sport in Society* (St. Louis, Missouri: Times Mirror, 1990), p. 235.

4. Jomills H. Braddock, "Sport and Race Relations in American Society," *Sociological Symposium* 9 (1989): 53–76.

5. See M. Ann Hall, "Towards a Feminist Analysis of Gender Inequality in Sport," in *Sport and the Sociological Imagination,* ed. Nancy Theberge and Peter Donnelly (Fort Worth: Texas University Press, 1984); Merrill J. Melnick, Donald Sabo, and Beth E. VanFossen, "Developmental Effects of Athletic Participation among High School Girls," *Sociology of Sport Journal* 5 (1988): 22–36; Michael Messner and Donald Sabo, eds., *Sport, Men, and the Gender Order: Critical Feminist Perspectives* (Champaign, Illinois: Human Kinetics, 1990).

6. Susan Birrell, "Racial Relations Theories and Sport: Suggestions for a More Critical Analysis," *Sociology of Sport Journal* 6 (1989): 212–27.

7. See John C. Gaston, "The Destruction of the Young Black Male: The Impact of Popular Culture and Organized Sports," *Journal of Black Studies* 16 (1986): 369–84; Gary A. Sailes, "The Exploitation of the Black Athlete: Some Alternative Solutions," *Journal of Negro Education* 55 (1986): 439–42.

8. Harry Edwards, "Educating Black Athletes," *Current* 257 (1983): 22.

9. Paul Hoch, *Rip off the Big Game* (New York: Anchor/Doubleday, 1972); Harry Edwards, "The Black Athletes: 20th Century Gladiators for White America," *Psychology Today* (November 1973): 43–52.

10. Birrell, "Racial Relations Theories and Sport," p. 214.

11. Barry McPherson, "Sport in the Educational Milieu: Unanswered Questions and Untested Assumptions," *Phi Delta Kappa* 6 (1980): 605–6; Melnick, Sabo, and VonFossen, "Developmental Effects of Athletic Participation."

12. Merrill J. Melnick, Donald Sabo, and Beth E. VonFossen, "Effects of Interscholastic Athletic Participation on the Social, Educational, and Career Mobility of Hispanic Girls and Boys," *International Review for Sociology of Sport* 27 (1992): 57–75.

13. See Jomills H. Braddock, "Race, Athletics and Educational Attainment," *Youth and Society* 12 (1981): 335–50. Michael Hanks, "Race, Sexual Status and Athletics in the Process of Educational Achievement," *Social Science Quarterly* 60 (1979): 482–96; Richard H. Wells and Steven J. Picou, "Interscholastic Athletes and Socialization for Educational Achievement," *Journal of Sport Behavior* 3 (1980): 119–28; Steven J. Picou, "Race, Athletic Achievement, and Educational Aspiration," *The Sociological Quarterly* 19 (1978): 429–38.

14. Wells and Picou, "Interscholastic Athletes and Socialization for Educational Achievement."

15. Melnick, Sabo, and VonFossen, "Effects of Interscholastic Athletic Participation on the Social, Educational, and Career Mobility of Hispanic Girls and Boys."

16. Merrill J. Melnick, Donald Sabo, and Beth E. VonFossen, "Educational Effects of Interscholastic Athletic Participation on African-American and Hispanic Youth," *Adolescence* 27 (1992): 295–308.

17. Hanks, "Race, Sexual Status and Athletics,"Wells and Picou, "Interscholastic Athletes and Socialization For Educational Achievement."

18. See, for example, Braddock, "Race, Athletics, and Educational Attainment"; Hanks, "Race, Sexual Status and Athletics"; Picou, "Race, Athletic Achievement, and Educational Aspiration"; Steven J. Picou and Sean Hwang, "Educational Aspirations of 'Academically-Disadvantaged' Athletes," *Journal of Sport Behavior* 5 (1982): 59–76; Wells and Picou, "Interscholastic Athletes and Socialization for Educational Achievement"; Steven J. Picou, Virginia McCarter, and Frank M. Howell, "Do High School Athletics Pay? Some Further Evidence," *Sociology of Sport Journal* 2 (1985): 72–76.

19. Braddock, "Race, Athletics, and Educational Attainment"; Hanks, "Race, Sexual Status and Athletics in the Process of Educational Achievement." Picou and Hwang, "Educational Aspirations of 'Academically-Disadvantaged' Athletes"; Wells and Picou, "Interscholastic Athletes and Socialization for Educational Achievement"; Picou, McCarter, and Howell, "Do High School Athletics Pay?"; Donald Sabo, Merrill J. Melnick, and Beth E. VonFossen, "The Influence of High School Athletic Participation on Post-Secondary and Occupational Mobility: A Focus on Race and Gender," *Sociology of Sport Journal* 10 (1992): 44–56.

20. Hanks, "Race, Sexual Status and Athletics"; Picou and Hwang, "Educational Aspirations of 'Academically-Disadvantaged' Athletes"; Wells and Picou, "Interscholas-

tic Athletes and Socialization for Educational Achievement"; Picou, McCarter, and Howell, "Do High School Athletics Pay?"

21. Picou, McCarter, and Howell, "Do High School Athletics Pay?"; Sabo, Melnick, and VonFossen, "The Influence of High School Athletic Participation on Post-Secondary and Occupational Mobility."

22. Melnick, Sabo, and VonFossen, "Educational Effects of Interscholastic Athletic Participation on African-American and Hispanic Youth."

23. Eldon E. Snyder and Elmer A. Spreitzer, "High School Athletic Participation as Related to College Attendance among Black, Hispanic, and White Males: A Research Note," *Youth and Society* 21 (1990): 390–98.

24. Melnick, Sabo, and VonFossen, "Effects of Interscholastic Athletic Participation on the Social, Educational, and Career Mobility of Hispanic Girls and Boys."

25. Ibid.

26. Coakley, *Sport in Society*, p. 245.

27. *Chronicle of Higher Education*, July 22, 1992.

28. D. Stanley Eitzen, "The Educational Experiences of Intercollegiate Student-Athletes," *Journal of Sport and Social Issues* 11 (1988): 15–30.

29. John W. Loy, "Social Origins and Occupational Mobility Patterns of a Selected Sample of American Athletes," *International Review of Sport Sociology* 1 (1972): 5–23.

30. Paul E. Dubois, "Participation in Sports and Occupational Attainment: A Comparative Study," *Research Quarterly* 49 (1973): 28–35.

31. Allen Sack and Robert Thiel, "College Football and Social Mobility: A Case Study of Notre Dame Football Players," *Sociology of Education* 52 (1979): 63–72.

32. Paul E. Dubois, "The Occupational Attainment of Former College Athletes: A Comparative Study," *International Review of Sport Sociology* 15 (1980): 93–108.

33. James R. Brown and Harold Green, "Social Mobility and Race of Former Athletes at State Supported Universities in Indiana," unpublished manuscript.

34. *USA Today*, March 19, 1991.

35. Gary Fallesen, "Blacks Need Not Apply," *Democrat and Chronicle*, September 27, 1992.

36. Kimberlee Jensen, "On the Verge of Extinction: Black Coaches in College Football," *CSSS Digest* 4 (1992): 2, 3.

37. R. Vivian Acosta and Linda J. Carpenter, "Women in Intercollegiate Sport: A Longitudinal Study—Fifteen Year Update" (New York: Brooklyn College, 1992); idem, "1992 Minority Study" (New York: Brooklyn College, 1992).

38. Jensen, "On the Verge of Extinction," p. 2.

39. George Eisen and Diana Turner, "Myth and Reality: Social Mobility of the American Olympic Athlete," *International Review for the Sociology of Sport* 27 (1992): 165–76.

40. Coakley, *Sport in Society*.

41. *USA Today*, March 21 and 22, 1990.

42. Wilbert H. Leonard and Jonathan E. Reyman, "The Odds of Attaining Professional Athlete Status: Refining the Computations," *Sociology of Sport Journal* 5 (1988): 162–69.

43. Barry D. McPherson, James E. Curtis, and John W. Loy, *The Social Significance of Sport* (Champaign, Illinois: Human Kinetics, 1989), p. 184.

44. Harry Edwards, "Race in Contemporary American Sports," *Phi Kappa Phi* 62 (1982): 19–22.

45. Braddock, "Sport and Race Relations in American Society."

46. Richard E. Lapchick and Jeffery P. Brown, "1992 Racial Report Card: Do Professional Sports Provide Equal Opportunities for All Races?" *CSSS Digest* 4 (1992): 4–9.

47. Edwards, "Educating Black Athletes," 25–36.

48. Lapchick and Brown, "1992 Racial Report Card."

49. Alison Dewar, "Incorporation of Resistance? Toward an Analysis of Women's Responses to Sexual Oppression in Sport," *International Review for the Sociology of Sport* 26 (1991): 15–23.

50. M. Ann Hall, "Gender and Sport in the 1990's: Feminism, Culture, and Politics," in Donald Sabo, ed., *Sport Science Review* (forthcoming); Yevonne R. Smith, "Women of Color in Society and Sport," *Quest* 44 (1992): 228–30.

51. Birrell, "Racial Relations Theories and Sport."

52. Loic J. D. Wacquant, "The Social Logic of Boxing in Black Chicago: Toward a Sociology of Pugilism," *Sociology of Sport Journal* 9 (1992): 221–54.

53. Mark A. Grey, "Sports and Immigrant, Minority and Anglo Relations in a Garden City (Kansas) High School," *Sociology of Sport Journal* 9 (1992): 255–70.

54. Douglas E. Foley, "The Great American Football Ritual: Reproducing Race, Class, and Gender Inequality," *Sociology of Sport Journal* 7 (1990): 111–35.

55. Ibid.

56. John Witosky, "Black Leaders Say U.S. Sports Don't Offer Equal Opportunities," *Democrat and Chronicle,* May 30, 1990.

57. Michael Messner, "Men Studying Masculinity: Some Epistemological Issues in Sport Sociology," *Sociology of Sport Journal* 7 (1990): 136–53.

58. Birrell, "Racial Relations Theories and Sport."

59. Ibid., p. 218.

60. Amateur Athletic Foundation of Los Angeles, "The Funding Crisis in High School Athletics: Causes and Solutions" (report from a Conference, April 23 and 24, 1992), p. 2.

Index

Contributors

GEORGE EISEN is a Professor in the Department of Kinesiology and Health Promotion at California State Polytechnic University, Pomona. He has published numerous articles and books dealing with such topics as the Olympic Games, religion and sport, ethnicity and sport, and the influence of social class on sport participation. His latest book, the highly acclaimed *Children and Play in the Holocaust: Games among the Shadows* was translated into five languages. He was awarded a Fulbright Scholarship to Estonia where he was assisting in developing an American Studies program.

DAVID K. WIGGINS is Professor and Director of Undergraduate Programs in Health Science at George Mason University. His research has focused primarily on African-American involvement in sport and physical activity. His most recent publications have appeared in the *Journal of Sport History, The International Journal of the History of Sport,* and the *Research Quarterly for Exercise and Sport.* He is currently working on an anthology dealing with the history of American sport.

ROBERT KNIGHT BARNEY is a Professor in the Faculty of Kinesiology and Director of the Centre for Olympic Studies at the University of Western Ontario. His research has focused primarily on Olympic history, the German-American Turnverein movement, and nineteenth-century baseball. He is a member of the Executive Council for the preservation of the Turnverein Heritage in America and served as President of the North American Society for Sport History.

CARMELO BAZZANO is a Professor in the Department of Human Performance and Physical Fitness at the University of Massachusetts, Boston. An immigrant from Sicily and former boxer and soccer player, Professor

Bazzano is especially interested in the history of boxing and the contributions of Italian immigrants to American sport. He is currently working to develop closer ties with Italian physical educators.

GERALD R. GEMS is currently serving as Chair of the Health and Physical Education Department at North Central College, Naperville, Illinois. His recent publications include articles in *Strategies, The International Journal of the History of Sport,* and *Illinois Journal of Physical Education.* He is currently working on a book dealing with sport in Chicago.

J. THOMAS JABLE is a Professor in the Department of Exercise and Movement Sciences at William Paterson College, Wayne, New Jersey. He has published in various historical and physical education journals, including the *Journal of Sport History, Canadian Journal of History and Sport,* and *Journal of Health, Physical Education, Recreation, and Dance.* He is currently working on a socioeconomic analysis of nineteenth-century Philadelphia through the medium of sport.

BRUCE KIDD is Professor and Director of the School of Physical and Health Education at the University of Toronto where he teaches and writes about the history and politics of sport. A former Olympic athlete, he is also Chair of the Canadian Olympic Associations Olympic Academy of Canada. He has published a number of articles in such journals as the *Sociology of Sport, International Review for the Sociology of Sport,* and *Olympika: The International Journal of Olympic Studies.* He is currently working on a history of Canadian sport in the 1920s and 1930s.

MERRILL J. MELNICK is Professor of Physical Education and Sport at SUNY, Brockport. His major teaching and research interests include social participation, sports fandom, and group dynamics in sport. His most recent publications have appeared in the *Journal of Sports Management, International Review for the Sociology of Sport, Sociology of Sport Journal,* and *Perceptual and Motor Skills.*

DONALD SABO is a Professor of Social Science at D'Youville College in Buffalo, New York. His numerous articles and books focus on sport, gender, race, and ethnic relations and social inequality. His most recent book, co-edited with Mike Messner, is entitled *Sport, Men, and the Gender Order: Critical Feminist Perspectives.* He is President-elect of the North American Society for the Sociology of Sport and ongoing consultant with the Women's Sports Foundation as well as a member of its Board of Trustees.

ERIC SOLOMON is Professor of English and University Librarian at San Francisco State University. He has written or edited four books, including two on

Stephen Crane and many articles on British and American fiction as well as contemporary culture. He is currently completing a book, *Jews, Baseball, and American Fiction.*

K. B. WAMSLEY is an Associate Professor in the Faculty of Physical Education at the University of Calgary. His research has focused primarily on hegemony, the state, and nineteenth-century Canadian sport and leisure practices. He is currently working on a book which examines the shaping of leisure in nineteenth-century Canada through legislation, expenditure, and revenue.

RALPH C. WILCOX is an Associate Professor and Chair of Graduate Studies in the Department of Health and Human Performance at the University of Houston. Educated in Canada, the United Kingdom, and the United States, he earned his Ph.D. in 1982 from the University of Alberta where he was recipient of an Izaak Walton Killam Memorial Scholarship. His research interests are in the sociocultural dimensions of sport, and he has published his work in a variety of national and international journals. He is currently editing a volume entitled *Sport in the Global Village,* a collection of essays addressing international issues in sport.

ALISON M. WRYNN received her bachelor's degree from Springfield College and her master's degree from California State University, Long Beach. She taught high school physical education in the Los Angeles area for four years and is currently in the process of completing her Ph.D. at the University of California, Berkeley, where she is a graduate student instructor.

ISBN 0-313-28814-3